In Secret Service of the Sacred Heart

remembering the life and virtues of
Denver's Angel of Charity

Julia Greeley, O.F.S.

recalled by her contemporaries
in their own words

compiled and edited by

Father Blaine Burkey, O.F.M.Cap.

Julia Greeley Guild
2760 Larimer St.
Denver CO 80205
2012

Nihil obstat:
>Rev. Christopher Joseph Popravak, O.F.M.Cap., Ph.D.
>Census Deputatus; Provincial Vicar, Capuchin Province of Mid-America

Imprimi potest:
>Very Rev. Charles Joseph Polifka, O.F.M.Cap., M.A.
>Provincial Minister, Capuchin Province of Mid-America

Nihil obstat:
>Professor R. Jared Staudt, Ph.D.
>Censor Librorum; Academic Dean, Augustine Institute

Imprimatur:
>Most Rev. James Douglas Conley, S.T.L.,
>Apostolic Administrator, Archdiocese of Denver

In obedience to the decree of Pope Urban VIII and conformity with the Apostolic Constitution of Pope Leo XIII, the author declares that he claims no more than a purely human consideration of the events and graces reported herein, and that he submits at all times and unreservedly to the judgment of the Catholic Church.

Cover art work by Isiah McGill, visual and musical artist of New Orleans and Denver (2012) [www.ArtbyIsiahMcGill.biz & IMHope Productions 720-628-0432 E-mail IsiahMcGill@yahoo.com]

'Taters from Heb'n'

Julia Greeley's charities took her through many a dark alley. One very cold night, after placing a sack of potatoes on a needy family's porch, she realized they would freeze and be useless, unless the householder took them inside. Julia asked a neighborhood child to knock on the door and run. "But don't dast say Old Julia sent ya." The toy fireman's helmet on the youth is McGill's subtle recognition of Miss Greeley's fondness for and parallel evangelical ministry to all of Denver's firemen.

ISBN: 978-0-615-61292-8

Published by Julia Greeley Guild, 2760 Larimer St., Denver CO 80205,
Phone 303-558-6685 / juliagreeleyguild @gmail.com

Copyright: Fr. Blaine Burkey, 2012.

Foreword

This is not an easy read. But I've been told it's a rewarding one, introducing to you Miss Julia Greeley, a most fascinating character of Denver's late 19th and early 20th centuries.

Aside from having an extra-ordinary subject, this study has four very serious goals which cannot be achieved without a certain amount of repetition and somewhat tedious examination.

This historical documentary study has been undertaken with the hope that it will help further the long-standing desire of many people in Denver and elsewhere that Julia Greeley's case for canonization be given an official hearing by ecclesiastical authorities.

For that reason, the book seeks to bring together everything that can presently be known about Julia Greeley and identify its sources.

Secondly, it proposes to follow chronologically the activities of the innumerable folk who since 1918 have labored to keep Julia's memory alive and to expand its orbit.

It also seeks to identify and expose misinformation that has been intermixed with Julia's story. <u>Such items and other cautions will further be called to the reader's attention by the use of underlining</u>.

Finally, yet primarily, the study seeks to enable other admirers of Julia to move her story forward, confident that they have the best information presently available.

Unfortunately striving to stay focused on the second goal has prevented, for now, the telling of Julia's story in one sequential order. For this reason, the reader may find it useful to consult at various points the Chronology given in the final pages — pages 111-115.

Enough said! Dig in, and judge for yourself.

Contents

The Day All Denver Knew	1
Connections with the Gilpins	13
Sacred Heart Apostolate	20
Renewed Interest of War Years	23
Julia and the Franciscans	31
The Empire Magazine	33
Letters to Fr. Kennedy	36
The Ryan House	43
Other Testimony Kennedy Collected	47
The Fire Houses	53
Dr. Currigan's 'Cure'	66
The Post-Kennedy Years	70
Some Special Surprises	73
In Superior and Supreme Courts	75
Divorce Case in a Nutshell	75
Julia's Pre-1887 History Revisited	77
Testimony of the Gilpins	82
Other Witnesses	98
Julia Greeley's Own Sworn Testimony	104
Julia and the Church's Court	109
Chronology of Julia's Life	111
Chronology of Julia's Cultus	116
Collaborators & Photo Credits	125
Bibliography	126
Index	136
Julia Greeley Guild and Prayer	141

Maps

Julia Greeley's Neighborhood	inside front cover
Mt. Olivet Cemetery	142
Julia Greeley at Ft. Logan & Environs	142
Julia Greeley's Denver	143

In Secret Service of the Sacred Heart

The Day All Denver Knew

Denver's very first suburb, to its immediate north, was known as Curtis Park,[1] probably because it contained the Denver area's first recreational park, also called Curtis Park.[2] Today it is part of the city's Five Points Neighborhood. The area quickly became the home of large numbers of Catholics, many of them Irish, but really a quite cosmopolitan group of Catholics; and in 1879, Denver's first Catholic bishop, Joseph Projectus Machebeuf, established Sacred Heart Parish at 2760 Larimer St. By April 25, 1880, the present church was opened.[3]

Jesuit residence and Sacred Heart Church in 1892.

Naming the city's third parish Sacred Heart was part of a distinctively Catholic devotion, developed through the centuries and particularly strong in Machebeuf's native France. The devotion was directed towards the physical heart of Jesus Christ, a living and beating symbol of His love for humankind, and ultimately towards Christ himself.[4]

Had you arrived in the Curtis Park district a century ago, you would have soon seen an old black woman who lived in the area. Everyone knew her as Julia Greeley. You well might have mistaken Julia for a common bag lady as she hobbled up and down Larimer and Lawrence streets pulling a little red wagon or lugging an old gunny sack. Sometimes they were filled with used clothing; at other times food stuffs or broken toys or firewood.[5] One time she was even seen carrying a mattress slung across her back.[6]

Often she was on the streets and back alleys at night, apparently unafraid of the dark. Julia's skin was a dark black, which frequently blended with her black dress and large floppy black hat. To

---

[1] Leonard 54.
[2] Leonard 58, 141.
[3] Noel 341.
[4] Catholics and many other Christians believe that Jesus Christ ascended into heaven and lives there in a living, albeit immortal and glorified, human body.
[5] Neil Horan to Kennedy 9-15-1978 in Kennedy papers, Archives, Archdiocese of Denver (hereafter AAD).
[6] Denver Catholic Review (hereafter DCR) 6-13-1918.

see her at close range could be somewhat daunting, as her closed left eye had been permanently destroyed in youth and usually oozed a fluid which she wiped away with a handkerchief.

You were in for a big surprise, however, when you found out who Julia Greeley really was. Actually the neighborhood had known Julia for years, and countless people had stories to tell about her. She had been in the area since Sacred Heart Parish was started. Very few, however, knew entirely who Julia was, not until that fateful weekend in 1918, when it finally came to light. Then the entire city knew.

Julia's rooming house at 2913 Walnut, built in 1902, as it looked in 1935-56 (top) and in 2011 (bottom). Julia lived there 1903-1916.

Julia was not homeless. The 1899 city directory had her living at 1421 28th St., a small one-room house on the northwest corner of the alley between Blake and Walnut streets.[7] From 1903 till 1916, she roomed at 2913 Walnut St.[8] Recently, however, she had moved to a room in the rear of 2821 Walnut St.,[9] the site of which is just to the south of today's Metropolitan Frame Company.[10]

The only one of these building still standing is fortunately the one where Julia lived the longest.

In a 1998 *Denver Catholic Register* article on Julia, Paul Hallett published a photograph of a two-story brick building at 2913 Walnut, which he identified at the house where Julia lived from 1903 till 1916. A careful comparison of the lines of the windows, doors, and especially the six brick pilasters of Hallett's photograph and those of the building still standing with the street number 2911 on front shows that the two, though considerably different in appearance, are indeed identical.[11] Real Property Records on the city web site list the building as erected in 1958, but other records in the Assessor's office show

---

[7] 1899 Denver city directory, 1903 Denver Sanborn insurance map.
[8] 1903 & 1905 Denver city directories, Sacred Heart Church and School Monitor 1:4 (Jan. 1907) 20; 3:3 (July 1913) 57; & 4:1 (July 1916) 44.
[9] 1916 & 1918 Denver city directories; Denver Post 6-10-1918.
[10] 1903 Denver Sanborn insurance map.
[11] The brick arches above the window were also still visible in the exposed interior brick work when the building was being rehabbed in January of 2012 as the new corporate offices of Spiremedia of Denver.

it was originally built in 1902. The later date is an artificially adjusted date based on further changes that were made.[12]

But back to Julia herself. On Friday morning, June 7, 1918, she left her room at 2821 Walnut Street headed to Sacred Heart Church on Larimer Street, just a block away. For years she had made this trip every morning. Today as she neared the church going along 28th Street, she became ill and went to the home of her friend Carrie Lindblad at 1221 28th St.[13] Mrs. Lindblad rushed her daughter across the street to the Jesuit residence to fetch a priest.

June 7 that year was the parish's

The triplex at 1221 28th St. was built in 1885. Julia Greeley was anointed there in the right end of building).

Br. John Echeverría SJ sent a priest to anoint Julia Greeley.

St. Joseph's Hospital (1910 view) where Julia Greeley died on June 7, 1918.

---

[12] Walter Sorrentino, assessor's office, phone conversation with Burkey, 6 Feb. 2012. The style of the brickwork ornamentation on the front of the building, the coarseness of brick exposed inside the building during January, 2012, remodeling, the appearance of the exposed lower surface of the upstairs flooring, and the footprint of the building (the width of which narrows by about four feet some 19 feet into the building) which is shown already on 1903 (with updates till 1928) and 1929 Sanborn Insurance Maps also make is quite clear that the building dates from Julia's time. From the fact that two private families were living in the building in 1924, when mixed private and commercial occupancy was first noted, and the fact that the building switched to strictly commercial use, as noted in 1926, it seems that the original building was a two-story structure, 50 x 20 feet, and that the other two-story part of the building and the one-story section, each about 46 feet wide, were added in the early 1920s or later. [Denver Householders Directory 1 (1924) 455, 2 (1926) 529].

[13] DCR 6-13-1918 & Sr. Mary Andrew Talle, S.C.L., to Kennedy 5-3-1974, in Kennedy papers, AAD. 1221 28th was the eastern third of the building, which still stands on the northwestern corner of the alley between Larimer and Lawrence streets. It is owned by Mrs. Angelica Renteria, whose relatives have lived there since the 1940s.

patronal feast of the Sacred Heart and a First Friday, a day also devoted each month to the Sacred Heart. Jesuit Brother John Echeverría (1862-1943) was opening the church for the big day, when he heard the doorbell ringing wildly over in the rectory. A little colored girl was crying, "Mama says bring the priest quick. Old Julia is dying." Father Charles A. McDonnell, an associate pastor, went and administered the last Sacraments. Julia was then moved to St. Joseph's Hospital at 18th and Humboldt, where Dr. Martin Currigan admitted her. She died at midnight[14] in Room 407.[15] The hospital's records listed Julia as "70, born in Missouri, single, a Catholic, a janitress." No diagnosis or race was given.[16]

As Julia had no known relatives, the Jesuit priests at Sacred Heart planned a funeral with the help of William P. Horan (d. 1930), local mortician, former county coroner, and prominent Catholic layman. Records at Mt. Olivet show that Julia had died from intestinal nephritis (kidney inflammation) and that Fr. William Lonergan, S.J. (1864-1925), the pastor, paid the $20 cost of the grave site and the $5 for opening the grave.[17] Records of Horan and Son Mortuary, preserved at the Denver Public Library, show charges of $20 for embalming, $65 for a casket, and another $37 for a motorized hearse, two limousines, and another car.

Fr. William Lonergan SJ, Julia's pastor, helped arrange her funeral.

Records of the ten burials before Julia's and ten after all show their accounts with Horan as settled. Julia's account showed a charge of $118, but with nothing shown as paid.[18] On the form for Julia's account, the three fields labeled *"Ordered by," "Charge to,"* and *"When rendered"* have been filled in with "Mrs. Joseph Walsh," "Miss Ryan,"[19] and "Rev. Fr. Lonergan." It would seem from all this that Julia's friends offered to pay for her funeral, but that Horan chose to cover it himself.[20]

Julia's death was reported on Saturday in the *Denver Post*, by a very short notice:[21]

---

[14] House diary, Jesuit residence, Sacred Heart Church, v. 3 p. 212.

[15] Hanna Nevin, R.N., who later served as a nurse in the old hospital building believed that Room 407 would have been just above the tree line and to the south end of the building, that is to the right side of photo above. [Nevin to Blaine Burkey, interview on Nov. 28, 2011].

[16] Sr. Mary Andrew Talle, S.C.L., to Kennedy 5-3-1974 in Kennedy papers, AAD. The building in which Julia died was torn down in 1964, soon after the present Twin Towers were dedicated. [Fishell 170 & 174].

[17] Mt. Olivet Cemetery, Interment Records, no. 8024.

[18] Horan Funeral Chapel, Funeral Records, p. 262.

[19] Probably Miss Jennie J. Ryan of whom much more will be said later.

[20] Julia's casket was an above average one. Caskets for the 21 burials studied averaged out to $57.68, with the range being from $0 to $225. Some other information given in Horan's record include Age: 70 — Occupation: Housekeeper — Birthplace: Carolina — Last place of residence: 1221 28th St. — How long resident of state: 35 years — Cause of death: Chronic intestinal nephritis. There is no indication where this information originated. It probably came from her friends. The last place of residence given was actually her friend's house from which she was taken to St. Joseph's Hospital. On both the 1880 and the 1910 census, Julia said that she was born in Missouri.

[21] Denver Post 6-8-1918, p. 9. The address given was not Julia's, but her friend Carrie Lindblot's.

> Died
> GREELEY—June 7, 1918. Julia Greeley, late of 1221 Twenty-eight street, at St. Joseph hospital. Remains at W.P. Horan and Sons funeral chapel. Funeral notice later.

The next day the *Post* had a new notice:[22]

> Died
> GREELEY—June 7, 1918. Julia Greeley, late of 2821 Walnut street. Funeral Monday morning at 8:30 from W.P. Horan & Son funeral chapel. Requiem Mass at 9 o'clock. Interment Mt. Olivet cemetery.

Loyola Chapel at 2536 Ogden, where Julia's body "lay in state" on June 9, 1918.

Julia's death was possibly mentioned at the Sunday morning Mass and maybe it was announced that, since Julia had only a small room, her body would be available for viewing in the parish's chapel of ease on Ogden Street on Sunday afternoon and buried from its main church on Monday morning, but it is really not known when the decision was made to move the viewing from Horan's chapel at 1527 Cleveland Place to the Loyola Chapel on Ogden Street.

What happened next surprised everyone. There was no email or tweeting in those days. Even television and radio were still in the future. Neither of the two daily papers had said anything about viewing in a church, yet when the body was placed there, huge crowds from all walks of life arrived and queued up to pay their respect. For five hours they passed by her body, quickly morphing the perception from her having "an ordinary wake" to her "lying in state."

Frances Belford Wayne of the Denver Post.

Frances Belford Wayne, social editor of the *Denver Post* and outspoken champion of victims of injustice and other suffering[23], wrote the first of scores of articles which would subsequently be written about Julia, and it appeared the evening of the funeral.

---

[22] Denver Post 6-9-1918, p. 8.
[23] Caroline Bancroft papers, DPL.

TRIBUTE IS PAID TO MEMORY OF JULIA GREELEY, NEGRESS

Body of Faithful Servant of Late Governor Gilpin Lies In State at Church of Sacred Heart—Woman Came Here in the Early Days

(By FRANCES WAYNE)

A plain casket under a blanket of flowers was rolled in place before the altar of the Church of the Sacred Heart Sunday afternoon at 3 o'clock. Then came a quiet crowd of men and women and children, some with flowers in their hands, to pay their last respects to the one who had closed life's accounts and entered into "the sleep that knows no waking" and whose body was lying in state before the church altar.

The people passing down the church aisle from 3 until 8 o'clock did not look on the face of one who had accumulated riches, or power, or place, or great fame flowering from high achievements.

They looked on the face of Julia Greeley, an aged negro woman, whose heritage when she entered life had been the shackles of a slave and whose bequest when she departed after eighty-five years of worthy living, is the memory of deeds kindly done; of unselfish devotion to those she loved; and a habit of giving and sharing herself and her goods, and the inspiring assurance often uttered by Julia that when she entered "the pearly gates she, too, would take her place before the throne of grace white and shining as the angels on the church altar."

Monday, a high requiem mass was sung in the Loyola chapel of Sacred Heart church by the Rev. A. Brucker and the choir in honor of Julia Greeley.

It was when Colorado was a territory that Julia Greeley came to Denver as a nurse and servant in the household of the late Governor William Gilpin. Until the Gilpin home was broken by death and the family dispersed, Julia was a faithful servant to Mrs. Gilpin and her children. In her will Mrs. Gilpin remembered "faithful Julia" with a gift of money that would have been enough to make her old age comfortable had she not had such an open hand, such a sympathetic ear.

But Julia gave until she reached her last cent—then did odd jobs here and there to earn more to give away. For, living in a room at 2821 Walnut street, her needs were few, and she had taken thought to lay aside just enough to pay for her funeral expenses.[24]

To the old-timers of Denver, Julia Greeley, with her deep lined, quizzical face, in which one eye was perpetually closed, was an institution.

Poor, old, alone, far from her native home, Julia Greeley did not ask charity or sympathy; she gave both in unstinted measure, and according to her giving she received the good will of those whose lives touched hers.

Julia Greeley was just an old black woman, who had been a slave and servant all her years.

---

[24] As mentioned earlier, others, Fr. Lonergan and William Horan, paid for Julia's funeral. She is reported to have made some provision for her funeral, but generously provided for a deceased pauper the burial plot she had owned. See the 4-13-1939 Register article quoted on p. 27.

> But because she was also a woman with a wide-winged spirit, she earned what few among the rich, powerful, mighty earn—the right to lie in state before a church altar, to have a high requiem mass sung in her honor and to be borne under flowers to her last resting place.
>
> "Old Julia" loved and lived a beautiful life. She loved kindness and was always kind; she was the symbol of fidelity and perhaps today "old black Julia" has slipped from under the burden of her years; has dipped into the waters of the river of life and is standing "white and shining before the throne of grace," glowing with happiness that all her hopes and dreams have come true and that she has been honored among people, regardless of color.[25]

What irony, that in the very act of saying that color did not matter, Ms. Wayne would suggest that Julia would no longer be black in heaven. A denizen of the 21st century might be tempted to scrap the whole article, but to do so would be a dishonest cover-up and at the same time an overreaction to something that had no intention of being offensive. To the contrary, it was meant to praise Julia, and Julia herself even took it as a compliment. One can find the concept as early as the time of King David, who prayed, "Wash me till I am whiter than snow."[26] It is still a clear example, however, of a subtle, totally thoughtless racism that hung over the entire white society of the time, even those most well intentioned. The reader should take note that similar disturbing words appeared in most articles praising Julia for many years thereafter; and when quoted in the present work, they shall appear just as they were presented to people of those other eras.

Six white angels guarded Sacred Heart's main altar.

Ms. Wayne's story was evidently not written from personal observation, as she had <u>the Sunday viewing of the body happening at Sacred Heart Church at 2760 Larimer and the Monday funeral Mass at Loyola Chapel at 2536 Ogden Street.</u> Actually it was the other way around, with the viewing being held on Ogden Street and the funeral on Larimer.[27] Wayne also had <u>Fr. Aloysius Brucker, S.J. (1851-1931), one of the parish's assistants, celebrating the funeral Mass.</u> However, Fr. Charles A. McDonnell (1875-1957), another assistant pastor, who less than a month later left for a military chaplaincy, was celebrant of the solemn high Mass; Fr. Walter A. Grace, assistant pastor at Annunciation Church, acted as deacon; and Mr. John F. Conway, S.J., a Jesuit scholastic assisting as senior class and junior debating society advisor at Sacred Heart College (now Regis University) acted as subdeacon.[28] All this is quite clear from Jesuit records.[29]

Father McDonnell gave Julia's first eulogy.

---

[25] Denver Post 6-10-1918.
[26] Psalm 51: 7.
[27] Loyola Chapel was built in 1909 and used by the parish until 1924 to accommodate its overflow crowds on Larimer St. The building is still standing and today is occupied by the Evangelist Temple Church of God in Christ.
[28] 1918 Catholic directory, p. 38.
[29] House Diary, Residence of the Sacred Heart, v. 3, p. 212, in Regis University's Jesuitica Collection. Fr. McDonnell was later the founding pastor of St. Ignatius of Loyola Church on Yale St. [Noel 353]. Grace later served time at the federal penitentiary in Leavenworth for forging a liquor permit and

The following day, the *Rocky Mountain News* ran an anonymous second story about Julia's funeral.

FORMER SLAVE DIES; BODY LIES IN STATE

—*—

Old Negress, Gilpin's Servant, Found Joy in Helping Others; Is Honored in Death

From a childhood of slavery in a Southern cotton field, to genuine honors in death, signalized by the body's reposing in state for forty-eight hours,[30] while a thousand white people filed by to pay tribute, is a far swing. There is really very little that Julia Greeley did not have in the eighty years of her life.

Yesterday morning a solemn requiem high mass was sung in Sacred Heart cathedral[31] for the much-loved black woman. The Rev. Father McDonnell of Sacred Heart was the celebrant, and acting with him as subdeacon was Prof. John Conway, whom the old woman had nursed when he was a baby.

Long a Faithful Friend

The church was filled with those whom she had served in one way or another; friends she had made while working in their households, and those she had made in the world service of charity.

Julia came to Colorado with the second Mrs. Gilpin,[32] who then was a bride. The black woman nursed the governor's children; was a faithful servant in the family until the last of them had left Denver.

To the time of her death, Mrs. Gilpin wrote to Julia, and visited her when in Denver. She remembered the black woman in her will.

Julia's later years were given to a wider service. All the money she earned, and whatever food or clothes she could beg from her many friends in high places, she gave to those in need.

---

did not resume ministry as a priest. According to Warden Walter White, Grace brought 152 prisoners into the church and was the greatest influence for good of any man who ever served time in the prison. He later was further disgraced by fathering a child by "Miss Colorado," Dulcy Burke. [Carberry 1-2]. Conway left the Jesuits in 1921 without being ordained. [Mary Struckel, Midwest Jesuit Archives, to Burkey, 2-3-2012].

[30] Other accounts speak of it being only five hours.
[31] Sacred Heart Church was not a cathedral.
[32] She did not come to Denver with Mrs. Gilpin, and Mrs. Gilpin was not the governor's second wife; he was her second husband.

Knew White Folk's Pride

A feature of Julia's charity was that she always dispensed it at night. She knew the white folk's pride—knew it would be hurt if the neighbors saw an old black woman bringing a basket of food, or carrying a mattress on her back to them. Father McDonnell tells of her calling him out of bed at midnight to carry a bucket of coal and a basket of food to a destitute family in the neighborhood.

Joseph Walsh and Joe Newman were pallbearers. The old black woman was buried at Mount Olivet cemetery with the church's highest honors.[33]

While these first articles on Julia were being discussed by local folk, the *Denver Catholic Register* was busy interviewing the local Jesuits and other people who knew Julia. The journalist who did so in all likelihood was the paper's editor, 27-year-old Matthew John Wilfred Smith, a native of Altoona, Pennsylvania. Though he became a priest in 1923 and later a monsignor and the most celebrated Catholic journalist of his day, Smith at that time was still a layman seeking to raise the quality of his paper. Later he founded and ran a nationwide chain of diocesan newspapers, all known as *Registers*.[34] Two days after Julia's funeral, Smith's front page carried a report less flowery than the Post's, but far more revealing of Julia's death and life. The *Register*'s article opened up with an extraordinary five-tiered banner headline:

Msgr. Matthew Smith, while still a layman, probably wrote the following article.

HIGHEST HONOR EVER PAID TO DEAD LAIC HERE GOES TO NEGRESS

Miss Julia Greeley, a Former Slave, Most Wonderful Apostle of the Sacred Heart

YEARS OF HEROIC PIETY BRING OLD COLORED WOMAN PRIVILEGE OF DYING ON HER LOVED PATRON'S FEAST DAY

Body Lies in State Five Hours Before Altar
While Throngs Pay Her Honor

---

[33] RMN 6-11-1918.
[34] DCR 2-2-2011.

HER CHARITY KNEW NO BOUNDS

The highest honor that has ever been paid to a Colorado Catholic layman immediately following death has been given within the last week to a negress, Julia Greeley, an aged woman who died in poverty in the Sacred Heart parish, but who is declared by the Jesuit Fathers of that church to have been the most zealous apostle of the Sacred Heart they have ever known.

And she died on the feast of the Sacred Heart. Her end came unexpectedly. But she received the full rites of the Church. The time of her death, considering the work she did in life, makes it look as if the very finger of God was present.

Body Lies in State in Church

She has the distinction of being the only simple Catholic layman in the history of Denver whose dead body lay in state in a Catholic church. From 3 until 8 o'clock on Sunday, her remains reposed in Loyola chapel, where they were viewed by a constant stream of people. There had been no great write-ups in the daily papers. How in the world all the people learned of her death and of the fact that she was to lie in state is astonishing. The fact that the news spread so quickly, without the assistance of the printed word, is proof of the great love which the Denver public had for this quaint and saintly old character.

Her life reads like that of a canonized saint. She was somewhere between 76 and 80 years old and was born in slavery, having been freed in the Civil War. She did not remember a great deal about her earlier life, but she lived at one time in Wisconsin, as is shown on her baptismal record. She was brought West from St. Louis by Mrs. Dickerson, a widow, a member of the family that led the social life of St. Louis. Mrs. Dickerson married Governor Gilpin, the great pioneer Governor of Colorado. She was a devout Catholic, and it was due to her influence, under God, that Julia Greeley became a Catholic. It is also interesting to note that Mrs. Dickerson's constant prayers finally won the conversion of her famous second husband. She constantly urged Father Brucker, S.J., of the Sacred Heart church, to pray to the Good Thief for Governor

Fr. Aloysius Brucker SJ (above) was one of Mrs. Gilpin's advisors. Julia Greeley was well known at St. Mary's (right), the proto-cathedral on Stout St.

Gilpin, since the Good Thief was Christ's last convert before his Death on Calvary. The priest gave her an approved prayer of the Church to this Good Thief, and the happy woman had the consolation of seeing Governor Gilpin receive the last rites of the Catholic Church shortly before his death.

In Parish Since Founding

After her conversion, Julia Greeley for a long time attended the old Cathedral on Stout street, and she is remembered by pioneer Catholics as a familiar figure there. But she had been identified with the Sacred Heart parish ever since its establishment in 1879. And no other layman has worked harder from that day to this for the upbuilding of the church.

She has been a daily Communicant practically ever since her conversion, said Father [Charles A.] McDonnell, S.J., this week. She was charitable to an astonishing degree and had a devotion to the Sacred Heart, the Blessed Virgin and the Blessed Sacrament that was marvelous. "It was not sentimentality, but real piety," said the priest.

No other Denverite has equaled her record in distributing Sacred Heart League leaflets. Denver is a big city and very widespread, but she used to visit every firehouse and hand out leaflets to the Catholic firemen. There was not a fireman, Catholic or non-Catholic, in Denver who did not know old Julia, for she never missed a month going the rounds with the leaflets. She took copies of the Messenger of the Sacred Heart to every firehouse monthly, and often gave the boys there other Catholic literature. As regular as clockwork every year, she got fifty subscriptions to The Messenger of the Sacred Heart and sold something like 200 Catholic almanacs. And she could neither read, write nor count!

Begged for the Poor

Her charity was so great that only God knows its extent. She was constantly visiting the poor and giving them assistance from her own slender means. When she found their needs so great that she could not help them with her own goods, she begged for them. Her charity was as delicate as it was great. She realized that white people, no matter how poor, might feel a little sensitive in receiving assistance from an old colored woman, so she went at night to their homes to deliver the goods she had begged, in order to keep the neighbors from seeing her. She had even been seen going thru the streets at night with a mattress on her back. Many and many a times she was seen carrying coal and groceries. Yet she was so poor herself that the city charity department had been furnishing her with fuel and groceries.

On one occasion, a priest of the Sacred Heart parish found her pushing a baby carriage along at night. She had found a poor family that needed it. So she had gone out and begged for it. On another occasion one of the Jesuits met her carrying a broken doll. In answer to his questions, she told him that she was taking it home to fix it up and intended to give it to some child.

Lover of Children

She loved children with that intensity found in the saints. When some woman of the neighborhood wanted to go shopping and Julia was around, Julia was always willing to look after the babies. Every door in the parish was open to her. Her marvelous piety and her constant charity made her the friend of everybody. She was known in every convent of Denver, for, as might be expected, she loved Sisters. And the Sisters loved her. It was a standing rule at the Sacred Heart rectory that Julia could come in and get a meal any time she wanted it. She could not possibly wear out her welcome.

She was left a little money by the Gilpins, but lost $900 in the failure of a Denver bank. Whatever else she had, she gave away. Nobody asked for help in vain from Julia Greeley. She was victimized many times by charity frauds. But Julia's rule seemingly was that it was better to give than to be too careful and deny assistance to someone who needed it.

She earned about $10 or $12 a month. She swept and dusted the Sacred Heart church every week and did other little odd jobs. With this little money and what she got from the city, she found enough to live and to help others. She had a little room on Walnut and Twenty-eighth. Here she lived alone, for Julia Greeley never married. She left no relatives so far as is known.

Fasted Frequently

She never ate any breakfast, except when she was going to do heavy work and it was absolutely necessary to have sustenance. This fasting was a religious act, and was not caused by her poverty, for her friends would gladly have given her this meal. She was asked various times by Father McDonnell, whether she had eaten breakfast and replied: "My Communion is my breakfast."

Last Friday, she was on her way to the Sacred Heart church to receive Communion and hear Mass. She became very ill and went to a colored friend's home across the street from the rectory. One of the priests was called. She was removed to St. Joseph's hospital and died late that day, after being fortified by a saintly life and all the last sacraments of the Church.

When her body lay in state, limousines and giant touring cars came carrying the rich to see her. The poor flocked to the chapel in throngs. When Father McDonnell recited the Rosary for her soul at 7:30, the chapel was well filled.

The Sacred Heart church was crowded Monday morning at her funeral. The prosperous and the poor, the educated and the uneducated, the prominent and the unknown were there—proud to pay homage to the aged negress.

Father McDonnell celebrated the Solemn High Mass, Father Walter Grace was the deacon and the Rev. John Conway, S.J., whom she had held often in her arms as a baby, was subdeacon. Father McDonnell spoke, bringing out most of the facts related above.

She was buried in the finest plot procurable in Mount Olivet cemetery. She had a splendid funeral. W. P. Horan, who managed it, gave her the best he knew how and was present himself at her burial and when her body was placed in the chapel.

Member of Third Order

She was a member of the Third Order of St. Francis at St. Elizabeth's church, and was buried in the Franciscan habit. She constantly worked for the upbuilding of Sacred Heart parish. Whenever a fair or a play or any other benefit was held, Julia always sold more tickets than anybody else.

She was not at all beautiful physically. One eye was gone and her face was wrinkled. But she had a smile that you could never forget. When Mother Pancratia Bonfils, founder of Loretto Heights academy, died a few years ago, Julia went to the Sacred Heart rectory and arranged to have a High Mass sung for her soul. "She was good to me," she said. "She told me that I would be white in heaven."

Her skin was black, but her heart was whiter than the purest snow. She would as soon have confessed her sins on the street as anywhere else, for she did nothing of which she could be very ashamed. So do you wonder that this old negro woman had the distinction of being called to the other life on the Feast of the Sacred Heart?[35]

The reader may have noticed: in five 1918 sources, Julia was referred to as being 70, 70, 80, 85, and 76-80. So how old was she? George Urquhart had asked Julia that very question. "Mr. George, I don't ask you any personal questions," she replied, and smiling added, "and I don't answer any." Urquhart felt it was because, being an ex-slave, she didn't know how old she was.[36] And that was indeed the truth of the matter.[37]

Connection with the Gilpins

Julia's age was not the only thing she did not know. The record of her entrance into the Catholic Church at Sacred Heart Church on June 26, 1880, less than two months after the dedication of the church, makes it clear that she did not know the full names of her parents, nor was she aware of whether or not she had been baptized before. Fr. Charles M. Ferrari, S.J. (1842-1914),[38]

---

[35] DCR 6-13-1918.

[36] Simpson to Kennedy, 6-23-1978, in Kennedy papers, AAD.

[37] George Hill Urquhart, an Episcopalian, was secretary and treasurer of the John McDonough Security Co. [1917 Denver city directory]. According to his granddaughter, Mary Anna Simpson, he helped St. Frances Cabrini find the site which is now the Cabrini Shrine in Golden and was the one who warned her there was no water available on the land, which led to her miraculous provision of a spring which is still producing. [http://www.ourbelovedjuliagreeley.blogspot.com].

[38] Fr. Charles M. Ferrari, S.J. (1842-1914), the priest who baptized Julia conditionally, was the son of a Neapolitan baron and descended from one of the doges of Venice. Ordained in 1874, he served in Philadelphia and rural Maryland before coming to Denver in 1879. His obituary in the *Register* said "he was the idol of the people, particularly the boys" and in his young days was "one of the handsomest men who ever occupied a Denver pulpit." Later on he completed the church in New Albuquerque; built the first church in Needles, Cal., and the one in Delta, Colo.; and built a Catholic hospital in El Paso and a Catholic school for Mexicans there. He also served in Ouray,

conditionally baptized her. Her parents were listed simply as George and Cerilda. Her sponsors were Celeste Tracy and Bernard Taylor, sister and nephew of Mrs. Gilpin. There is nothing in the baptismal record to support the *Register*'s claim that the record says "she lived at one time in Wisconsin." The record does, however, say she was born in Hannibal, Missouri.[39]

Julia surely knew who her slave master was and where she got the name Greeley, and when she became a free woman, but all that has remained her secret. There are at least three suggestions as to when she got the name Greeley. Fr. Kennedy wondered if she had taken it from her former master. Considering the brutal treatment she is said to have received from her master,[40] this does not seem at all likely. Richard S. Brownlee, director of the State Historical Society of Missouri, who grew up in the Hannibal area, told Fr. Kennedy, "It was not necessarily customary for a slave to assume the name of their former owner. More often than not, they selected the name of persons they admired, or someone famous."[41]

Someone later suggested she got the name Greeley while working for the second wife of Horace Greeley, the great opinion maker of his day, who brought her to Denver.[42] But that never happened! Horace Greeley's only wife died less than a month before he did, and she never lived in St. Louis or Denver.[43]

It is more likely that Julia took the name Greeley from Horace himself, who endeared himself to many black people of his day by strongly urging Lincoln to emancipate the slaves.[44] Various notes by Fr. Kennedy suggest that some people (for example Agnes Hines Erger, No. 28 on p. 55) confusedly identified the Gilpins as Greeleys.[45]

From both obituaries given above, it obviously was the common opinion nearly a century ago that Julia Gilpin (1836-1912) brought Julia Greeley with her to Denver.[46] Mrs. Gilpin was the scion of a wealthy French-Creole Catholic family in St. Louis, and a great, great granddaughter of the founding father of St. Louis, Pierre de Laclede Ligeste.[47] A granddaughter of General

---

    Cañon City, and Pueblo. At Albuquerque, he is said to have done "wonderful work among the consumptives, sweeping out their cabins, carrying their fuel and doing all sorts of menial service. At Cañon City, he instituted the practice of saying Mass in the penitentiary." Father was fluent in seven languages and exceedingly humble. At some point later in life he left the Jesuit community. He died in Mercy Hospital, Denver, on June 10, 1914 [DCR 6-1-1914], and is buried at Mt. Olivet Cemetery (sect. 2, block 2, grave 58) [Interment Records, No. 5957] amid numerous diocesan priests.

[39] Sacred Heart Church, baptismal records, v. 1, p. 9; Beckwith 107-108.

[40] Testimonies of Eleanor Pavella Castellan, No. 22 on p. 48; Agnes Hines Erger, No. 28 on p. 55; Marguerite Graves Stephens, No. 40 on p. 64.

[41] Brownlee to Kennedy, April 8, 1974, in Kennedy papers, AAD.

[42] DCR 2-7-1990, quoting Paul N. Stewart, founder of the Black American West Museum; Mason 9.

[43] Greeley Family History web site.

[44] Ibid. The 1870 U.S. census for Missouri showed six black men named Greel(e)y, of whom three were named Haris, Harris and Horace.

[45] Noel Collection, Blair-Caldwell African-American Research Library (hereafter BCAARL) & Castillo Collection, Archives, Capuchin Province of Mid-America (hereafter ACPMA).

[46] The common opinion was only partially correct. This will be explained much later.

[47] Pratte 59-60, Cannon 267.

Bernard Pratte, Sr., cofounder of one of West's largest fur trading companies, and daughter of General Bernard Pratte, Jr., a St. Louis mayor, Julia spent the years 1851, 1852, and 1853 at St. Elizabeth Seton's St. Joseph Academy in Emmitsburg, Maryland.[48] When she was about 20 years old, Colonel William Gilpin (1815-1894), a reputed veteran of Fremont's second expedition and of the Mexican and Indian wars,[49] proposed to her. Miss Pratte declined, however, as he was 23 years her senior,[50] and she did not love him.

Instead, she married Captain John H. Dickerson at St. Francis Xavier Church in St. Louis on Mar. 27, 1860. The Dickersons had four children—Louise, Sidney, Julia, and Elizabeth—before the Captain died on March 2, 1872.[51]

By then William Gilpin had served for a year (1861-1862) as the first territorial governor of Colorado and then amassed a large fortune in Colorado real estate. It was thought, moreover, that he did more than any other person to promote the settlement of both Kansas and Colorado.[52] Gilpin's ardor for the widow Dickerson had continued to burn for much of two decades, and after he had proposed several more times, Julia accepted.[53] She married him on Feb. 16, 1874, at the home of her uncle, U.S. Senator Lewis V. Bogy (1813-1877), with John Patrick Ryan (1831-1911), coadjutor archbishop of St. Louis and later archbishop of Philadelphia,[54] officiating.

---

[48] Sr. M. Felicia, S.C., to Kennedy, Emmitsburg, 4-4-1974, in Kennedy papers, AAD.

[49] Though Gilpin's obituary in the Denver Republican 1-21-1894 speaks of his being a 2nd lieutenant in the 2nd Dragoons in the Florida war, a major with Colonel Doniphan in the Mexican war, and commanding colonel of a regiment raised in 1847 to combat depredations along the Santa Fe Trail, and was generally known as Colonel Gilpin, he is nowhere listed in Heitman's register of 18th and 19th century U.S. army officers.

[50] William Gilpin Collection, MS268, in Colorado Historical Society Library.

[51] Dickerson was born in Ohio in 1821 or 1822 and graduated from West Point 11th in his class. He then served in the 4th and 1st Artilleries in the War with Mexico 1847-48, the Florida hostilities against the Seminoles 1850-51 and 1852-53, and the Civil War 1861-64. Among other things, he was Acting Adjutant General of the Department of New Mexico 1848-49, constructed the road from Omaha to Ft. Kearney 1856-57, was quartermaster in the Utah expedition 1856-57, and was chief quartermaster for the Department of the Ohio 1861-62 and 1863-64. After resigning from the Army Mar. 31, 1864, he was Commission Agent for Army quartermaster supplies in Cleveland 1864-65 and commission merchant in St. Louis 1866-71. In 1865 he was breveted major for effective and meritorious service in the Department of the Ohio. He died at St. Louis, Mar. 2, 1872. [Cullen 2: 312, Heitman 373] Mrs. Gilpin said Dickerson died in 1870, but this was given from memory while under stress on the witness stand.

[52] Garrigan 3: 84.

[53] Mrs. Gilpin said that after several proposals, she finally gave in when the Colonel said he had already planned a trip to China, but would cancel it if she would marry him.

[54] Archbishop Ryan was later the advisor and ecclesiastical superior of St. Katherine Drexel (1858-1955), whose passion was the evangelization of native Americans and Afro-Americans. The only known connection of Julia and St. Katherine is that among her papers, St. Katherine had a typed copy of the *Register*'s 6-13-1918 obituary of Julia, so she apparently knew of her. [Dr. Stephanie Morris to Burkey, Bensalem, Pa., Sept. 9, 2011] Mother Drexel was in Denver on Oct. 18, 1911 and in the afternoon visited Sacred Heart College, just across the street from where Julia Greeley was cooking for the Ryan sisters. [Jesuit House Diary, Sacred Heart College, Oct. 18, 1911, p. 108]

According to the former governor's biographer, Thomas Karnes, "The couple left that same evening, February 16, 1874, for a honeymoon in Colorado and California. They were accompanied by Julia's eldest, nine-year-old Louise Dickerson, and a nurse, an ex-slave known as One-Eyed Julia Greeley."[55]

The Friday *Rocky Mountain News* announced the new family's arrival in Denver under Personal Notes:

> GILPIN — Ex-Governor William Gilpin returned to Denver yesterday. He brings with him a wife, and child. He was married on Monday last in St. Louis by Rt. Rev. Bishop Ryan to Mrs. Julia Dickerson nee Pratt [sic]. Many friends of the governor will be rejoiced to hear of his return and his marriage.[56]

The following Thursday, the same paper announced that "Ex-Governor Gilpin started for San Francisco, with his family, last night."[57] Based on Karnes assertion that Miss Greeley was with them, one might presume she also went along on the honeymoon in San Francisco, but that never happened. Forty days later the paper carried another Personal:

> GILPIN — Ex-Governor William Gilpin and family returned from California yesterday and are domiciled at the American house.[58]

Professor Helen Cannon claimed that Julia was "an important and beloved member of the household" the Gilpins set up at 1743 Champa St. in Denver.[59] According to Karnes the other three Dickerson children came to Denver,[60] and in due time there were also three Gilpin children.[61] The 1880 U.S. Census for Denver shows Julia Greeley and two much younger Irish-born servants living with the Gilpins at 443 Champa St., which was later renumbered 1743 Champa.[62]

name	race	gender	state	age	relationship	occupation	birthplace
Gilpin William	W	M	M	57		ex-Gov. of Colo.	Del.
Julia P.	W	F	M	41	wife	keeps house	Mo.
William	W	M	S	5	son		Colo.
Mary L.	W	F	S	5	daughter		Colo.
Louis B.	W	M	S	3	son		Colo.
Dickerson Louisa F.	W	F	S	15	stepdaughter	attends school	Mo.
Sidney J.	W	M	S	13	stepson	attends school	Mo.

---

[55] Karnes 331-332, based on Cannon 271. The couple and Mrs. Gilpin's oldest daughter did come at that time, but Julia Greeley was not with them. More about this later.
[56] RMN 2-20-1874.
[57] RMN 2-26-1874.
[58] RMN 4-7-1874.
[59] Cannon 267.
[60] Karnes 332.
[61] Baptismal register, St. Mary's Church, Denver, 1: 137 & 2:69. Mary Louise had actually been baptized earlier, presumably in danger of death, and Matz supplied the ceremonies.
[62] 1880 U.S. Census, Colorado, series T9, roll 88, p. 232; 1888 Denver city directory.

Julie		W	F	S	11	stepdaughter	attends school	Mo.
Elizabeth		W	F	S	9	stepdaughter	attends school	Mo.
Greeley, Julia		B	F	S	40	servant	domest.serv.	Mo. illiterate[63]
McDonald, Cecilia		W	F	S	20	servant	domest.serv.	Ireland
McCarty, Eliza		W	F	S	21	servant	domest.serv.	Ireland

Colonel Gilpin saw to it that his Dickerson stepchildren all went to St. Mary's School and other Catholic schools, but sent his own children to public schools.[64]

Julia Gilpin helped bring Julia Greeley into the Church and through the Church to the people of Denver. It has been suggested that the inspiration came to the Gilpin <u>nurse when she witnessed the baptisms and other sacramental events of the Dickerson and Gilpin children</u>.[65] It was also thought she was <u>present also when her employer sang in the choir</u> at the proto-cathedral on Stout Street, between 15th and 16th streets.[66] More about these false claims later.

Miss Greeley's *Register* obituary made it clear she was "remembered by pioneer Catholics as a familiar figure at Old St. Mary's."[67] Julia herself acknowledged Mrs. Gilpin's role in her conversion. When someone suggested she ask her employer to leave her some money, she replied very simply, "Oh, she gave me sumpin more'n money; she gave me my faith."[68]

Col. William Gilpin, Colorado's first territorial governor, 1861-1862 (Photo courtesy of Colorado Historical Society).

Julia Greeley's obituary in the *Register* also said <u>that Julia Gilpin brought her husband into the Church</u>.[69] If this indeed happened, it was done very secretly, and even Bishop Nicholas Matz was unaware of it. In his graveside eulogy, he made it very clear that he was there as the Colonel's friend, and not as his minister, and that the ex-governor was not being buried in consecrated ground.

Julia Pratte Gilpin, Greeley's first employer in Denver (Photo courtesy of Colorado State Historical Society, which received it from her great grandson, John H. Dalrymple of Brooklyn).

Just the same, Matz said that when he came to Colorado 20 years earlier, "Governor Gilpin, though not a Catholic, came every Sunday with his family to the cathedral; whether in the church or out of it, he always manifested the greatest respect for the church <…> His noble wife and

---

[63] By 1887, Julia was able to say she could read a little, but not write (see p. 104) On the 1910 Census (see p. 45), Julia answered "Yes" to both the ability to read and the ability to write.
[64] Karnes 333. St. Joseph's Hospital had been built in 1876 on land donated by the Gilpins. [Fishell 42-44, DCR 11-7-1968].
[65] Kennedy 1974, pp. 13-14, citing Theodora O'Donnell Arnold.
[66] Porchea 101, RMN 12-24-1880.
[67] DCR 6-13-1918.
[68] Testimony of Agnes Hines Erger, No. 28 on p. 55.
[69] DCR 6-13-1918; also Hafen-Hallett 383 & 387.

family, being such devoted Catholics, this formed a link binding us in a manner also to the governor."[70]

Life in the Gilpin house was far from that of a utopia, and Julia Greeley had to seek employment elsewhere. It is really beyond the scope of this study to go deeply into the marital woes of the Gilpins. It's enough to say that divorce proceedings which began in 1887 were widely followed by the press.[71] This went on for four years, and the Colonel won his case before a superior court jury and gained custody of his children, whom he forcibly removed to a newly-purchased house at 1321 S. 14th St., now known as (North) Bannock St.[72]. On an appeal to the Supreme Court *on error*, the superior court was overturned and the case remanded. The Colonel chose not to have the case retried, and eventually husband and wife were reunited in the Colonel's new home on South 14th St.[73]

Commenting on the reunion, Fr. Kennedy said, "One cannot help wondering how much they were helped by the prayers of Julia Greeley."[74] Of course, there is no way of knowing that, but as later will become clear, it doesn't seem likely!

During the time of the Gilpins' separation, the Colonel's maiden sister, Mary Sophie, took care of Gilpins' three children who were in his custody.[75] During the same time, Julia Gilpin's children by Dickerson became adults.

Marguerite Graves Stephens later said that her mother had told her that during the divorce proceedings Julia Greeley had testified on behalf of Mrs. Gilpin, which prompted the Colonel to blackball her so that she couldn't find work and that the Jesuits at Sacred Heart had hired her as cook.[76]

The Gilpin's son Willie, was killed in a fall from a cliff on a fishing trip in Platte

Graves in Mt. Olivet Cemetery of William, Willie, and Julia Gilpin.

---

[70] Matz, Denver Republican 1-24-1894. A note found in the Kennedy papers, Noel Collection, BCAARL, suggested that a reference to Julia Greeley's being a Catholic was found in AAD by Fr. Edward Woeber in Matz's correspondence with Msgr. Percy Phillips. A very careful examination by the present study of a catalog of Matz's extensive correspondence failed to turn up a single hint of any such letter.

[71] Denver Republican 6-18-1887, 7-2-1887, 12-9-1887, 12-10-1887.

[72] 1903 Denver Sanborn insurance map v. 1, p. 39.

[73] Kennedy 1979 p. 33; Karnes 334-336; 1888 Denver city directory.

[74] Kennedy notes, Noel Collection, BCAARL & Castillo Collection, ACPMA.

[75] Karnes 336.

[76] Testimony of Marguerite Graves Stephens, No. 40 on p. 63.

Canyon in 1892,[77] and was one of the first people buried in Mt. Olivet Cemetery. He was buried from the Catholic cathedral.[78] His father died intestate of heart disease at the age of 80 on Jan. 20, 1894, and was buried in Mt. Olivet three days later.[79]

Julia Gilpin survived for another 18 years and left a bequest for her former domestic servant. She maintained a residence in Denver, but spent most of her time visiting children in New York and St. Louis, where she died of a chronic gastric problem on Dec. 21, 1912[80] and was buried next to Willie, on the other side from her husband, on Dec. 24.[81].

Both Frances Wayne and the *Register* referred to Mrs. Gilpin's legacy towards her former servant. Mrs. Wayne said it was "a gift of money that would have been enough to make her old age comfortable had she not had such an open hand, such a sympathetic ear."[82] The *Register* said she lost $900 of it in a bank failure.[83] Such information probably came from Fr. McDonnell's eulogy or from Br. John Echeverría (see. No. 27 on p. 54). It was repeated later on by Mrs. Arnold (see No. 1 on p. 36); Fr. Kennedy, who said she left $1,000 to "faithful Julia;"[84] Mary O'Sullivan;[85] and Mary Ann Simpson who even identified the Hibernian Bank as the one that failed.[86]

Mrs. Gilpin appears to have gotten a lot more credit than was warranted. Extensive records of her estate paint a whole other picture. Her will, written three years before her death, said that, if the estate of her deceased sister Celeste Tracy [Julia Greeley's godmother] was not settled before Julia Gilpin's own death, then from this legacy once settled they should give to "Julia Greeley, colored, the sum of one hundred ($100) dollars, if she be living." Deputy Sheriff Robert L. Owens personally informed Miss Greeley of this contingent legacy on Dec. 30, 1912.

The estate was not settled for another 32 years. Meanwhile, however, on Mar. 30, 1914, the administrator of the estate informed the probate court that at the time of Mrs. Gilpin's death Mrs. Tracy's estate had already been settled and Mrs. Gilpin had already been paid. As a result, Julia

---

[77] Denver Republican 7-17-1892; Colorado Sun 7-20-1892

[78] Willie was the 12th person buried there on July 18, 1892, just 13 days after the cemetery's first interment. He was buried from the Catholic cathedral. He is entered in the Mt. Olivet Cemetery Interment Records, as both Nos. 12 and 412. From this, a reference to a removal, and the explicit testimony of Bishop Matz, it is certain that Willie was first buried in section 2, block 19, row 1, and moved to section 9, block 1, row 1, grave 2, on May 23, 1894, three months after his father was buried in section 9, block 1, row 1, grave 1, on Jan. 23, 1894. At the Colonel's funeral, Matz said that Willie "reposes in yonder consecrated spot. In due time we propose reverently to raise him and consecrate for him a resting place alongside his father." [Matz, Denver Republican 1-15-1894] .

[79] Denver Republican 1-24-1894. In the Mt. Olivet records, Colonel Gilpin's funeral was at first listed as being from the Catholic cathedral, but this was struck through and St. Mark's Episcopal Church substituted. Interment Records No. 361.

[80] Denver Post 12-23-1912; Karnes 340.

[81] Mt. Olivet Cemetery Interment Records, No. 5213 (sect. 9, block 1, row 1, grave 3).

[82] Denver Post 6-10-1918 .

[83] DCR 6-13-1918.

[84] Kennedy (1974) 14.

[85] DCR 2-22-1995.

[86] http://www.ourbelovedjuliagreeley.blogspot.com.

Greeley received exactly nothing from Mrs. Gilpin's estate.[87] Mrs. Gilpin could have already given Miss Greeley the money herself, but Deputy Owens reported nothing about the contingent legacy already being fulfilled.[88]

Returning now to 1918 — a month after Julia's funeral, the *Register* carried two more items relating to her. The one took notice of an article in *Ave Maria* magazine, which, commenting on the honors paid Julia, said: "Worldly philosophers will see in the demonstrations thus recorded a striking instance of the democracy of the American Catholic Church; Scripture students will look on them as exemplification of the dictum of Proverbs: 'Favor is deceitful and beauty is vain; the woman that fears the Lord, she shall be praised'."[89]

The other item was a short piece titled, "People Deem It Honor to Distribute Leaflets Colored Julia Handed Out." It told how several people wanted to take over Julia's ministry of distributing leaflets of the League of the Sacred Heart to the firehouses of the city and other places that "the saintly old colored woman" used to care for every month. "It is no small thing to visit every firehouse in Denver monthly," the Register noted.[90]

Sacred Heart Apostolate

The leaflets and other literature mentioned here and in the *Register*'s June article were literature of the Apostleship of Prayer which was being promoted internationally by the Jesuits and their coworkers. The Apostleship had begun in France in 1844, when Fr. Francis X. Gautrelet told a group of Jesuit seminarians eager to work on the missions: "Be apostles now, apostles of prayer! Offer everything you are doing each day in union with the Heart of our Lord for what He wishes, the spread of the Kingdom for the salvation of souls."

Members of the Apostleship, known also as the League of the Sacred Heart—today there are at least 40 million members—consecrate their daily work to the Sacred Heart and thus join their daily prayers for a specific monthly intention. The leaflets which Julia distributed named the month's intention and explained the urgent need to include it in prayer. By 1909 the pope himself was regularly involved in the selection of these intentions, but it is not known exactly when that practice began.[91]

---

[87] Probate case 15579, City and County of Denver, Colo., Colorado State Archives.

[88] There is a copy of an earlier "last will" by Julia Gilpin, written Dec. 10, 1886, but it contains nothing relative to Julia Greeley. [Julia Gilpin Collection, MS2544, Colorado Historical Society Library].

[89] Proverbs 31: 30; DCR 7-18-1918 p. 2. Ave Maria magazine, published at South Bend, Ind., was in 1900, "the most popular English-language Catholic magazine in the world." [https://www.avemariapress,com/about/ (cited 3-1-2012)].

[90] DCR 7-18-1918, p. 5.

[91] Jim Kubicki, national promoter, Apostleship of Prayer, to Burkey, Milwaukee, May 18, 2011. On May 25, 1899, Pope Leo XIII published "Annum Sacrum," an encyclical letter encouraging consecration to the Sacred Heart. In 1900, Denver's Bishop Matz announced indulgences for the Feast of the Sacred Heart and for the litany and other prayers honoring the Sacred Heart [Matz to the clergy, Denver, June 4, 1900, in AAD]. A couple months later he forwarded the pope's letter to the Denver church. [Matz to clergy and laity, Aug. 10, 1900 in AAD] Several years later, in a

The first magazine called the *Messenger of the Sacred Heart* was published by the Apostleship in 1861, and eventually various parts of the world started their own magazines with the same title. Today there are at least 50 different Messengers of the Sacred Heart, as well as 40 other periodicals sponsored by the Apostleship of Prayer. Each of them basically promotes devotion to the Sacred Heart and tries to develop an awareness of the needs of the Universal Church.

Shown here is a copy of the 4-page Apostlehip of Prayer leaflet which Julia would have distributed in January of 1909, if her distribution ministry had started by that time (actual size 5 3/16" x 3 7/16").

Since Julia Greeley was somewhat illiterate, one has to believe that someone informed her each month of the general content of the leaflets she was recommending to others, and that she also was consecrating her own daily activity to the intentions set forth by the Apostleship. This surely was one of the secrets of her own spirituality: to place all of her day's activities into the secret service of the Sacred Heart.

The League of the Sacred Heart at the Larimer St. parish had a meeting of its promoters at 3 o'clock on the third Sunday of each month. It also had a Communion of Reparation every First Friday.[92] That's where Julia was headed the day she died.

---

letter concerning the annual clergy retreat, he announced a papal blessing and a consecration to the Sacred Heart. [Matz to Msgr. Robinson and Rev. Brethren, May 26, 1907, in AAD].
[92] Sacred Heart Church and School Monitor 4:5 (July 1918) 6.

On the last page of the July 1918 issue of Sacred Heart Parish's semi-annual publication, Julia's recent passing was recalled in a short paragraph: "Old 'colored' Julia is gone to her reward. She died a beautiful death on the Feast of the Sacred Heart — a fitting close to forty years of untiring labor as an apostle of the Sacred Heart."[93]

"Uncle Tom" Mullen cooked at St. Thomas Seminary.

Memory of Julia no doubt remained long in the mind of her contemporaries and probably weaved its way in and out of many conversations over the years, but its first reappearance in the public press was four and half years later, when shortly before Christmas of 1922, another ex-slave and Secular Franciscan, Uncle Tom Mullen, died and was buried in a Third Order habit and, because of his extraordinary service as cook at St. Thomas Seminary, he was buried with a Pontifical Requiem Mass at St. John the Evangelist Church (on the northeast corner of 5th and Josephine).[94] The *Denver Catholic Register* titled a front-page article "Two Laics Most Honored by Church at Burial in History of Denver Were Humble Negroes." Recalling Julia's extraordinary charitable work and her promotion of devotion to the Sacred Heart, the article revealed, "When death claimed Julia Greeley..., priests who had known her well declared her the most saintly character they had ever met."[95]

On the 10th anniversary of Julia's death, a "Listening In" column in the *Register* noted that the "last issue of the St. Elizabeth chronicle, magazine of a St. Louis [Missouri] Negro parish" had reprinted verbatim the *Register*'s own lengthy 1918 obituary. The editor went on to call Julia "an ugly one-eyed woman" whose soul "was like a lily." He then gave some illustrations of her charity and apostolic spirit and revealed possibly for the first time that she made her rounds of the fire houses on foot. "After her death," he recalled, "there was a scramble to get a share of the work she had made eminent in the distribution of those leaflets."[96]

Renewed Interest of the War Years

It was another 11 years then till Julia's cult surfaced again in the public media. On Feb. 23, 1939, Fr. Eugene P. Murphy, S.J. (d. 1973) of the Radio League of the Sacred Heart at St. Louis University asked students at St. Mary's Academy in Denver to help him find information on Julia Greeley for a radio program he hoped to air.[97] He must have contacted the *Denver Catholic Register*, too, for just a week later, the paper announced that her life would be reviewed in a series of radio programs to be broadcast on a new radio program, The Sacred Heart Hour, which Fr. Murphy was about

Fr. Eugene Murphy SJ made Julia known nationwide by radio.

---

[93] Sacred Heart Church and School Monitor 4:5 (July 1918) 60.
[94] Two other articles, one by Albert W. Stone, found in the James Harrison scrapbooks, v. 1, at BCAARL, noted that Mullen was the only black person present in a church packed with church dignitaries.
[95] DCR 12-21-1922.
[96] DCR 6-14-1928.
[97] Murphy to Machebeuf History Club, 2-23-1939 in Kennedy papers, AAD.

to begin airing on station WEW at St. Louis University, beginning Sunday, March 19. The *Register* said, "Her story will be used to exemplify the eleventh promise made to St. Margaret Mary: 'Those who shall promote this devotion shall have their names written in My Heart never to be blotted out'." The paper used the occasion to repeat much of the content of its 1918 article, adding a few new items, such as avowing, "When Julia Greeley died, Denver lost a woman whom everybody believed to be a saint," and calling her the Apostle of the Sacred Heart. It ended saying, "There was nothing beautiful about Julia Greeley—except her soul and her smile. She had only one eye, her face was wrinkled and probably ugly, but her smile showed forth the charity of Christ and her soul was white as white."[98]

The article was immediately effective. The very next week, the paper gave its younger readers their first glimpse of the visage of Julia Greeley — the now familiar photo of her in a white dress and her large black hat, seated and holding her "Little White Angel," as she called her tiny charge. The photo, taken in McDonough Park across Federal Boulevard from St. Catherine's Church in April of 1916, was taken by Father William W. Ryan, the church's founding pastor. The little girl holding the rosary was Marjorie Ann, seven-months-old daughter of George and Agnes (Rooney) Urquhart. To date, it is the only known photo of Julia Greeley.

Fr. William W. Ryan, founding pastor of St. Catherine's, who took the photo.

Marjorie Ann was by now 24, living at 1361 Bannock St. (across the street from the present site of Denver Art Museum and just up the block from where the Gilpins had lived at 1321); and she and her mother provided the Register with both the image and something of its history:

The only known photo of Denver's Angel of Charity, shows her with Marjorie Ann Urquhart, who first made it available in 1939.

---

[98]DCR Mar. 2, 1939.

Saintly Negress Nurse
'To Little White Angel'

[....] Even when Marjorie was so small she couldn't sit up, her mother recalls, Julia begged Mrs. Urquhart to let her take the baby on the streetcar to Sacred Heart church. The mother compromised by allowing Marjorie to be wheeled in her buggy to St. Catherine's church, which was within walking distance of the Urquhart home.

So anxious was Julie for her little charge to be a practical Catholic that she placed a rosary in the infant's tiny fingers when she was four months old and diligently attempted to teach her to pray.

Julia's coming to the Urquhart home was quite accidental. Mrs. Urquhart, who desired to employ a maid, was sitting on her front porch one day more than 20 years ago when she saw an old Negress walking slowly down the street. She called to her, asking if she would come in and wash the floors. The woman accepted her offer and entered the house. She immediately noticed the holy pictures in the rooms, and remarked, "You must be a Catholic."

Julia told Mrs. Urquhart how she distributed leaflets of the League of the Sacred Heart throughout the city and how she worked at Sacred Heart church. She remarked on the absence of children in the home—the Urquhart's only child, a boy, had died thirteen years previously—and said that before long they would have a girl. Her prediction was true, and after Marjorie's birth she came regularly to the Urquhart residence.

A daily communicant, Julia never ate until she came to take care of Marjorie about 11 o'clock each morning. She stayed until 7 o'clock in the evening. All day long, as she went about her work, Julia prayed and sang songs to the Sacred Heart.[99]

George and Agnes (Rooney) Urquhart lived at 4270 Hooker. The church Julia visited in St. Catherine's Parish, built in 1912-1913, was demolished in 1934 and eventually in 1952 replaced with the present one.[100] Many years later, Marjorie added an important detail which was left out at this time, perhaps by the paper. That is that Mrs. Urquhart had told Julia that "she was not able to have any more children," and Julia responded, "There will be a little white Angel running around this house. I will pray, and you'll see."[101]

Five weeks after the remarkable photo appeared, the *Register* revealed that the Urquharts were not alone in remembering Julia. The *Register* ran back-to-back two more articles revealing recollections of another five Denverites.

---

[99] DCR 3-9-1939.
[100] Noel 347.
[101] Simpson to Kennedy, July 10, 1978, in Kennedy papers, AAD. See No. 13 on p. 42.

Capt. George S. Young, U.S. 7th Infantry, employed Julia at Ft. Logan prior to the Spanish-American War. Capt. Young's officer's quarters in 1898 (No. 19) were in the left or south half of the huge duplex, identified as No. 10) which stands just to the left of the Field Officer's Quarters which house the Friends of Historical Ft. Logan. Servants lived in the attic. According to Sharon Catlett, occupants of these duplexes "typically included the officer, his wife, children, and four live-in servants – butler, cook, upstairs maid, and downstairs maid. The officers, not the army, paid the servants." [Catlett 182]

Secret Charities of Julia Greeley Are Recalled by Denver People

In a world where saints are often forgotten sooner than sinners, the memory of Julia Greeley, saintly and beloved Negress, refuses to die. An example of the great respect this woman commands is revealed in the report of a Boulder resident that a novena was made in honor of Miss Greeley and a small favor resulted. Old-time Denverites, stirred by recent articles about Julia in the Denver Catholic Register, have disclosed hitherto unpublished anecdotes about this charitable apostle of the Sacred Heart.

Julia Greeley, an ex-slave and the first lay person whose body rested in state in a Denver church, became widely known in Catholic homes in the city because she earned her livelihood by doing odd jobs.

It was while she [Julia] was working as a cook for a Captain Young at Fort Logan[102] that Mrs. H.E. Gallagher, now a member of Annunciation

---

[102] Capt. Young was George Shaeffer Young of the 7th. Infantry, who was stationed at Fort Logan from September, 1890, till April, 1898, and the only officer named Young there during that period. [Ft. Logan Post Returns, National Archives, RG 94, M617 series, roll 641] During Young's brief time in Cuba, his wife Edyth Field Young and son Harold (and possibly his daughter Polly, and maybe even Julia Greeley) remained at the Fort. Young rejoined his family there briefly during postwar convalescence. [Denver Evening Post 8-10-1898] Born in Jefferson County, Va., in 1858, he was commissioned a second lieutenant in the 7th Infantry on Jan. 20, 1873, and served in innumerable conflicts with Indian tribes on the Western frontier before coming to Ft. Logan. He was with Brevet Major General John Gibbons' Montana Cavalry during the 1876 Campaign and carried dispatches to Gen. George Crook's column. While stationed at Ft. McKinney, Wyo., in 1880,

parish, first came to know the pious Negress. Mrs. Gallagher recalls how Julia, as a member of the small band of faithful who attended services at the basement chapel in Logantown, was constantly working to better the tiny house of worship for the parishioners. Once when the chapel was in need of an organ for Divine services, Julia volunteered to purchase the musical instrument for the chapel. She instructed one of the Sisters of Loretto at Loretto Heights college to select the organ, and she paid for it.

It didn't cost Julia more than $30, according to the Rt. Rev. Richard Brady, chaplain at the college, but $30 was a small fortune to her.[103]

At the outbreak of the Spanish-American war [in 1898], Captain Young was transferred; and Julia came to Denver, where she again worked by the day, the hour, the job. She earned enough to keep herself and devoted the rest to her works of charity. Among the many who hired Julia was Mrs. Michael Howard, Mrs. Gallagher's mother. Mrs. Gallagher related that Julia was past her 60th birthday when she learned to play the piano. On one occasion she called at the Howard home and at the request of the family demonstrated her musical ability. She played and sang a Gregorian Mass in its entirety, much to the enjoyment of her listeners.[104]

The Lee home (built 1888), where Julia named a child in 1905, still stands at 3239 Champa.

Mrs. Thomas Lee [Ellen Madden Lee], a Sacred Heart parishioner, also recalled Julia's love for Church music. According to Mrs. Lee, the Colored devotee of the Sacred Heart would often play and sing at services at Sacred Heart church when the White girls would fail to appear.

Mrs. Lee also recounted how Julia named one of her sons. The elderly Negress had

---

Young led a party which moved 112 casualties of the Fetterman Fight from Ft. Phil Kearney to the Custer National Cemetery at the Little Big Horn site. [Young to William Camp, Mindanao, Philippines, June 13, 1911, in Camp 120-121] While in the Philippines in 1904, Young served on a court martial which acquitted a soldier, whom a civilian court headed by William Howard Taft afterwards convicted. The later decision, however, was reversed by the U.S. Supreme Court. Young participated in the Battle of El Caney in Cuba during the Spanish-American War and died as a full colonel on Jan. 5, 1919. [New York Tribune 1-8-1919].

[103] The parish near Ft. Logan was begun in 1894 and named St. Patrick's. Fr. Brady was assigned there in 1896. [Noel 369] The basement church at 3290 W. Milan Ave. in Sheridan was torn down in 1959 and the present church erected by 1961, at which time the parish was renamed Holy Name Parish. [DCR 5-4-2011] Logantown is today part of the city of Sheridan, a small enclave totally surrounded by Denver and Englewood (once known as Orchard Place). See more on Julia in Sheridan at Fr. Anthony Weinzapfel's Testimony, No. 44 on p. 66.

[104] When paraphrasing this in Kennedy 1974, p. 18, Fr. Kennedy substituted "Mass of Angels" for "a Gregorian Mass."

come to the Lee home after the family had been trying to decide on a name for the infant, but had come to no agreement. Upon Julia's entrance, Mrs. Lee immediately suggested that the ex-slave settle the dispute. At first Julia refused, believing it was all a joke, but at last, and with definite finality, she pointed at the unnamed boy and said: "I name you Francis Xavier!" Thus there is a Denver man proudly bearing the name, Francis Xavier Lee.[105]

One of Julia's least known but kindest deeds was the surrender of her burial plot to a deceased elderly Negro. The ex-slave owned a lot at Mt. Olivet cemetery and had planned to use it as a last resting place, but, when word reached her that the remains of the old Colored gentleman, known by various names (but as "Uncle Ambrose" to a few), were headed for a potter's field, she insisted on giving up her plot. Her charity in this case was repaid by the silent tributes of the hundreds who attended her last rites.[106]

Thus the tales of Julia Greeley continue to come to the fore. Many of her charitable acts will probably remain hidden forever, but the modest "Nigger Julia," as she called herself, continues to be a saint to hundreds of Denverites—and as one Denver woman put it, "more of a saint every year."[107]

Sacred Heart statue above the main altar in Julia's church.

St. Anthony of Padua's statue in Sacred Church's north transept.

---

[105] The naming of the Lee boy happened at 3239 Champa [1924 city directory] in 1905, sometimes between the child's birth on Sept. 14 and baptism on Oct. 1. [Sacred Heart parish, Baptisms, v. 2, no. 3464].

[106] An unsuccessful effort was made to locate Julia's first lot at Mt. Olivet. Records of the more than 8,000 burials there before Julia's produced only three Ambroses and one Tighe (another named suggested for the elderly gentlemen), but no connection has yet been made for any of them with Miss Greeley: Ambrose Hickey, aged 2, #1449; Ambrose Chapla, aged 58, #4522; Patrick F. Tighe, aged 66, #5539; and Ambrose Mathes, aged 51, #7436. And all four of them were first buried in Mt. Calvary Cemetery. [Lloyd Swint to Burkey, Wheat Ridge, Aug. 10, 2011].

[107] DCR 4-13-1939.

Mrs. Hagus Recalls Julia's Kind Deeds
(By ROSE M. HAGUS)

One-eyed, shiny black Julia Greeley knew nothing of the moral and social problems of youth. Nor could she discuss in high-sounding phraseology "The Prevention of Delinquency," "Girl Welfare," "The Need of Youth for Ideology," "The Well-Directed Enthusiasm of Youth," but she did know that girls love to dance and that danger lurked in the public dance halls.

She knew of some girls working for what could not be termed a "decency wage" and bearing on their young shoulders burdens of financial responsibility—an invalid sister, a widowed mother, younger brothers and sisters to keep in school. But youth was in their hearts and its call was heard over more serious things.

Sodalities and clubs provided pleasure in the monthly socials in the school hall. On these occasions the girls present were prettily dressed. The girls in whom Julia became interested, she learned, could not dress so well as the others and vanity prevented them from attending. Here was another "joy" for Julia. She never thought of her deeds as charity. She had friends who never failed her. The Sacred Heart and St. Anthony would show her the way.

She elicited the interest of some girls and young women in a far part of the city who would not be expected to attend these socials. She told them of "her girls," but not their names—those were Julia's secrets. She asked the more fortunate not to wear their pretty clothes for too long a time, but to give them to her, so that "her girls" could go to nice dances.

The young women to whom she appealed entered into the spirit of making other girls happy, and many a dress was discarded before it would have been otherwise. These garments were always given to Julia, all freshened—cleaned and pressed—with perhaps new bits of ribbon and lace. How happy Julia was to carry these packages to her "White girls,"—after dark of course.

Julia was present at these social affairs behind the scenes, dishing up ice cream, and getting a peek at her particular protege. Next day she would report to the donor of the dress; "She was the purtiest girl on the floor and no wallflower."

One day there was a wedding dress to supply. A young matron gave up hers which had, for sentimental reasons, been packed away.

Julia's "joy" was more constructive than almsgiving.[108]

---

[108] DCR 4-13-1939. Rose Mary Hagus (1876-1943), widow of Joseph Hagus and sister-in-law of Msgr. Charles Hagus, was the aunt of Fr. Gerald Kelly, S.J., famous medical ethicist. [DCR 2-22-

Later that year, as World War II was beginning in Europe, Madelyn Nicholds, a senior at Loretto Heights Academy,[109] published an article in the Academy's publication, *T'Akra*. Alluding to the evils of the segregation of Jews in Germany and that of Negroes in the United States, she argued for an end to all racial intolerance. Of interest to the present study, she spoke of Julia Greeley at the beginning, middle, and end of her full-page essay:

Tolerance

There may, someday, be a Saint Julia Greeley of Denver. Another saint in the great catalogue of the Church is not so significant as the fact that Julia Greeley was a negro and a former slave. Julia's great charity is remembered tenderly by many Denverites, not because she did anything so great, but because she did so many little things with her whole heart. "Love Thy Neighbor" wasn't just a platitude to Julia. It was a commandment. Second only to "Love Thy God." Everything she did, everything she said, found its roots in the two great commandments. And because love begets love, Julia's black and white friends would make her a saint [....]

Madelyn Nicholds Alixopulos

Pigment may be different, racial traits may be different, but difference does not mean inferiority. Julia Greeley knew that. Julia was a real democrat. She ignored the barriers of color and gave help where help was needed. She ignored the barriers—so there were none. Julia may yet have to intercede before the throne of God, for those white people whose floors she scrubbed [....]

We cannot be good citizens in this democracy unless we are willing to be catholic as well as Catholic. Unless we are able to throw aside our petty prejudices and acknowledge that the fatherhood of God and the brotherhood of man, makes no stipulation whatsoever for the brotherhood of white with white and black with black. May Julia Greeley show us the way![110]

In November of 1942, Sr. M. Lilliana Owens, S.L., teacher of history at St. Mary's Academy in Denver, had an article published in the *Sacred Heart Messenger* entitled "A Negro Apostle of the Sacred Heart," which was based on previously published articles. The article mistakenly said

---

1943]. Mrs. Hagus was buried at Mt. Calvary Cemetery, but later transferred to Mt. Olivet, sect. 18, blk. 6, lot 14, grave 1.
[109] Madelyn was born in Denver in 1917, later married Hedrick Alixopulos, and passed away in Texas in 2005. [Gwen Mayer to Burkey, Denver, Sept. 22, 2011].
[110] T'Akra, April 1939 p. 3, in Kennedy papers, AAD.

Julia had lain in state in the Loyola University Chapel. Also it repeated the Register's misinformation about Wisconsin being mentioned in Julia's baptismal record. And it also spoke of Governor Gilpin's being involved in leaving a legacy to Julia. Col. Gilpin had died intestate.[111]

As the 25th anniversary of Julia's death approached in 1943, the Register announced the publication of a pamphlet written by Fr. Murphy entitled *My Name Written in His Heart*. The pamphlet again reflected on the 11th promise of the Sacred Heart to St. Margaret Mary Alocoque: "Those who promote this devotion shall have their names written in My Heart never to be blotted out." Murphy's work, which would be in its 8th edition of 39,000 copies by 1958,[112] began by reviewing the career of Julia Greeley as an apostle of the Sacred Heart from the time of her coming to Denver in midwinter of 1874 "until her saintly death" in 1918.

The *Register* not only announced the pamphlet; it reprinted all but one paragraph of its nine pages on Julia. The pamphlet introduced a fair amount of fictionalized dialogue, but contained very little new information. Unfortunately even some of that was incorrect. The pamphlet did, however, serve to preserve and spread to a whole new audience interest in Julia's story.[113]

For the record, Murphy spoke of Julia Greeley's employer, the widow Julia Dickerson, coming from St. Louis with her four children and nanny to marry Major William Gilpin, first territorial governor of Colorado. Actually Dickerson had already married ex-Governor Gilpin in St. Louis on Feb. 16, 1874, and then came to Denver with him and her oldest child. Murphy spoke of Julia Greeley's living in a two-room cottage, which possibly would have been the last site where she roomed, at 2821 Walnut. St.

Fr. John LaFarge SJ listed Julia an example of sanctity.

The same year that Murphy published his pamphlet, his confrere, Fr. John LaFarge, S.J. (1880-1963), an editor of *America* magazine and founder of the Catholic interracial movement in the United States, mentioned Julia Greeley in his seminal study of Catholic doctrine on interracial justice. He included her in his list of black "examples of that moral triumph which we call sanctity" and further called her and New York's Ven. Pierre Toussaint (1766/1780-1853) "hidden martyrs of charity."[114]

In September of that same year, Sr. M. Lilliana published a second article on Julia in the journal of the Colorado State Historical Society. Her new article incorporated materials from other recently published articles.[115]

---

[111] Owens (1942) 34-35.
[112] Copy in AAD.
[113] DCR 4-29-1943.
[114] LaFarge 40.
[115] Owens (1943) 176-178.

Julia and the Franciscans

In the midst of the Civil Rights movement of the 1960s, Paul Hallett published a "Registorial" entitled "Julia Greeley Saintly Negro." "When Julia Greeley died," Hallett wrote, "Denver lost a woman everybody believed to be a saint. Perhaps no other Coloradan had that distinction, except possibly Father Leo Heinrichs, O.F.M., the pastor of St. Elizabeth's, who was shot while distributing Communion the morning of February 21, 1908."[116]

Paul H. Hallett, longtime Register reporter

St. Elizabeth Church, now on the Auraria Campus, was where Julia attended regular meetings of the secular Franciscans.

It is safe to assume Julia Greeley knew the Servant of God, Fr. Leo Heinrichs (1867-1908), since she had been a member of the secular Franciscans at St. Elizabeth's Church since 1901, and she not only attended regular meetings at St. Elizabeth's, but encouraged many others to do so.[117]

Every August 2, Julia was at St. Elizabeth's Church on 11th Street (now St. Francis Way) from the time the doors opened till when they closed. She spent the day there gaining plenary indulgences for the Poor Souls.[118] St. Francis of Assisi obtained the Portiuncula indulgence from Pope Honorius III in 1216. Visitors to the tiny chapel of Our Lady of Angels in Assisi were thus enabled to obtain a plenary indulgence for themselves or the poor souls as often as they visited the church and prayed for the Pope. The privilege was later extended to every Franciscan church on the anniversary of the dedication of the Assisi church.

An exile from Germany, Fr. Francis received Julia into the Franciscan family in 1901.

Fr. Francis Koch, O.F.M., had been the friar who received Julia into the Third Order under the name Elizabeth on Feb. 24, 1901.[119] Koch and Julia were kindred spirits. Noel wrote of him, "Father Koch's shabby brown habit embarrassed some parishioners. They showered him with clothes, but would next encounter him in his tattered old garments. 'I met a poor fellow suffering from the cold,' Fr. Koch would explain. 'What else could I do?'"[120]

---

[116] DCR 6-17-1965.
[117] Testimony of Eleanor Pavella Castellan, No. 23 on p. 51.
[118] Kennedy 1974 p. 17.
[119] Kennedy 1974, p. 17. This information was from the "red bound Book of Professed Members." [Kennedy notes, Noel Collection, BCAARL]. The present study has not yet located this book.
[120] Noel 350.

Francis came to America as the result of Otto von Bismarck's closing all religious houses in northern Germany. On the Feast of Our Lady of Angels, Aug. 2, 1875, he preached his last sermon in the famous Recollect Franciscan Church on Our Lady's Hill in Fulda. With five other friars, he arrived in New York later that month a homeless exile with little money and no place to go.[121] During the next 12 years Francis was a tireless evangelizer and church builder in northern New Jersey. He came to Denver in 1887 and built the present church which was dedicated in 1898 and consecrated in 1902.

Fr. Leo also left Germany because of Bismarck's *Kulturkampf,* but he came as a seminarian and joined the Order in this country in 1886. Ordained in 1891, he became pastor at St. Elizabeth's in Denver in 1907.[122] It still remains to be verified, but quite likely as pastors both Francis and Leo were spiritual assistants of the local fraternity of the secular Franciscans.

Fr. Leo Heinrichs, who was martyred while distributing Communion, was probably Julia's spiritual assistant as a secular Franciscan.

Fr. Leo was shot by Giuseppe Alia, an anarchist bent on killing priests, possibly because of some perceived offense by a priest in his native Italy. Even when he was about to be executed for Leo's murder, Alia expressed regrets that he hadn't killed more priests. In 1927 the dioceses of Newark and Denver and the archdiocese in Cologne, Germany, opened informative processes in Leo's cause for beatification as a martyr.[123] The process closed in 1933 and was forwarded to the Vatican, where it still awaits action.[124]

Julia's choice of Elizabeth as a Third Order name is especially noteworthy. Her new patron, St. Elizabeth of Hungary and Thuringia, one of the patrons of all Secular Franciscans, was a royal princess who spent most of her life serving the poor and disabled of her adopted country, often in great secrecy.

There was a gentle irony to Julia's being buried by her Jesuit friends in a Franciscan habit. It is interesting that it was a Jesuit, Fr. Eugene Murphy, who caught the symbolism of the event. "Julia was clad in the habit of a Franciscan tertiary," he wrote. "Here was the secret of her influence: She had taken Christ literally, as had the Poverello of Assisi. Like him she had given away all to the poor and had gone about making melody in her heart unto the Lord."[125]

---

[121] They had travelled on the same voyage of the"Culand," the very steamship which brought the first Capuchin Franciscans to the present compiler's home parish in Cumberland, Maryland.
[122] DCR 10-28-1909, pt. 2, p. 55.
[123] DCR 2-22-1927, 3-1-1927; RMN 3-4-1927.
[124] Joyce 7, Cicognani 98-104; http://newsaints.faithweb.com/year/1908.htm.
[125] Murphy 10-11.

But back to Hallett's article, after retelling then the main points of Julia's life, the *Register* writer went on to say,

> Long before the days when sympathy with Negroes became fashionable, people from all walks of society flocked to Loyola chapel to pray before the little Black body as it lay in state. This testimony was not to her race, but to sanctity...
>
> Julia Greeley will never be commemorated in Civil Rights history. She occupied a lowly position most Whites of her day were quite willing to see her in. If she were ever eager to break out of it, tradition has left us no complaint.
>
> She did perform a great service for both her people and the Whites in showing that sanctity is possible for all in whatever condition. Perhaps very few are alive today who remember Julia Greeley. When these are gone, her name may be known only from the yellow files of the Register. But the sanctity of her life can never become uninteresting, irrelevant, or unimportant.[126]

The Empire Magazine

The information provided by the *Register* was soon greatly complemented by a considerable wave of research begun by Eleanor Pavella Castellan (1888-1978). In 1969, the *Denver Post*'s Sunday supplement called *Empire Magazine*, ran a series on some notable members of Denver's black community. This prompted Mrs. Castellan to ask the *Post* if it could add some information on Julia Greeley, who was a part of Castellan's growing up. "She was old when I first knew her," Castellan wrote. "She was very poor and worked at whatever she could get, most of the time for 50 cents a day. But Julia was happy and never complained. Every first Friday of the month she made the rounds of the fire houses (there weren't very many at that time), and she would distribute leaflets of the Sacred Heart. It made no difference to her whether the firemen were Catholics or not. She would always say, 'They are all God's children.' I called many people who knew her, and they would always say, 'Yes, I knew Julia, but I don't remember anything about her. It's too bad someone hasn't written about her.' So I thought perhaps you could fill in some of the details I'm sure we all would like to know."

Eleanor Castellan, who was 30 years old when Julia Greeley died, helped collect many recollections of Julia in the years before her own death in 1978.

The *Empire* recounted many details of Julia's life previously published, adding, "Cemetery records show that the cause of death was a form of nephritis" and that "although she was popularly regarded as a 'saint,'

---

[126] DCR 6-17-1965.

Empire could find no record of any canonization proceedings." It also noted that she was buried in Section 8, Block 7, Lot 5 at Mt. Olivet.[127]

Five weeks later, the *Empire* carried another letter from Mrs. Castellan saying she had received several telephone calls from various people and a letter from Theodora Arnold, which she then shared. Mrs. Arnold's original letter was recently discovered among research material in the Denver Public Library.[128] It revealed that numerous minor editorial improvements had been made before publication.

Most of the substantive omissions made dealt with family history rather than Julia Greeley. Mrs. Arnold did, however, say in her original letter: "Father Higgins of St. Philomena's Parish was gathering all the evidence for her canonization at one time. I never heard what happened?" Since nothing further has turned up relative to research on Julia by Msgr. William Higgins (d. 1967), it might be useful to note that Higgins was a member of the ecclesiastical court which collected such information in the cause of Fr. Leo Heinrichs. So were Msgrs. Matthew Smith and Richard Brady and Jesuit Fr. Aloysius Brucker, S.J., all of whom are mentioned elsewhere in this study.[129] Perhaps Mrs. Arnold remembered this well-publicized investigation of sanctity, by then 42 years past, and understandably believed it had been about Julia.

This is Arnold's letter, as published:[130]

> Dear Mrs. Castellan,
> Your letter brought to mind many pleasant memories of my childhood days and Julia Greeley's kindness to all the family upon the death of my mother in 1893.
> My father, Thomas O'Donnell, was operating a dairy. Among his milk customers were many to offer him advice and help. One suggested he get Julia Greeley to keep house for him as she was looking for work.[131] He did, and my sister Margaret, James and I were able to continue in school [at Cathedral on Logan Ave.] The Empire article failed to mention she was blind in one eye because of cruel treatment when she was a slave. She would never eat with us at the table—always in the kitchen. I used to think it was on account of her eye. It seemed to be running water at all times and did seem rather repulsive until her kindness made one forget it.
> But as soon as we gathered around the table to say the Rosary for Mother, she was one of us who answered.
> I'll never forget our first Christmas without Mother. Julia told us she was going to ask Father if she could take Margaret and me down town at night to see the display of lights and all the toys in the basement

---

[127] Empire 9-21-1969.
[128] Arnold to Castellan, Denver, 9-29-1969, Kennedy papers, Noel Collection, BCAARL, & Castillo Collection, ACPMA.
[129] DCR 3-1-1927.
[130] Empire 10-26-1969.
[131] The O'Donnell's lived on the southwest corner of 5th and N. Boulevard (now Federal) at the time that Julia was with them. [1893 Denver city directory].

of the Denver Dry Goods.[132] When there, she told us to pick out anything we wanted for Christmas. I remember my sister picked out a three-piece toilet set—comb, mirror and brush—while I, after hearing so much about the hard times, looked at the price tag and picked a little wooden bucket and shovel, all for 10 cents and only suitable for a 2-year-old child. Julia said, "Oh, no, child, you want something better than that." And then she bought me a doll's trunk costing a dollar and also the bucket... She was getting $10 a month in wages.

She remained with us until school closed in June ... After that we often saw Julia on the streets, delivering the Sacred Heart League leaflets to the firemen. And when I graduated from Cathedral High in 1901, who did I see after the exercises but my old friend, Julia. She came to see me and wish me well. That was the last I ever saw of her.

Wouldn't it be nice if all who knew her would join into a circle or league of friends, donate a dollar a month or a week, have a Mass for her every First Friday and let the Jesuit fathers distribute any money left over for her own poor in their parish?

Sincerely,
Mrs. Theodora Arnold
St. Elizabeth Retreat
Denver

Fr. Pacificus Kennedy OFM, gathered much of what is known of Julia Greeley.

When this short conversation in the *Empire* failed to surface additional testimonials, Mrs. Castellan and Mrs. Arnold enlisted the assistance of Fr. Pacificus Kennedy, O.F.M., a priest at St. Elizabeth's Friary.[133]

By 1974, Fr. Kennedy and his helpers had located numerous other admirers of Julia Greeley. According to him, "Half a century after her death more than thirty people beamed as soon as they heard her name."[134] Kennedy told their stories in the December 1974 issue of *Friar* magazine, published in Butler, N.J.[135] By 1979, he and his associates had obtained additional testimonials, and in June he published a supplement to his earlier article.[136]

Kennedy seems to have collected his reports mainly in two ways. Several he obtained in the written form of letters, while others he recorded manually from oral interviews.

---

[132] The magnificent Denver Dry Building still stands on the southwest corner of 16th and California and houses among others stores TJ Maxx.

[133] Kennedy 1979, p. 30, in AAD. Kennedy, who often shortened his name to Fr. Pax, was stationed in Colorado all but four of the years from 1943 till 1977. The first eight years he was on the Franciscans' Western Mission Band and from 1969 till 1972 he was chaplain at Penrose Hospital in Colorado Springs. [Kennedy to Sr. Mary Hughes, Boston, Sept. 29, 1994, in Kennedy papers, AAD].

[134] Kennedy 1974, p. 30

[135] Kennedy 1974, pp. 12-19, in Kennedy papers, AAD.

[136] Kennedy 1979, pp. 29-38, in Kennedy papers, AAD.

Father later deposited in the archdiocesan archives the actual letters of people mentioned in his articles. Kennedy's recordings of the testimony of many of his other informants have been found among a large, unorganized collection of his notes written on mismatched scraps of paper. They were found among Dr. Thomas Noel's research materials on Julia Greeley preserved at the Blair-Caldwell African-American Research Library, a branch of the Denver Public Library (hereafter BCAARL) and a nearly identical collection presented by Max L. Castillo to the Archives of the Capuchin Province of Mid-America (hereafter ACPMA). These notes are all photocopies, and the location of their originals remains unknown.[137]

This drawing appeared in Fr. Kennedy's 1974 article in Friar magazine. The drawing on the title page is from his 1979 article.

Much, but not all, of the information in Kennedy's notes has been paraphrased in his articles; conversely the source for some parts of Kennedy's articles are not found in his notes.

In the 30-page compendium which follows, priority will be given first to the letters, then to the raw testimony in Kennedy's notes, and only then to the passages of his articles not found in his notes.

Letters to Fr. Kennedy

1. Theodora O'Donnell Arnold, Denver, undated letter

"My mother died Oct. 24, 1893, and in a short time, possibly two weeks, my father engaged Julia Greeley to keep house for us, as he thought my sister Margaret and I would be unable to do house work and attend school too. She worked for father 'til school closed about June 15th 1894. — I was under the impression Julia received the $1,000 from the Gov. Gilpin's estate until I recently read the life of Gov. Gilpin and knew he was still alive when Julia was with us. History tells us the Gilpins did not get along too well on account of Mrs. Gilpin's extravagance. Maybe this was accumulated wages <paid> to Julia and <then she was> let go? I am sure she never returned to work for them, as we would see her frequently in the streets and visit going to and from school. — I will pray for Julie as one of God's saints, canonized or not."[138]

---

[137] All of Fr. Kennedy's materials, including the original negative of the famous photo of Julia and Marjorie Ann, were obtained from him by Mary Frances O'Sullivan and given for safekeeping to the AAD, Dr. Thomas Noel, and Max L. Castillo. Since then the negative has disappeared; but thanks to digital scanning, the photo is not ever likely to disappear.

[138] Kennedy papers, AAD.

2. Theodora O'Donnell Arnold, Denver, March 28, 1974:

"I am a little tardy in answering your letter. However I thought it might help me in being sure which eye was gone. It didn't settle the matter however. As I look back 80 years it seems first the right eye was missing and then again it seemed the left eye ball was gone. I know she always carried a cloth to wipe the water off her face as it seemed to drain from the tear duct continually."[139]

3. Eleanor Pavella Castellan (1888-1978), Denver, March 19, 1974:

"...I telephoned Miss Eva Walsh [1882-1980, sister of Judge Joseph Walsh, see No. 43 on p. 65], ... Her family were <sic!> very active in the Sacred Heart Parish, and I asked her about Julia Greeley. — She said she did not know very much about Julia except that she was an awful beggar, not for herself but for other poor people in the Parish. — Miss Walsh said that Julia asked Father Swift[140] to write a letter for her. After Father finished, Julia looked at it and told him to write 'Please excuse the poor penmanship and spelling.' — Father Swift must have told this story.

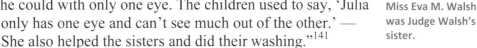

Miss Eva M. Walsh was Judge Walsh's sister.

"I never heard it before, but I know that Father [Swift] did not like Julia and when she was doing the cooking at the rectory he happened to go to the kitchen and chased Julia out. — Then he went to Father Barry and told him, and he said he wasn't going to eat anything the dirty old nigger cooked. Then he had to do the cooking until they found someone to take Julia's place. — When we asked Julia why Father got mad at her, she said, 'He sure was mad, he was mad,' but she never told us what happened. ... — I'm sure she did the best she could with only one eye. The children used to say, 'Julia only has one eye and can't see much out of the other.' — She also helped the sisters and did their washing."[141]

Sr. Ann Gertrude Cronin SC.

4. Sr. Ann Gertrude Cronin, S.C., (1900-1986), Colorado Springs, March 26, 1974:

"At the time of Julia Greeley's death I was a student at Sacred Heart High School and had always lived in Sacred Heart Parish. Julia was well known to all of us. I was at her funeral at the then Loyola Chapel. She was a third order Franciscan and as she had no home as such she was laid out in the center aisle

---

[139] Kennedy papers, AAD.
[140] Fr. Henry J. Swift, S.J. (1862-1935) entered the Jesuits in 1881 and taught at Jesuit colleges in Las Vegas, NM, Morrison, and Denver before being ordained in 1896. Besides his ministry at Sacred Heart Church in Denver, he served on the staff of *America* magazine, taught at Loyola Prep School in Chicago, and served parishes in Albuquerque and El Paso. He took the Jesuits' 4th vow Aug. 15, 1905, and died in El Paso on June 27, 1935, a member of the New Orleans Province. [Mendizábel 357 no. 19.751]. No photo could be found.
[141] Kennedy papers, Noel Collection, BCAARL, & Castillo Collection, ACPMA.

at Loyola Chapel after her death and until her funeral. She was dressed in the Franciscan habit. Many hundreds came to visit her remains. She was well known to all the Firemen and Policemen as she distributed the Sacred Heart leaflets badges and Apostleship of Prayer to so many of them."[142]

5. Fr. Martin Currigan, S.J., St. Louis, Mo., undated

"My dad died in 1948. I've been trying to recall anything he told me about Black Julia. Actually I can't answer any of your clear questions. Wish I could. — I recall his saying that the old S.H. church was filled the day of her funeral. She had helped so many poor people. (I was 4 years old and lived in the parish but was not at the funeral)."[143]

Fr. Martin Currigan SJ

A red-bordered Sacred Heart badge similar to the one that Julia handed out to firemen, and perhaps others.

6. John F. Healy, Jr., D.A. in Breckenridge, son of Denver's legendary sixth fire chief, July 26, 1978:

"I do remember Julia, but if you recall, I left Sacred Heart School after the 8th grade and went out to what is now Regis for high school. So my recollection of Julia is very limited.

"I do vividly remember the goodly supply of Sacred Heart badges as I would call them, and it seems to me they were on a red felt background. I do know that she hit my father frequently at the black fire house at 26th and Glenarm where he kept his automobile."[144]

Chief John F. Healy, Sr., (1873-1945), when named fire chief in 1912.

---

[142] Kennedy papers, AAD. Sister was the daughter of David & Annie (Sullivan) Cronin.
[143] Kennedy papers, AAD. Martin was the son of Dr. Martin Currigan who admitted Julia to St. Joseph's hospital and certified her death.
[144] Kennedy papers, AAD.

7. Sr. Ellenora Louise Hilbers, S.C., (1894-1986), Mt. St. Joseph, Ohio, March 22, 1974:

Sr. Ellenora Louise Hilbers SC

Sr. Margaret Clare Blucher SC

"I am very happy & interested in anything concerning the saintly life of Old Black Julia Greeley. Only information I have to offer is that as a grade school student at Sacred Heart, Denver, between 1900-1908, I met good Julia almost daily as I passed her on my way to or from school. At the time our family parents, Mr. Herman B. Hilbers and Mrs. (Ella) H.B. Hilbers lived at 3320 Larimer St. and also at 3311 Larimer Street. I remember Julia Greeley as she knocked on our back door faithfully every month to distribute the Sacred Heart leaflets of the Apostleship of Prayer.... From St. Sebastian Convent, Chicago, Sister Margaret Clare (Blucher, 1896-1975)[145] wrote to say that she remembered that Julia Greeley went to Church every day and prayed a lot."[146]

8. Chief Judge Neil Horan (1899-1992), Denver, Sept. 15, 1978:

"I have a very vivid boyhood recollection of her. I went to old Sacred Heart School and Church and over the years on my way to either place, I would meet Julia pulling a little red wagon loaded with clothes that she had collected. Some times she would greet me with 'Hello, Sonny,'

Chief Judge Neil Horan

and a few cheery remarks. Other times she would have a little black book and she and the wagon would be stopped in front of a house where she had made a collection, then she would say, 'Sonny, would you please write that number (pointing to the number of the house) in this book — I left my glasses at home and I can't see too well without them.' I was always happy to comply — I doubt if she could write, even if she could see. Little did I realize that I was helping a person who I hope will someday be canonized. — I often saw her mopping the floor of the old church, but when I saw her on the street she would be pulling the little red wagon. She never seemed to use any of the clothes for herself. The old clothes she wore were always the same. God must have loved her greatly, because in her poverty she was always happy, seeking only to help others whom she considered less fortunate than herself. — It was incongruous to see that lovely smile while a tear dropped from her poor blind eye."[147]

9. Sr. Antonita Klein, S.C., Mt. St. Joseph, Ohio, April 10, 1974:

"Sr. Florita (French, S.C., 1894-1980) says she never knew her personally but she remembers seeing her and says that she only heard good things about her; like she was good to the poor and tried to help them when she was poor herself. She went to Mass and Holy Communion every day. Came to the convent for

Sr. Florita French SC

---

[145] 1914 graduate of Sacred Heart High School.
[146] Kennedy papers, AAD.
[147] Kennedy papers, AAD. Horan was retired chief judge of the Denver district court. [RMN 1-7-1973].

breakfast. Every fireman and policeman in Denver knew her. She went to jail to visit people. Passed out Sacred Heart leaflets to them. — She lived just a block from the sisters and whenever they saw her they would ask her to come to the convent for meals. When she was sick, the sisters took her food and went to her room to take care of her. She was patient and accepted her illness beautifully. — She lost her eye in the Civil War, but they do not know which one. She never talked about it to them."[148]

10. Sr. M. Irene Lally, S.C.L., Leavenworth, May 6, 1974:

Sr. M. Irene Lally
SCL

"When I was a small girl I saw Black Julia many times in the church praying. She went out on the street with gunny sacks filled with wood, coal, clothes and food and medicine and would make her rounds to the desperately poor for whom no one else provided. She took care of and administered what supplies she could beg for them. Policemen and firemen would give donations to her and recommend her wherever she went because she was taking care of the forgotten poor. She, in turn, provided them with Sacred Heart badges and medals for those with whom they came in contact. Sister M. Irene doesn't know where Black Julia stayed because people always saw her in the church or on the streets delivering things to the poor."[149]

11. Missionary Sisters of the Sacred Heart, Golden, undated:

"There is no Sister left that had been here way back then. Going through several of the writings that were left we do not find any mention of Julia or anything that would give us an inkling that Mother Cabrini and Julia ever met. Of course, way back then there was hardly ever a thought or to be more forthright, time to record such incidents. Sadly, we are the losers!"[150]

---

[148] Kennedy papers, AAD. The Sisters lived just north of the parish school on Lawrence St. The convent building is now a women's shelter called Sacred Heart House of Denver, and the school building is now Centro San Juan Diego.
[149] Kennedy papers, AAD.
[150] Kennedy papers, AAD.

12. Marjorie A. Urquhart Simpson (1915-1983), Mission Viejo, Calif., June 23, 1978:[151]

St. Catherine of Siena parish's first church was torn down to allow for the building of the present church.

Marjorie Urquhart Simpson, the child photographed with Julia Greeley, later shared with Fr. Kennedy the photo and her recollection of what her mother told her of Julia.

"I have the original picture, carry it in my Rosary Novena - also the Pastor Father Ryan, then pastor of St. Catherine's Church, who took the picture of Julie & me. If he was only alive but that's many years ago. He left St. Catherine's for Michigan, his maiden sister, Clara, was his housekeeper. — I recall Mamma mentioning how Julia would arrive early in a.m. Bathe me, dress me, feed me my bottle, & then off to visit St. Catherine's in my baby-buggy sometimes my mother was afraid because of Julie's not seeing with only 1 eye - the other eye was lost by a whip from a slave master - on one occasion my dad asked Julie how old she was & she replied, 'Mr. George, I don't ask you personal questions and I don't answer any' - and smiled at him. He felt it was because she didn't know how old she was - being an ex-slave. — My mother would give her a few dollars (we were not wealthy people) and food to take back to the many people that depended on her for food and whatever. — She was very black and unattractive however when she would come to take care of me in the morning, my Mother said I would kiss her cheeks, eyes, ears, mouth and hug her to let her know how I loved her - I recall my dad saying how he liked corn bread & Julie would make it for him on various occasions at our house. — This episode is one I vaguely recall my mother mentioning; the details are very scant, so I trust I am not getting too far off, as I am praying to Julie, Mom and my sister to help me. Julia did menial work for a brothel — a prostitute — fallen away, Catholic girl was dying. She was calling for priest. Julie ran to the church (could be Sacred Heart Parish) brought back a priest who attended her. He called to Julia to come to the room and the bed posters were shaking & bed was jumping from side to side — this was felt

George Urquhart

The Urquhart home (built 1911) is still at 4270 Hooker

---

[151] All of Mrs. Simpson's testimony is based on her mother's accounts, as Marjorie was only three years old when Julia died. Marjorie herself died Feb. 10, 1983, in Los Angeles. See also testimony contained in the DCR article of 3-9-1939 on p. 24.

by Julie a fight with devils — This I believe but cannot prove or give any more light on this episode. It sounds so much like the picture show. I trust my version of recall is not getting mixed."[152]

13. Marjorie A. Urquhart Simpson (1915-1983), Mission Viejo, Calif., July 10, 1978:

"I am not having much luck in finding out the date of birth of my brother (Billy) William Urquhart - will try through the Birth Certificates in Denver. We believe he was 12-15 to 17 years older than me. He was born Jan. 18th. I remember my mother mentioning this date when a friend of ours had the same Birthday (but the year?). I know from mother (we called her mamma) he (Billy) starved to death, no food would agree with him, her milk or formula. And also my dad's 2 brothers would take turns at nite <sic!> carrying (Billy Baby) trying to reserve his strength till they could find some formula to feed him that would stay down. Dr. Danahey MD delivered me, I don't know if he was the family doctor for Billy's time. My dad's family wanted this baby boy so badly to carry on the Urquhart name - he died and was mourned greatly. I have no date of his death.

Marjorie was born the following year.

"Julie (in my prayers to her I call her Blessed Julia) was walking past our home in North Denver - 4270 Hooker St. We had a full length front porch - my mother was sitting out there, probably in a rocking chair, or straight chair, I'm not sure. She called to Julia, asking her if she would mop our kitchen floor, which colored Julia agreed to. While in our house, she (Julie) noticed the Holy pictures on the walls also a crucifix over my mother and dad's bed. It must have been because there always was one when we were small children. She (Julia) mentioned the fact that you must be a Catholic & Mamma acknowledged. why aren't there any little children running around this house. My mother said she was not able to have any more children. I'm sure mamma must have told Julia about my brother - He was named William (Billy) after my dad's oldest brother who we all loved (a bachelor). Julia replied to my mother there will be a little white angel running around this house. I will pray and you'll see."[153]

---

[152] Kennedy papers, AAD. See also Urquhart testimony contained in DCR article of 3-9-1939 on p. 29.
[153] Kennedy papers, AAD. William George Urquhart died in 1904, ll years before Marjorie's birth.
   [Horan Mortuary Records, DPL, p. 404. Though in the index, the record itself cannot be found at DPL]. Marjorie also had a younger sister named Virginia Rose Urquhart Maroney, born 1919).

14. Fr. Harold L. Stansell, S.J., Regis University historian, Denver, July 6, 1978:

"I went through practically everything that we have by way of diaries, minutes, etc., along, of course with correspondence. Sorry to say that there were no records about the building at 5158 <sic!> Lowell Blvd. I do know, however, that the building belonged to Regis in the 1920s; in fact I lived in it during my senior year in high school. I did see a brief note that indicated that Father Robert Kelley purchased the building; he had become Rector in 1920. After I left for Florissant the Jesuits loaned the building to the Christian Brothers. The boys who had finished the eighth grade at St. Vincent's Home and St. Clara's were housed there and attended classes at Regis.... Sometime after 1935 the Jesuits sold the house but I could not find any reference to the purchaser. Unfortunately, I could find no reference to the Misses Ryan or Julia Greeley. It is too bad that this request did not come while some of the older Jesuits were still around; but they are all gone and there is no one who knew about these things around anymore."[154]

The Ryan House, which still stands at 5127 Lowell Blvd., was another site where Julia was employed as a servant.

The Ryan House

The house Fr. Stansell wrote about was a large brick residence, still standing at 5127 Lowell (not 5158 Lowell), where Julia Greeley is reported to have worked for the Ryan Sisters. As late as 1930, it was the only building on the southern half of Block 177 of Berkeley Subdivision of Denver. The building, erected in 1895, was quite possibly a farm house before the land was made part of the city.[155]

The first recorded urban owner of the lots on which the house stood (lots 29 to 35) was Fr. Joseph Marra, S.J., superior of the New Mexico-Colorado Mission of the Jesuit Province of Naples, Italy. Marra obtained title thereto on Aug. 11, 1893, and turned it over to Sacred Heart College (forerunner of Regis University) on Oct. 28, 1908.[156]

---

[154] Kennedy papers, AAD. Fr. Stansell wrote *Regis: On the Crest of the West* in 1977.
[155] 1930 Denver Sanborn insurance maps, v. 8, p. 739.
[156] City & County of Denver Assessors Lot Index 1860-1917, v. 1, p. 335, roll 1 in DPL. Sacred Heart College was renamed in 1921.

Meanwhile, Miss Jennie J. Ryan (1850-1923) and Miss Maggie A. Ryan (1853-1936) occupied the house from 1902 until 1912.[157] The two single sisters had previously lived for years at 2720 Lawrence, just two blocks from Sacred Heart Church on Larimer St. and three and a half from Julia Greeley.[158] In the 1902 directory, the sisters were listed as residing "at the Jesuit College," and in 1903 as living on the northwest corner of Homer Blvd. and W. 51st Ave., both addresses referring to the house on Lowell, since there was no other house between there and 51st St., and the house was the property of the Regis Jesuits. In 1904 and 1905, the Ryans were listed "on the west side of Homer Blvd between 51st and 52nd Ave." Finally in 1906 the address was given as "5127 Homer Blvd (Lowell Blvd.)." By 1913, the sisters were no longer living there, but instead were residing at 2459 Lafayette, on the southwest corner of 25th and Lafayette, less than four blocks east of Loyola Chapel at 2536 Ogden, where they were pew holders.

It is not known what further connection the New York-born Ryan sisters might have had with the Lowell Blvd. property, but on Mar. 14, 1914, Jennie signed a quit claim deed for Lots 25 to 28, just south of 5127 Lowell.[159]

Jennie J. Ryan

Maggie Ryan was a seamstress, and Jennie taught at Washington School, a block west of St. Elizabeth's Church on 11th Street, for more than 40 years. When Jennie died of pneumonia at the age of 73 in 1923, five years after Julia Greeley, she had just begun her 41st year of teaching in a new location, Perry School in Barnum Neighborhood. The *Denver Post* called her "the oldest teacher in service in the Denver public schools and one of the most widely known and beloved characters in church and social circles here." She died at her home at 2604 Downing[160]. The *Post* said Jennie was "one of the first parishioners of Sacred Heart church and a charter member of the Altar and Rosary society and the Tabernacle society there."[161] Of special interest in Julia Greeley's story, Jennie was also secretary of the League of the Sacred Heart, of which Julia was one the chief promoters.[162]

The *Denver Catholic Register* carried a lengthy article by W.S. Neenan entitled "Saintly Catholic Woman Who Dies Here Had Taught 5000 in 40 Years." Neenan referred to Jennie as "one of the clearest witnesses of God's grace the writer has ever known." Referring to Jennie's long service, Neenan said she served "with a measure of unstinted devotion known best by God. She arose daily at 5:30 and the stroke of six found her at Sacred Heart church or Loyola chapel, a guest at the Table… Long stretches of hours were spent in loving labor for God's Church and for his poor.

"At the close of many a hard day, she never once failed in attendance at long drawn out sessions of charitable and benevolent organizations of which she was ever a leader and a beacon of light. For forty years the refined little lady bore a strain few men we have ever known would care to

---

[157] 1902-12 Denver city directories; Jesuit House Diary, Sacred Heart College, Denver, Feb. 19, 1902, p. 42: "The Misses Ryans [sic] became our tenants in the house vacated by the Peytons last week." On Feb. 15, 1902, the building was referred to as "our widows' home."
[158] 1885 and 1901 Denver city directories.
[159] Denver County Land Records, v. 2380, p. 375, copy in Jesuitica Collection, Regis archives.
[160] The house stood where the Whittier School's playground equipment is presently located.
[161] Denver Post 5-14-1923.
[162] Sacred Heart Church and School Monitor, 4:5 (July 1918) 6.

face."[163] Jennie was especially associated with the Women's Catholic Order of Foresters, and served many years as its secretary and chief ranger.[164]

Records from 1885 till 1923 show the Ryan sisters living in four different locations, all of them within four blocks of the Jesuits. This was probably no mere coincidence, but the full meaning of their fascination with the sons of Ignatius remains a mystery.[165]

The house at 5127 Lowell was used by the Jesuits of Regis for many different purposes in the years that followed. In 1918 John F. Conway, S.J., whom the *Register* said Julia Greeley had held in her arms as a baby, was living there as a scholastic.[166]

It was Sr. Celine Hayden (No. 33 on p. 58-59) who told of Julia Greeley's working for the Ryan sisters on Lowell Blvd. and even suggesting that she lived with them. The number of years she worked for the Ryans is not known, but it appears she was already working for them in 1910 and continued doing so until they moved back into the Five Points neighborhood in 1912 or 1913. It is somewhat questionable whether Julia lived with the Ryan sisters, since during the time Julia was working for them, the Sacred Heart Church and School Monitor and the Denver city directories listed her as living at 2913 Walnut. The 1910 U.S. Census also lists Julia on April 15 as a servant for a private family, but living at a boarding house run by John Conway's parents at 2913 Walnut Street:[167]

name	relationship	gen.	race	age	state	birthpl.	occupation/workplace
Conway Michael	head	M	W	65	M	Ire.	shoemaker/shop
Katherine	wife	W	W	60	M	Ill.	keeper/lodginghouse
Harborne Mary D.	daughter	F	W	41	Wid	Ill.	laundress/handlaundry
William A.	grandson	M	W	9	S	Co.	none
Katherine N.	granddgt	F	W	8	S	Co.	none
McGraw Anna	head	F	W	75	Wid	Can.	none
Kelley Elizabeth M.	head	F	W	80	Wid	Eng	none
Greeley Julia	head	F	Mu	60	S	Mo.	servant of a private family
Steward Samuel	head	M	W	47	S	Mo.	carpenter
McCoy David W.	head	M	W	69	M	Ind.	own income

The Conways had already lived at 2913 Walnut for at least 10 years. The 1900 U.S. Census shows the parents and eight children living there, including 10-year-old John, who later as a Jesuit served as subdeacon at Julia's funeral. Besides the Conways, 10 other people from two different families lived there.[168] As John was born in 1890 in Georgetown, the family must have moved to Denver soon afterward for Julia to have held him as a baby.   By Blaine Burkey.

---

[163] DCR 5-17-1923.
[164] DCR 3-16-1903, 3-30-1906, 1-8-1914.
[165] The Ryan sisters are buried at Mt. Olivet in Sect. 4, Block 2, Row 8, about 30 feet west of Bozo the Clown and about 150 feet southwest of Julia Greeley.
[166] The son of Michael and Catherine Conway, John was born 24 Mar. 1890 in Georgetown CO, entered the Jesuits 14 Aug. 1906, and left the community 20 Jul. 1921 [Mary Struckel, Midwest Jesuit Archives, to Burkey, 3 Feb. 2012.
[167] 1910 U.S. Census, Series T624, Roll 114, Page 165B, line 91.
[168] 1900 U.S. Census, Series T623, Roll 117, Page 344.

15. Sr. Catherine Regina Taylor, S.C., Denver, sometime shortly before April 25, 1974:

"I am racking my brain trying to recall all the good works of good old Julia Greeley. The one thing that stands out in my mind is her great love for the Sacred Heart. Every First Friday or oftener she would walk to the different fire stations to see that each fireman was fortified with a badge of the Sacred Heart. If they didn't have one, she was sure to supply them with the same."[169]

Sr. Florence Wolff SL interviewed S. Mary Anthony Haberl SL

16. Sr. Florence Wolff, S.L., archivist, Sisters of Loretto, Nerinx, Ky., Nov. 4, 1977:

"I did ask one of our octogenarian sisters, Sr. Marie Anthony Haberl, who attended old St. Mary's and whose mother was the first president of the alumnae, if she remembered anything about her [Julia]. She immediately responded that Julia used to work at St. Mary's, at Sacred Heart, and in their home. She added that Julia never knelt down to scrub, but did a superb job by just bending over. Also that she [Julia] told her [Sister's] mother one time that she often had her people say that she looked like a fly in a pitcher of buttermilk in those white churches."[170]

17. Sr. Florence Wolff, S.L., archivist, Sisters of Loretto, Nerinx, Ky., Dec. 9, 1977:

"Have been trying to get a little more about Black Julia from Sister Marie Anthony (Haberl). Here are some of the things she remembers and relates every item with a smile in her eyes and in her voice. She loved Black Julia you can be sure. — She recalls how almost every Saturday, Julia would come to their house. Made jelly bread sandwiches for the children and played with them. The Haberls had other help, but Mrs. Haberl knew Julia from her own school days at St. Mary's or at least from her daughter's school days. Sister said she was always where she was needed, and when she was helping about their house she always ate with them. — Here are a few dates on the Haberl family which might help you locate Julia. <The> Mrs., Fannie Darrah, was born in Denver, July 1, 1865, and attended the first St. Mary's - the old white house. In 1888 she married Anthony Haberl, and they had three girls and four boys, born between 1890 and 1906. Sister Marie Anthony had her 85th birthday yesterday. — The first St. Mary's was a white frame building on 14th and California, which had belonged to George Clayton. In 1867 a west wing was built, but it was partially destroyed by fire in 1869. In 1872 the east wing was built and in 1880 the middle building. We have picture of this completed building. We were always on [the south side of] California between 14th and 15th. In 1911 they moved to

85-year-old Sr. Marie Anthony Haberl SL enjoyed reminiscing about "Black Julia."

---

[169] This was contained in a letter written to Sr. Ellenora Louise Hilber, which the latter sent to Fr. Kennedy from Mt. St. Joseph, Ohio, Apr. 25, 1974, in Kennedy papers, AAD.
[170] Kennedy papers, AAD.

California [should read Pennsylvania] Street and rented the land [on California] to the public market."[171]

18. Francis O. Worland, Denver, April 20, 1974:

"I never graduated from SH[H]S, nevertheless did attend SH grade school from 1916-1922. Graduated from Regis High School in 1930. Made my First Communion while in the first grade of Sacred Heart Grade School 1916. ....I remembered Julie Greeley's funeral in 1918. She was a slave they told me, worked for the Sisters of Charity doing cooking and house work, also worked for the Poor People of Denver. Julie <u>lay in State in Sacred Heart Church</u>, and the school children attended her Mass. <u>Was dressed as a nun with the Sisters of Charity habit.</u> Was well thought of by the Sisters, the Priests, and the Laity. Well known in Denver. Most People thought Julie a Saint — So do I. To this day I never forgot Julie, although I never knew Julie personally. As everyone knew, Julie was a colored woman, a former slave, worked for the Sisters of Charity in their convent, for the Poor in Denver. I'll never forget her."[172]

Other Testimony Kennedy Collected

19. Mildred Connell Arkins (1908-1987):

"My First Communion Day — was it 1915? — Julia came to our house (2837 Josephine in Sacred Heart parish).[173] She came and wanted to shake hands and I foolishly said my right hand would turn black. My mother laughed and said 'Don't be foolish.' Julia did not mind. She kissed me on the cheek and said, 'This is a holy child.' — She was the first Catholic black lady in Denver. — Julia cleaned house for my mother on Fridays — her head would be wrapped in cloths. She beat rugs. She was a small slight woman, with large feet. Her right eye was the blind one. She worked for many. What I remember most is how her face always glowed."[174]

The Arkin home (built 1896) still stands at 2837 Josephine, now in St. Ignatius of Loyola parish.

---

[171] Kennedy papers, AAD. Anthony F. Haberl lived at 1106 Colfax Ave. [1917 Denver city directory].

[172] Kennedy papers, AAD. Worland, who was only about six in 1918, was mistaken about the habit. Julia was wearing the habit of the Secular Franciscan Order (O.F.S., at that time called the Third Order of St. Francis). A Sister of Charity, Sr. Ann Gertrude Cronin, S.C., No. 4 on p. 42, testified to this.

[173] This is now in St. Ignatius of Loyola Parish. Mildred was the daughter of Edward Cornelius and Catherine Higgins.

[174] Arkin Recollections, Kennedy papers, Noel Collection, BCAARL, & Castillo Collection, ACPMA., paraphrased in Kennedy 1979, pp. 34-35, in Kennedy papers, AAD.

20. Theodora O'Donnell Arnold:

How did Julia become interested in the Catholic Church? Theodora O'Donnell Arnold suggested she <u>may have been attracted if and when she witnessed the Baptism of the Dickerson and Gilpin children</u>.[175]

21. Sr. Catherine Rita Besson, S.C., (1888-1982):

"Yes, I knew Julia very well. She was very devoted to the Sacred Heart. Her job was mopping, sweeping and keeping the Church clean. She always had a pocketful of orange peel and chewed on this while working. She always had a cute little expression/ greeting when she met you. I don't remember what it was. ... Many times Julia could be seen going through the alley carrying a chair or a mattress to some poor person. Believe it was the left eye that was blind."[176]

Sr. Catherine Rita Bessin SC

22. Eleanor Pavella Castellan (1888-1978):

"Julia had been a slave and was blind in one eye, caused by a cruel mistress when she was child. She was too young to remember how/when it happened. Perhaps it was an accident. Julia did not know how old she was.

"Julia was as simple as a little child, trusting in everyone, and forever a faithful member of the Catholic Church. She earned very little in those days. But would always share what she had with others. Had a keen sense of humor and could always laugh at herself when she found herself in a ridiculous situation — like the time she made a commotion among the children when she came into church with her skirt inside out. The nun quieted the kids, then scolded Julia. But all Julia said was, 'Ah know, Sister, ah know.'

"Every First Friday Julia made the rounds to all fire houses in Denver to distribute leaflets of the Sacred Heart. Made no diff to her whether they were Catholics or not. They would get a leaflet of Sacred Heart and she would always say 'God bless you all.' The men would joke with her and tease her, but she would just laugh and go on her way.

"Julia was loved by everyone & was a welcome guest in every house in the parish. She always knew where she could get a good meal. She had her faults too. Many a time if the mother of the house was not home, she would go to the pantry and help herself to whatever was there — as she had been told to do. When the mother returned she would find that what she intended to serve that evening was gone.

---

[175] Kennedy 1974, pp. 13-14, in Kennedy papers, AAD. Actually she never attended any of the baptisms, but more on that later.

[176] Besson Recollections, Kennedy papers, Noel Collection, BCAARL, & Castillo Collection, ACPMA; used partially in Kennedy 1974, p. 14.

"Julia lived in one room in rear of house. People in front often drank, fought, quarreled. Julia never would say anything except, 'That their business.'

"When Julia heard of a sick child she would go there and make the mother rest while she herself would sit up all night with the child. Had a way with children & they loved her. As she crooned softly it didn't take long before the baby fell asleep.

"When there was a death in the family, you could always find Julia working in the kitchen. If family was poor, she would go out asking for clothes so they would look nice when they went to the funeral. She made friends with everyone, rich and poor.

"Julia arranged a picnic for children at City Park. She would round up as many as she could at one time (9 or 10) and would take them on the trolley car. Of course she always joshed with the conductor that they were all her children. I remember because I was one of them. We each had a nickel or a dime to spend, and Julia always provided and brought along lunch for all of us. We would come home happy and tired, Julia the happiest of all because she had spent the day with the children. ....

"Whenever I go into the old neighborhood I wonder if Julia's ghost still walks the familiar streets. She was too active to lie quiet and still in her grave. I can see her shuffling along, with her rosary & hear her say: 'How's you are, Honey'?"[177]

23. Eleanor Pavella Castellan (1888-1978):

"Julia could not read or write. She would say: 'Please read this for me — my glasses aren't good enough.'

"Let's face it: Julia looked pretty tacky because of the old clothes she wore. Some said they didn't like her — but when Julia smiled, something to see.

"When in need of help everybody called on Julia. Fr. Edwin Barry <Fr. Edward Barry, S.J., 1853-1922> needed a cook. Julia supplied. At end of month the grocery bill was astounding. Father phoned grocer and said: 'Must be some mistake.' Grocer presented itemized bill. It was correct — and high. Father asked Julia: 'Did we order all this stuff?' 'Oh, yes.'
'But what happened to it?' 'Well you know that widow. I had to give her some groceries. Then that family with the drunken father. I couldn't let his wife and chillun starve, etc.' Julia was actually surprised Father had to pay. She thought the priests got everything for free.

"When new baby arrived for the poor family that had no baby buggy, Julia would scout around and find a family that had a used baby carriage & no baby in prospect. She would deliver at night when nobody could see her.

---

[177] Castellan Recollections, Kennedy papers, Noel Collection, BCAARL, & Castillo Collection ACPMA; partially used in Kennedy 1974 pp. 15-16, 19.

Fr. Edward Barry SJ was Julia's patron and defender.

"Julia put a sack of potatoes on porch of poor family right in front of door. She watched from across the street unobserved. It was very cold — nobody came out that door — Julia was afraid potatoes would freeze & get mushy. She went next door & got little child to ring the door bell — 'But don't dast say that Old Julia had anything to do with it.'

"Yes, Julia had a pew with her name on it, as Agnes Erger says. It was up front on left side — what we used to call Gospel side. It was right in front of communion rail, just big enough for one or two. So Julia didn't have to sit with the white folks, or vice versa. But some of them complained. Some of the wealthy used to bring their friends to high mass — for the music. Let's face it, Julia cold look pretty tacky in her hand-me-downs, and she had big feet and shoes that hardly fit, and she would be flopping them up the aisle. Well, when they complained to Father Barry he said emphatically, 'As long as I'm pastor here, Julia is going to keep her pew.' When Julia heard about this, she went to Father and said she could come to some other Mass. He said, 'Julia, you're going to keep your regular seat and come to high Mass like you always do, because I know you want to. Julia can sit any place in this church she wants to.'[178]

The interior of Sacred Heart as it looked at the time of Julia's death. Julia's pew was right at the foot of the huge crucifix in front of the left end of the Communion railing.

"In those day kids played under arc light at night, singing and dancing. We entertained ourselves — not like today. Julia would come along, pick up <the> sides of her skirt, and sing and dance and laugh with us.

"I think <the> blind eye was the left eye - always watering - you could see some red in the eye.

---

[178] The importance of this pew to Julia is further emphasized by the fact that there were 600 families in the parish at the time, but only 75 pew holders. [Sacred Heart Home and School Monitor 1:1 (Aug. 1905) 27] It should also be noted that, while in the reporting of this there is no indication given of racism being involved in the complaint against Julia, for many years in other parts of the country, black Catholics were required to sit in the back of white churches, and they would not be given Communion until all the whites had received. [Linda Marie Chase, interview with Burkey, Feb. 16, 2012; Raboteau 119 & 124].

The corpus Julia gazed upon now hangs on a side wall of the church. It was badly broken when it fell from the wall, but has now been faithfully restored.

"Julia belonged to the Third Order at St. Elizabeth and she was always getting people to join. I was 16 and Julia got me and Julia Higgins and a few others to go with her to the Third Order at St. Elizabeth's. Julia belonged & wanted everybody to join. My mother said: 'Julia, you're foolish - they are too young - wait till they get older.' We went once and that was all.

"When Julia Higgins' mother died, Old Black Julia got hold of everything she could and sewed for the lil chillun there.

"Julia lived in one room at 28th & Walnut, behind people who were always drinking, quarrelling, etc. Everybody wanted to know what went on there. Julia kept mum. 'That's their business, not mine.'"[179]

24. Anna Catherine Cronin (1908-1989), sister of Dan Cronin, the fire chief:

Cronins lived 28th & Curtis. My Mother said Julia Greeley would take goods etc. to white families at night, so nobody would see a black entering the home. She was waked in S.H. Church. One of SJs [Jesuits] said: "Sacred Heart Church was the only home she had known so she was waked in church."

Ann Cronin went 12 years thru grade/high school at Sacred Heart. Graduated h[igh] [school] 1926.

My mother would give her cup of tea and a sandwich. Julia was humble and bashful about coming into home — we'd sit in kitchen. Mother would sit with her. Julia was a wonderful person. "I can not see/say which eye was blind." "Yes, I think I remember Julia with corncob pipe."

Saw her in church a lot — like all kids. I did not pay attention to what she did.

Brother John S.J. belonged to Spanish nobility.[180]

---

[179] Castellan supplementary recollections, Kennedy papers, Noel Collection, BCAARL, & Castillo Collection, ACPMA; partially paraphrased in Kennedy 1974, p. 15-16, in Kennedy papers, AAD; Kennedy 1979, pp. 34-35, in Kennedy papers, AAD. Eleanor's parents were Emilie and Nicholas Pavella. [James Castellan to Burkey, Jan. 5, 2012]. Mrs. E. Pavella lived at 2640 Larimer. [Sacred Heart Home and School Monitor 4: 3 (July 1917) 39].

[180] Ann Cronin Recollections, Kennedy papers, Noel Collection, BCAARL, & Castillo Collection, ACPMA. Ann and Dan P. Cronin were children of Patrick and Sarah (Clarke) Cronin. Their uncle

Pat and Sarah Cronin and three of their children, who would have been in Cronin house at 2815 Curtis when Julia Greeley made her visits there. The house is still standing, but has obviously seen better days. Timothy stands in front of his father, and Anna beside her mother. The infant is Daniel, who later served the city as fire chief and safety manager.

25. Daniel P. Cronin (1912-1998), Denver's Fire Chief (1968-1970) and a Manager of Safety:[181]

Left eye / Corn Cob Pipe / Visited Mrs. Pat Cronin (Sarah) at 2815 Curtis / tea and talk

"In the first two decades of this century there were about 15 or 16 Firehouses scattered all over the city. Each month she traveled to every fire house in advance of the First Friday."

Denver safety manager
Dan P. Cronin

Daniel was Denver's police chief. While still a simple policeman this elder Daniel attended the Mass at which Fr. Leo Heinrichs was shot and killed, and he subdued and arrested the murderer.

[181] Dan Cronin Recollections, Kennedy papers, Noel Collection, BCAARL, & Castillo Collection, ACPMA. Daniel P. Cronin was a Denver fireman for 34 years (the last three as fire chief) before becoming Manager of Safety in 1971.

The Fire Houses

By the time Julia died, there were 20 fire houses in Denver.[182]

Engine Co. No. 1 — 1326 Tremont
Engine Co. No. 2 — SW corner Colfax & Santa Fe
Engine Co. No. 3 — NW corner 26th & Glenarm
Engine Co. No. 4 & Hook & Ladder Co. No. 2 — 2026 Curtis
Engine Co. No. 5 — 1817-1823 Blake
Engine Co. No. 6 & Hook & Ladder Co. No. 1 — SW corner 14th & Market (Central Sta.)
Engine Co. No. 7 — W. 36th & Tejon
Engine Co. No. 8 — 1618 Marion
Engine Co. No. 9 — 47th & Gilpin
Engine Co. No. 10 — NE corner 33rd & Arapahoe
Engine Co. No. 11 & Hook & Ladder Co. No. 3 — W. 3rd & Cherokee
Engine Co. No. 12 — W. 26th & Federal
Engine Co. No. 13 — SE corner Center & S. Broadway
Engine Co. No. 14 — E side Oneida near Colfax
Engine Co. No. 15 & Hook & Ladder Co. No. 4 — 11th & Clayton
Engine Co. No. 16 — S. Ogden & Iowa
Engine Co. No. 17 — W. 38th & Osceola
Engine Co. No. 18 — 2207 Colorado
Engine Co. No. 19 — S. Pecos & W Alameda
Engine Co. No. 20 — W. 6th & Knox Court

Fire station No. 3 at 2563 Glenarm (built in 1885) is now vacant. The four unidentified firemen shown could be the ones killed in 1895 in the St. James Hotel fire, but there is no way of knowing.

Stationhouse #7 is still standing at Tejon & 36th Ave. It is now used as a beauty parlor and apartments.

Whether Julia actually went to all of them is not known, nor is it known when she started going. Fr. Kennedy suggested one occasion which might have played some role in calling her to this ministry. On Saturday night, March 23, 1895, four of the five men at

---

[182] 1918 Denver city directory.

> Engine Co. No. 3, about 11 blocks from Julia's residence, were killed in a fire at the St. James Hotel at 1528 Curtis St. When the floor under the rotunda of the three-story building collapsed, Harold W. Hartwell, Frederick Brawles, Richard Dandridge and Steve Martin were hurled into the blazing inferno. Three of them were black men. The lone survivor was off-duty that night.[183] Julia, of course, knew that there was no better preparation for such a dangerous occupation than embracing a life of prayer.[184]
>
> By Blaine Burkey.

26. Ralph and Charles DeOrio, stonecutters

Since the tiny rose-colored stone on Julia's grave appeared to be rather new in contemporary style, Fr. Kennedy asked the DeOrio brothers to check their records. The answer received was, "It was ordered and paid for in 1956 by Agnes Rooney Urquhart and her daughter Marjorie. All they wanted carved on the stone was 'Beloved Julia Greeley'."[185]

The gravestone on Julia Greeley's grave in Mt. Olivet was put there 38 years after her funeral.

27. Br. John F. Echeverría, S.J. (1862-1943), lay brother at Sacred Heart for 40 years:

Julia Greeley became a convert through the efforts of Mrs. Gilpin. The Gilpins left Julia $1,000 in their will. She lost $900 of this in a bank failure. With the little money she received from her labors, housework and taking care of children she purchased leaflets and Sacred Heart badges which she gave to Denver firemen. She sold 100 Sacred Heart Almanacs every month. She was daily communicant and was taken ill in the Sacred Heart Church -- from here she was taken to St. Joseph's Hospital where she died on the Feast of the Sacred Heart 1918. She is buried in Mt. Olivette Cemetery in Denver. She came to Denver from St. Louis with Mrs Gilpin.[186]

28. Agnes Hines Erger (1894-1981), aged 80, niece of Rose Stetter Fisher:

Mother Pancratia had surgery at St. Joe's Hospital. Julia went there and said to RNs, "I want to see her, you tell her Julia is here." RNs: "No, nobody can see her." JG: "You go ahead and tell her. And then tell me what she says." Pancratia was anxious to see her.

---

[183] Nakkulaa 55, Kreck 55-71, Dorgan-Ross 66. Dandridge and Martin are both buried among the 16 firemen surrounding the Fireman's Memorial in Fairmount Cemetery.

[184] The old No. 3 station at 2563 Glenarm (which was once known as Lincoln) was replaced nearby in 1931, and the old building became the Wallace Simpson Post #29 of the American Legion. [Kreck 69] Today it seems to be empty.

[185] D. DeOrio & Sons, contract, June 2, 1956, in Castillo Collection, ACPMA; Kennedy 1974, p. 19, in Kennedy papers, AAD. This was 38 years after Julia's death.

[186] Collected by Machebeuf History Club, St. Mary's Academy, in 1939, in Kennedy papers, AAD. Re the legacy, see p. 19. Her coming to Denver will be discussed later.

"Julia told my aunt, Mrs. Rose Fisher, that she took her name from Judge and Mrs. Horace Greeley. Mrs. Greeley, Catholic, instructed Julia. In Mountain town near Denver. When somebody said, 'They ought to leave you a little money,' Julia said, 'They've given me more than money — they gave me my faith'."[187]

Young Ladies Sodality was having a popularity/beauty contest benefit of S H Church: 10 cents vote. To show JG's humility, just to make money for the church, she went to the firemen and got them to vote for her. Collected about $350. Julia won contest.

Julia came back for Portiuncula — flopping big shoes —her big handbag — Uncle Frank Fisher said, "Julia, look out, somebody will take that bag." "Mr. Fisher, they'll have to tickle me pretty hard to get it." — Julia not afraid to go home on Larimer Street.

Julia always had bunch of broken old rosaries — she could take to Fred across St & he could fix/repair them.[188]

Agnes Hines Erger heard Julia say that an infuriated slave master blinded her eye by either a shot or a blow. Julia always kept a cloth handy to wipe away the discharge.[189] Agnes Erger said, "When Julia was three years old, she was sick, and her mother stayed away from the fields to take care of her."[190]

29. Rose Stetter Fisher, S.F.O. (b. ca 1871), who ran a grocery and boarding house across from St. Elizabeth's church:

On August 2, Feast of the Portiuncula, Julia would cross the street from St. Elizabeth's church to Mrs. Fisher's grocery and cafe to get something to eat. On one occasion the kitchen girl had already finished the dishes and tidied up. "Oh, get something for Julia anyhow," Mrs. Fisher told her. "All right," said Mary, "but you'll have to pray for me, Julia." That prompted Julia to say, "Mary, I'll put you in a canoe with a lot of others I pray for. But I'll pray special for Mrs. Fisher, all by herself."[191]

30. Wilma Gerspach, singer-organist at Holy Ghost church for over 50 years:
When I was 11 years old ... 1917 Julia Greeley gave me an Easter egg, dyed purple. I kept it till 1950. It became dehydrated. You know how every year we'd put all our Easter stuff out on the table — every year I'd shake it — it was like a marble inside.

---

[187] This is a good example of how some people came to confuse the Gilpins and the Greeleys.
[188] Erger Recollections, Kennedy papers, Noel Collection, BCAARL, & Castillo Collection, ACPMA; partially used in Kennedy 1974, p. 17. Fred, Rose Fisher's husband, ran a religious goods store on 11th St. (now St. Francis Way).
[189] Kennedy 1974, p. 13, in Kennedy papers, AAD.
[190] Kennedy 1979, p. 35, in Kennedy papers, AAD.
[191] Kennedy 1974, pp. 17-18, in Kennedy papers, AAD. Fred & Rose lived at 1037 11th St. Rose was also an eyewitness to the martyrdom of Leo Heinrichs and said he died smiling at the foot of the Blessed Virgin's altar.

When I was 4 or 5 I have a vague but real memory of Julia Greeley holding me on my <her!> lap at my grandmother's home 3231 Champa Street -- where Downing cuts across Champa.

I remember how people always said, "You remember Old Black Julia." Mother Cabrini was in Denver <at the> same time.[192]

left: Grandma Gerspach's home at 3231.Champa, where Wilma sat on Julia's lap. *right:* The home of Otto and Julia Gerspach (possibly Wilma's parents) at 3241 Champa. The houses were built in 1886 and 1884.

31. Helen Hyland Griffin:

"Yes, I knew Julia. Darling person. We were all in choir and Sisters could not come out at night. They'd say 'We'll send nigger Julia to stay with you.' — to keep us from misbehaving. I remember her there at Tenebrae on Good Friday Night. Julia didn't have many teeth in front. Her left eye was blind.

"Grandma [Mrs.] Edward Kennedy loved her — 3263 Curtis Street[193] that's where first meeting was held for formation of Sacred Heart parish. Julia was such a good friend of Grandma's she must have been there. Fr. Guida [the founding pastor] was there, too."[194]

Grandma Kennedy's home was built in 1887.

---

[192] Gerspach Recollections, Kennedy papers, Noel Collection, BCAARL, & Castillo Collection, ACPMA; paraphrased in Kennedy 1974, p. 15. Mary and Albert Gerspach lived at 3231 Champa in 1920. They were probably Wilma's aunt and uncle. Otto Henry and Julia Gerspach of 3241 Champa were probably Wilma's parents. [U.S. Census for 1920].

[193] The U.S. Census for 1910 has the Kennedys at 3263 Arapahoe, which casts some doubt on the Curtis St. address.

[194] Griffin Recollections, Kennedy papers, Noel Collection, BCAARL, & Castillo Collection, ACPMA; used partially in Kennedy 1974, p. 16. That Julia was there is, of course, pure speculation and not likely, since she had not yet entered the Church.

32. Agnes Day Grosheider (1892-1983), Sacred Heart high school class of 1911:

Agnes Day Grosheider

Margaret Ducey Day

"My mother was president of Altar & Rosary Society at S. H. for years. Julia Greeley had lunch at our house many and many a time.[195] We always enjoyed her. She had wonderful smile. Everybody knew Julia. My mother loved her. Julia had a band (of Altar and Rosary) to collect 25 cents a month dues from. People would give her change because they knew she was poor and she'd pass it on to someone next house she went to. — A cosmetic saleslady came to front door of Sacred Heart. Fr. Barry in collar answered door. Lady could see he was priest but she gave her sales talk anyhow. Barry said: 'Wait a minute. I'll get the housekeeper.' He brought Julia out. Saleslady disappeared in hurry."[196]

33. Sr. Celine of the Trinity [Mary Catherine] Hayden, O.C.D. (1900-1985), San Diego:[197]

"The profound holiness of Miss Julia Greeley was recognizable by all and sundry. Her delicious sense of humor; delicateness about taking greenbacks, baskets of food and clothing to a side door, and disappearing in the darkness, never spending a cent on herself; and the lavish heavenly-interior favors, known only to the Jesuits of Regis College and Sacred Heart." §§§

St. John's Church at 5th and Josephine, where Julia attended S. Celine's First Communion. The building is now divided into lofts.

"The twenty-eighth of May, 1910, in the vestibule of the Church of Saint John the Evangelist [at 5th and Josephine] Aunt Julia Greeley offered me a dainty corsage. A voice of harmonic overtones lured by vision to ascend. Ebony hair in tight twists beneath a coarse net: pearly teeth with gaping wide-open spaces; a winsome smile; and 'Phantom-of-the-Opera' countenance — one eye gouged out in a fury tantrum by the master <u>whose name the slave had assumed</u>, because it was the only one known to Miss Greeley..." §§§

---

[195] Thomas W. and Margaret Day lived at 3347 Arapahoe. Margaret was born about 1856.

[196] Grosheider Recollections, Kennedy papers, Noel Collection, BCAARL, & Castillo Collection, ACPMA; partially used in Kennedy 1974, p. 14; Friar 1979 p. 37. Mrs. Grosheider's mother, Margaret Ducey (Mrs. T.W.) Day (b. ca 1856), later presented copies of the Sacred Heart Church and School Monitor to the Denver Public Library. One issue of this semiannual publication listed the hundreds of members of the Altar Society and indicated that Julia was one of the 14 directors of the Society and had 25 other women in her group, the fourth largest group in the Society. [Sacred Heart Church and School Monitor 2:7 (Jan. 1912) 9].

[197] As there are at least 12 typed pages of Sister's recollections, given on numerous occasions, and often repetitiously, the following extractions, always in her own words, are compiled from various pages with an effort to include as much information as possible.

Sr. Celine Hayden OCD

"I was ten. She presented a dainty bouquet to me in the shadowed vestibule, not advancing nearer, not touching. The first glimpse of that scarred visage was such a shock that instinctively I drew back and hesitated. Mother came to the rescue by an introduction." §§§

"Mother introduced her as Aunt Julia, universally loved and revered, and later explained that she was the cook for two maiden ladies who owned the house at 5150 Lowell Boulevard,[198] across from Regis College, eventually transformed into a residence for senior students."[199] §§§

"August 1, 1913, farewell dinner for William H. Hayden [Sister's brother], entering the Novitiate at Florissant. Reverend John J. Brown, S.J., said the Annex would be used for Seniors. Laughingly, Charles K. Hayden [another brother] remarked: We shall call it the 'Bughouse,' and thus it was termed by sedate ladies. He resided there until launching upon his Jesuit career the summer of 1914." §§§

"Julia appeared young, tall, slender, erect, stepped briskly, with evident purpose, knelt motionlessly with perfect posture, intently absorbed in the adorable Eucharist..." §§§

"Following the schedule of Forty Hours' Devotion, Julia walked to every Parish, participating in the Masses, Litanies, Benedictions, and worshiping for hours at the Court-Throne of Incarnate Love."[200] §§§

"Walked 10 miles from 50th & Lowell to 5th & Josephine <for> the three days of 40 Hours Devotion, arriving early with flowers for the altar of Exposition, remaining until the closing cadence, then disappearing into the darkness, with a brisk step. At night she may have boarded the 6th Ave. car, changed at the loop, 15th & Lawrence, for the Rocky Mountain Lake streetcar. That was a demanding journey. Mr. & Mrs. Charles H. Hayden, informants." §§§

"Altar Society Ladies everywhere were acquainted with "Aunt Julia," because of her luxurious donations of flowers, prevalent on Lowell, where she was in residence in 1910,[201] as cook for the Misses Ryan." §§§

"First Thursday of every month WALKED full circuit of fire-stations, distributing Propagation of Faith leaflets; Colorado Catholic; Western Watchman; red Rosaries; pamphlets; yarn and knitting needles. Started from 50th and Lowell and returned on foot. Recent firemen retain no memories of that generation." §§§

---

[198] The Ryan sisters lived at 5127 (and not 5150) Lowell and did not own the building.
[199] See "The Ryan House" text block after No. 13 on pp. 43-45.
[200] In the 1885 Denver city directory, six Catholic churches were listed: St. Mary's, St. Elizabeth, Sacred Heart, St. Patrick, St. Ann, and St. Joseph. By the time of Julia's death in 1918, the directory listed 21 parish churches in Denver, plus Loyola Chapel which it labeled "sucursal [the Spanish word for *branch*] of Sacred Heart."
[201] She probably did not live in the Ryan House.

"Crisscross was necessary for fire-stations. Rather than waste cash, the Apostle of the Sacred Heart traversed on foot, pulsing to the Mysteries, fingering beads. A one-man show to encourage knitting, was more of a challenge than for Fitzsimons General Hospital after World Wars. If weather failed to cooperate, she resorted to the trolley for distant parishes (Exposition), but 50th Avenue was the city limit, and with cars slow, and at long intervals, it was a taxing trip, requiring a transfer." §§§

"She moved to downtown Lawrence Street, near the Church of the Sacred Heart, and by catering became acquainted with the upper echelon, who contributed to her charities. She was pardonably proud of the sobriquet 'Everybody's Aunt,' claiming to be naught but a 'dark spot in a bowl of cream,'" while paradoxically boasting of her girls 'as the most modishly chic of Denver,' regardless of race or type. Why not? It was the truth.

"Thence she traversed the city, twenty-two miles on foot, the first of every month, distributing Propagation of the Faith leaflets, brochures, Catholic literature, instructions and materials for arts and crafts, to entice firemen from useless card-games. The project was successful." §§§

"Thoughtful Sisters of Loretto, who conducted a boarding and day academy for the élite at Fifteenth and California, saved fashionable dresses and coats. Periodically Julia would tread the trellised arbor for the promised treasure trove.

"Miss Greeley supplied help of any kind, wherever, whenever required, tirelessly, late, or early, in heat, or bitter cold."[202] §§§

34. Rose Ann Honeyman:

We lived at 35th and Humboldt. Old Black Julia visited Catholics all over. She came to our house to hand out her Sacred Heart Leaflets. — She ate with us. Always left a happy feeling. But that doesn't mean she didn't have ups and downs. She seemed to prefer Mary and Con to Frank and me.[203] But there was a good reason. First time Frank saw her he started to cry. He had never seen a black person before. There weren't many blacks in Denver. I think Julia was the first black Catholic, but I am not sure. There was a reason I may have turned Julia off. She carried a big black bag. If you gave her an apple or an orange or candy it went into the bag, and somebody got it at the next house she visited. Now I didn't like the looks of the bag and didn't like to take anything out of it. Somebody gave me

The Honeyman family's home (built in 1888) still stands at 3524 Humboldt, a half block from Annunciation Church.

---

[202] Hayden Recollections, Kennedy papers, Noel Collection, BCAARL, & Castillo Collection, ACPMA; partially used in Kennedy 1979, pp. 36-37. A Margaret R. Hayden, possibly Sister's mother, directed the Loyola Choral Club in 1911. [Sacred Heart Church and School Monitor, 2:5 (Jan. 1911) 47].
[203] All siblings.

this beautiful big doll and Julia thought Mary should have had it. Julia went out and bought a bigger, more beautiful doll for Mary. We all knew she couldn't afford it. I think Julia was first black person admitted to St. Joe's Hospital. Was it Fr. McDonnell or Fr. Lonergan who got her in?[204]

35. Lucille Hagus Imherr (Mrs. George Imherr):

Julia Greeley was small slender person, not over 5 ft. — always had a lovely smile — she lived close to the church (S.H.) — I think her right eye was the blind one. Her face was V shaped — rather pointed chin — always dressed in black — black hat with brim on it — black coat. Always bid everybody good day. — Julia Greeley lived (1916) 2821 Walnut one block west of Sacred Heart & opposite side of church.[205]

36. John McNulty:

11 years old in 1918. Julia swept church (he did not see her sweep). "I was coming from old church and I can remember exact spot — between Lawrence and Larimer — on 28th St — where we met and talked. She was so cheerful — she had time to talk to kids — not many people do that — she was liked by kids — If there's ever a saint in heaven, she was out of this world.

"Julia lived on Stout in 2700 or 2800 block — house set back.

"Fr. Casey tore out old pews where Julia sat. I'd like to know one where Julia sat.

Originally there were at least 20 of these two-seaters in Sacred Heart Church. Three remain today, but there is no way of knowing if any one of them was Julia's.

"She made impression on me — spent her money on somebody who had more than she did.

"I pray to that woman every night to intercede with Sacred Heart for me. I know she's not at that stage, but to me she is.

"Some called her nigger, but I thought [that] pretty offensive.

"Large hat that covered her face — long dress — decided limp — see a block away."[206]

---

[204] Honeyman Recollections, Kennedy papers, Noel Collection, BCAARL, & Castillo Collection, ACPMA; partially used in Kennedy 1974, p. 16. Honeyman's father, Frank, a watchman at the Denver Athletic Club, lived at 3524 Humboldt, a one story brick house still standing, but now painted brown. [1914 Denver city directory].

[205] Imherr Recollections, Kennedy papers, Noel Collection, BCAARL, & Castillo Collection, ACPMA; partially used in Kennedy 1974, pp. 14.

[206] McNulty Recollections, Kennedy papers, Noel Collection, BCAARL, & Castillo Collection, ACPMA; paraphrased in Kennedy 1974, p. 34. Fr. John E. Casey, S.J., was pastor at Sacred Heart from

37. Terrance F. Owens (b. ca 1856/57), Denver's fifth fire chief (1903-1912):

After enrolling many firemen in the League of the Sacred Heart, she went downtown to see Chief Terry Owens.[207] "What you selling now, Julie?" he asked. "Tickets for the Orphans Ball or the Orphans' Picnic?" She sold more tickets for church affairs than anyone else in Denver. — "Dese tickets are for Heb'n, Chief, and I wanna give 'em to all your men." — Terry looked over a leaflet and said "That's fine, Julie, but don't forget me." — "No, suh! You not the foist memba, but you the chiefest."[208]

Fire Chief Terry Owens

38. Frank Reynolds:

Julia spent almost all her time in church.

Dave was a black man who worked around Sacred Heart Church and helped Brother John Echeverria, S.J. Dave and Julia were <the> only colored you'd see in church.[209]

Julia Greeley cooked in the early days at St. Mary's Academy at 1440 California St.

39. Sr. Alice Carlene Roche, S.L.

Mother Pancratia, S.L., built Old St. Mary's Academy, 14th and California, where present (1970) Denver Post stands. Building started 1872 and Lorettines operated that boarding/dayhop school till 1911 when they moved to Pennsylvania Ave.

In October 1915 Pancratia was sick and dying in St. Joseph's Hospital. No one was permitted to see her. The nurse came in and whispered to Pancratia that an old black woman was there and wanted to see

---

1948 to 1973. He possibly removed the pew in 1948, when he gave the church a "new look," by covering the entire interior with white paint trimmed with gold. The exterior of the church and rectory were also painted white (or yellow), possibly at the same time. Fr. Marcus Medrano, a later pastor, had all the paint on the church removed, and Fr. Gene Emrisek, O.F.M.Cap., similarly had the rectory exterior restored. There is no other indication than this that Julia Greeley lived on Stout St. There are years however when the Denver city directories do not say where she was living, e.g. 1888, 1889, 1892, 1896-1898, 1900-1902.

[207] Owens' office was in the city hall [Denver Republican 10-12-1911] which at the time was at the northwest corner of 14th & Larimer. Owens was a fireman 1881-1912.

[208] Kennedy 1974, pp. 14-15. It is presently unknown where Kennedy got this information, as Owens himself was born 112 years before Kennedy was collecting recollections and was clearly no longer living.

[209] Reynolds Recollections, Kennedy papers, Noel Collection, BCAARL, & Castillo Collection, ACPMA.

her. "Oh that must be Old Julia." RN: "Yes, how did you guess."

"Oh, dear Julia cooked for us at the Academy for so long. Please bring her in. I know how far she has walked here just to see me. Keep out the rest of Denver high and low — but not dear Julie." Pancratia died Oct. 12, 1915.[210]

40. Marguerite Graves Stephens (1900-1988), O.F.S.:[211]

Marguerite Graves Stephens

Grandmother insisted upon our showing deep respect to her revered friend — Miss Julia Greeley, who came to our home often and singingly rocked the current baby to sleep.

Grandmother Anna Graves lived at 1421 — 28th St., Denver, not quite two blocks from Sacred Heart Church.[212] She raised her seven grandchildren by her deceased daughter by herself. — The old directory lists Julia as living at 1421 — 28th St. in 1897. From 1897 to 1903 no mention of her is in the directory. It lists her as living at 2913 Walnut in 1903-4-5.

On a below-zero night Mother and Father encountered Julia and wondered how she could balance her bundles destined for the needy, but jokingly she pursued her path, slipping and sliding across icy pavement into the darkness.

My parents, the current baby[213] and I visited Grandmother this cold freezing snowy evening. Going home about 9 o'clock we met Julia, she was pushing a baby buggy which she used to carry clothing & such for the needy. She called from across the street to my Dad, "Mr. Graves

Nora and Edward Graves, with daughter Marguerite.

---

[210] Roche Recollections, Kennedy papers, Noel Collection, BCAARL, & Castillo Collection, ACPMA.

[211] Mrs. Stephens was reportedly born in Hartford, Conn., Aug. 18, 1900. At the time she knew Julia Greeley, she lived with her parents, Edward and Nora Graves at 2721 Lawrence St.

[212] This building was a small one-room building on the northwest corner of 28th and the alley between Blake and Walnut streets. [1903 Denver Sanborn insurance maps] Julia herself was listed as living there in 1899 [1899 Denver city directory], at which time Anna Graves was living at 2633 Larimer. [1898-1900 Denver city directories]. Marguerite herself was living at 1421 28th in 1918. [Sacred Heart Church and School Monitor, 1918].

[213] Madelyn G. Graves (1907-1991). The baptismal record lists her as Mary Madeline Graves, born 8-11-1907. At the time, Ed and Nora lived at 2635 Walnut. John and Julie Higgins were the godparents. Sacred Heart Parish, Baptismal Records, 2: 88.

you got anything on your hip?"[214] I think Sister[215] didn't mention it because perhaps saints aren't supposed to be human. I think this was about 1908.

She [Julia] lived with a family that had abandoned the practice of religion. Through her prayers and example, all of them returned to the Sacraments.

She lived with the family of John and Annie Higgins. They were loose living people. Eight of them. They all died receiving the last Sacraments.

Youth hummed verses about ridding the city of negroes. A little girl repeated the rhyme, and for a lifetime has regretted hurting inadvertently the sensitive Southerner, who never returned to that locale.

Julia used to drop in anytime and rock the current baby while Mother did her work. One day I was singing this: "Hurray, hurray, we'll knock the niggers down, Hurray, hurray, we'll run them out of town." Julia asked "Child, who taught you that?" I answered, "Momma," though she hadn't. We were always taught to respect negroes. Julia never returned to our home.

When a couple by whom she was employed sued for a divorce, Julia had the backbone to testify in favor of the wife. The infuriated husband blackballed her against the possibility of another position, but the Jesuits of Sacred Heart Parish took her as cook, decidedly more to her taste, and the proximity of the adorable Blessed Sacrament, her Love and Life.

This was Governor Gilpin and wife. I have heard this from Mother (deceased) that Julia testified favoring his wife. I don't know the charges. He blackballed Julia & she couldn't find work.[216]

The upper echelon told her to refrain from the altar railing at the ten o'clock Mass. Father Barry, S.J., invited Miss Greeley, and delivered a homily to the women on the Mystical Body of Christ and the Spiritual Banquet of grace for souls of every race.

Father Barry refused to ask Julia to refrain from going to the communion rail at 10:00 o'clock Mass on Sunday. The fashionable ladies didn't want to brush elbows with her I guess. Julia fasted until that time as a penance. Father put them in their place but not from the pulpit.[217]

With Sacred Heart leaflets for firemen in every station, and scores of children, Aunt Julia gave red rosaries generously, saved and used for decades.

---

[214] From the following sentence, it seems likely that "anything on your hip" was a reference to hip flasks in which many men carried distilled spirits.

[215] Mrs. Stephen's testimony was taken in two stages, first by an unidentified Sister given to flowery interpretations (therefore probably Sr. Celine Hayden), who seemed intent on concealing identities, and later by Wilma Gerspach who attempted to draw out greater details. In the present study, Sister's version is in italics and Wilma's in regular type.

[216] Actually the Governor had taken this action long before the divorce trial, but Julia did indeed testify at the trial. Much more about this a little later.

[217] Fr. Edward D. Barry, S.J., while pastor of Sacred Heart Church, was also architect for the first buildings at Sacred Heart College [Stansell 48].

Julia delivered Sacred Heart badges, leaflets to firemen in nearby stations and to many others. I don't know how many red rosaries Julia gave. I know I had one from her & Grandma also. She didn't have much money so I doubt she could afford very many.

Her LEFT eye had been cruelly removed by an irate master.

Her left eye was destroyed by a master's whip when she was three years old. I presume she was clinging to her mother's skirts & her mother got the whipping.[218]

I do not believe Julia ever called herself "nigger Julia." She had too much dignity for that.[219]

41. Sr. Catherine Regina (Katie Laetitia) Taylor, S.C., (1898-1988):

Sr. Catherine Regina Taylor SC.

Katie Laetitia lived at SH parish 1907-15 and then she went to Mt. St. Joseph, Ohio.

There was row of short pews on left side of church as you faced altar. Julia had one of these with her name on it — so she wouldn't have to sit near white people.

I saw the prizes Julia gave other children whose sponsor she was at Confirmation, just a little holy picture..... But I wanted one. Told my mother I wanted Julia for my sponsor because she was holy. "I don't care how holy she is, you're not going to have a colored woman for a sponsor."[220]

42. Benjamin Palmer Van Hille:

Ben saw her dusting the pews in Sacred Heart.[221]

---

[218] Charlene Scott reported in 1990 that there are different tales of how Julia lost her eye. "One story [given without attribution] is that her mistress slapped her so hard that she was blinded." Scott then went on to tell the prevailing story of the whip. [DCR 2-7-1990].

[219] Stephens Recollections, Kennedy papers, Noel Collection, BCAARL, & Castillo Collection, ACPMA, partially used in Kennedy 1979, p. 35-38.

[220] Taylor Recollections, Kennedy papers, Noel Collection, BCAARL, & Castillo Collection, ACPMA; paraphrased in Kennedy 1974, p. 16. The only person found thus far with Julia as a sponsor was Helen Cecilia Durkin, who was confirmed by Bp. Nicholas Matz on May 20, 1909 at Sacred Heart Parish.

[221] Van Hille Recollections, Kennedy papers, Noel Collection, BCAARL, & Castillo Collection, ACPMA.

43. Agnes Gavaghan Walsh (1898-1989),[222] widow of Judge Joseph Walsh (1888-1955):

12 years at Sacred Heart; graduated 1917. "We had nothing but love and respect for Julia." Julia was "part of Church." "Left eye was blind one. — Yes, I remember her corncob pipe."[223]

Agnes Loretta Walsh was one of Julia's closest friends

Judge Joseph Walsh was one of Julia's pallbearers.

44. Fr. Anthony Weinzapfel (d. 1976), pastor Holy Name Church (1942-1970):[224]

Fr. Anthony Weinzapfel

Mrs. Agnes Padan lives with her brother Tom Skeahan. Says "Julia was short, fat, pleasant."

Ft. Logan Army Post built 1884. Logantown was popular name of section near Fort where retired soldiers lived. Two names interchanged.

St. Patrick's basement church built 1895 of Castle Rock stone; flat roof; ground came up to windows; purpose was to build on top of it, but never done. Torn down or up 1960 when Holy Name was built. Msgr. [Richard] Brady took care of

St. Patrick's Church in Logantown was on the site of today's Holy Name Church in Sheridan, but faced on Mansfield Ave.

---

[222] Agnes graduated from Sacred Heart High School in 1915. She helped arrange Julia's funeral, and her husband was one of the pallbearers. [RMN 7-11-1918].

[223] Agnes Walsh Recollections, Kennedy papers, Noel Collection, BCAARL, & Castillo Collection, ACPMA. Mrs. Joseph Walsh lived at 2831 Champa. [Sacred Heart Church and School Monitor 4: 3 (July 1917) 38] For more information from her sister-in-law, Eva Walsh, see under Eleanor Pavella Castellan, No. 3 on p. 41.

[224] Fr. Weinzapfel Recollections, Kennedy papers, Noel Collection, BCAARL & Castillo Collection, ACPMA, partially used in Kennedy 1974, p. 18. It is not clear what part Agnes Padan (1897-1991), postmistress at Ft. Logan, played in these recollections. She was just an infant at the time. Her mother, Cecilia Skeahan (1875-1957) could have had some connection with the Church during this time, but she was not a member of the Church until just prior to her death in 1957. [Holy Name Church, Sheridan, death records, July 1, 1957] Mrs. Mary Hoolahan Jensen (1859-1944), who is quoted, seems the likely source of the rest of the information as she was still living two years after Fr. Weinzapfel became pastor at Holy Name. [op.cit, Sept. 12/13, 1944].

St. Pat's 1895-1942 with Mass twice a month. Fr. A. Weinzapfel took over in 1942.[225]

Msgr. Richard Brady was Julia's pastor at Logantown.

Julia Greeley lived on Federal, little settlement of Blacks, Federal near Oxford.[226] She bought a little pump organ which lasted till 1925 ($30). She cooked at Sliney's Hotel (run by Sliney).[227] SL nuns taught catechism at St. Pat's which would account for J.G. asking them to pick out the organ. Mary Jensen said Julia was a saint. Black construction men living Franklin/Grant were ex-slaves.[228]

Mountain View Hotel was earlier known as the Star Hotel and operated by Patrick Sliney.

Dr. Currigan's 'Cure'

Fr. Kennedy seems to have been the first to report a seemingly unusual event which had happened 37 years earlier, shortly after the U.S. became involved in World War II. As it has been referred to several times since then and suggested as some confirmation of Julia's sanctity, it behooves that it be treated here as thoroughly as possible. Fr. Kennedy began and ended his second article in *Friar* magazine with the story,[229] but the source of his story was the following letter from Sr. Margaret Ann Noonan, S.C.L., to another Sister of Charity of Leavenworth:[230]

---

[225] Logantown's subterranean church (St. Patrick's) was 21' by 60' and seated about 130, mostly Ft. Logan personnel. [Noel 369]. In 1959 this old church at 3290 W. Milan Ave. in West Englewood was demolished and replaced by the present Holy Name Church. The new church was dedicated in 1961 [Noel 369-370, DCR 5-4-2011].

[226] This settlement was known as Ft. Logan Homes and was between S. Federal (then Military Rd.) and Clay, and Jersey (Mansfield) and Oxford. It is now part of Sheridan [Hutcheson 6].

[227] Patrick Sliney (also Saliney and Seliney) had a saloon near the southeast corner of S. Lowell and Mansfield in Sheridan, directly north of the train station. The Colorado State Business Directory lists him from 1893 till 1915. In 1902 they started listing it as the Star Hotel. It was later renamed the Mountain View Hotel and burned down in the 1960s [Hutcheson (1998) 5, Hutcheson to Burkey, phone conversation, Sept. 8, 2011].

[228] In *Register* 4-13-1939, Mrs. Gallagher spoke of Julia cooking for Capt. Young at Ft. Logan before the Spanish-American war. Her cooking at Sliney's was possibly after Young was moved from Ft. Logan.

[229] Kennedy 1979, pp. 29-30, 38, in Kennedy papers, AAD.

[230] Kennedy papers, AAD. Another letter from Sr. Margaret Ann, this one to Sr. Perpetua, is in the archives of St. Joseph's Hospital, Denver. Mailed Apr. 28, 1998, from Leavenworth, it says only the following related to the present subject: "Thank you for sending the *Denver Register* [Oct. 13, 1982]. I was there in the crowd outside Helen's room when Dr. Currigan came in crying like a

Sr. Margaret Ann Noonan SCL

Dr. Martin Currigan, who attended Julia

May 25, 1974

Dear Sister M. Andrew[231]

I had never heard of Black Julia until my sister's critical illness in the 40s.

Dr. Courigan [sic] operated on Helen & diagnosed the case as hopeless—cancer throughout. He gave her a colostomy and told my mother to get the family together, that Helen had about 2 weeks to live.

When Dr. Courigan was driving home that rainy night, he kept seeing an ugly, black, scarred face in the windshield. He was terribly puzzled about who it was. Finally it dawned on him that it was the face of Black Julia, whom he hadn't thought of for years. He took care of [her] as a young intern in her last illness. I think he was with her when she died.

He turned his car around (rainy night and all) and drove back to the hospital. The family and relatives were all sitting in the hall outside Helen's room.

He told them all to have Novena of Masses said honoring Black Julia for Helen's recovery. We went to all the parishes—many waved their present Masses so that these could be said immediately.

Msgr. Mac [Hugh L. McMenamin] at the cathedral told his young assistant Father Fred McCallin (my cousin) that he smelled a miracle. He was sure of it.

Helen stayed in the hospital a couple of weeks, but at Dr. Courigan's insistence she went home. He thought the home environment would be more cheerful for her last days.

She was coming along fairly well—but being a nurse she realized her temperature increase was indicative of something wrong. She went down to Dr. Courigan's office. He was going away so he sent her to Dr. Cheeley (sp?)

Dr. Cheeley operated and found no cancer. He diagnosed it as peritonitis of the intestines. He treated her, but did not close the baby. He felt terrible about Helen. He asked each of us to offer a novena of Masses. All, of course, did. Some parishes were unable to take all nine Masses, but many did. All (nearly) Denver was praying. For me there was no doubt that Black Julia is a saint, no matter what happens — nor there is no doubt that Helen was a saint. Her life was a reflection of Julia's."

[231] Sr. M. Andrew Talle, S.C.L.

> colostomy until he was sure all was all right. He closed it in about 2 months. She has led a very active life ever since.
>
> Dr. Courigan should have taken a biopsy. He was so sure that he didn't do it. Sister Louise de Marillac [Blain], S.C.L. was in surgery at the time. She felt the same way about the cancer....
>
> Sincerely,
> Sister Ann Margaret

Helen Noonan, R.N., was the daughter of Emmett and Helen Noonan and had worked with Dr. Currigan in previous years. Dr. Martin Dominic Currigan, Jr. (1887-1949), who received his M.D. in 1912, had done his internship at St. Joseph's Hospital, was at the time of Julia's death chief resident physician of the City and County of Denver. He was later chief physician of the city and a regent of the University of Colorado.[232]

In subsequent years this event has been described as a cure verified by Dr. Currigan[233] an event smelling like a miracle,[234] a miracle,[235] and a reported miraculous cancer healing[236] The present study, however, needs to point out that, while a miracle may have been involved, this claim would never pass the scrutiny that the Church would apply in judging it, and there is nothing to be gained in citing it further. Suffice it to quote the report which Ruth L. Reed of the medical records department of St. Joseph's Hospital sent Fr. Kennedy on July 2, 1974 (boldface added):

> We have checked our records for the information which you requested from Sister Ascella [Asella Delaney. S.C.L.,] regarding Helen Noonan, R.N.
>
> Dr. Currigan was indeed her physician in August, 1941, **he did not take a biopsy of tissue and a diagnosis of cancer was not positively made.** The patient later, after a rising temperature over a period of time, was referred by Dr. Currigan to a Dr. Cheley. Dr. Cheley did an exploratory operative procedure. The pathological diagnosis on tissue obtained at this procedure was that this was an inflammatory process.
>
> From information we can obtain from this old record it seems that Mrs. Noonan's condition improved after this abscess was cleared.[237]

Wilma Gerspach, Fr. Kennedy's research assistant, later spoke to Mrs. Noonan and informed Fr. Kennedy:

---

[232] Stone 2: 868-870.
[233] DCR 2-7-1990; Noel 342.
[234] DCR 10-13-1982 and 4-15-1998.
[235] Hawkins web site.
[236] Fishell 100-101, DCR 4-15-2009 & Catholic Review 2-18-2010.
[237] Reed to Kennedy, 7-2-1974, Kennedy papers, AAD.

> Emmett's wife Helen says that the family really didn't want Dr. Currigan to operate, as they felt that he & Helen were too closely associated in working together, so much for that little bit.
> Dr. Currigan died in 1949, at age 61, so was 30 years old in 1918 & in practice. Helen was 38 years old, and the operation was in 1942. There were 3 people in the waiting room, her Father & Mother and a cousin. — As in Sisters letter, Dr. Cheley operated a few months later. Helen did nursing at St. Joes for 12 years. — I didn't call Sr. Ascella as Helen said she is very confused & mixed up. She sees her often I guess — so I didn't think she would be of much help. — Helen, the one with the operation is alive but having poor health & glaucoma. — Sr. was in the convent at the time of operation so was not with the family.[238]

There is another claim that needs to be dealt with for the sake of future writing about Julia. Several articles of fairly recent date have stated that, when her body was moved in the 1950s, it was found to be incorrupt. Mary O'Sullivan (in 1995) is the first known to make this statement in print.[239] Pam Pedler repeated it in 2009, calling it "another saint-like quality."[240] Asked where she got this information, Ms. Pedler cited material on a Find A Grave website posted by Dennis Hawkins, and Hawkins said he got it from his notes of a 1992 centennial tour of Mt. Olivet led by Dr. Tom Noel and Jan Parsons, director of the cemetery.[241]

The fact of the matter is that the 1918 interment records of Mt. Olivet and Horan's mortician's records, show that Julia's body was buried in the exact same spot where it lies today, and there is no evidence that it has ever been moved or even disinterred, so there is no way anyone could know whether or not her body is incorrupt.

How then did this myth arise? It probably arose from a mishearing of what Noel, or more likely Parsons, said in 1992. A brochure she had had prepared for the centennial, as part of the cemetery's walking tour, on p. 9 briefly told Julia Greeley's story and on p. 4 told of the relocation in 1950 of the bodies of about 7,000 people from the old Mt. Calvary cemetery at 900 York Street to Mt. Olivet. The brochure added on page 4, "Another astonishing tale from the men who worked on the project relates that when the grave of an Irish lass from Leadville was uncovered, the scent of rose petals filled the air. There was great consternation that the body of a saint might have been disinterred. Sanctity terrified all and created great problems for Church officials who had to verify or deny the saintliness. Despite intensive research by the *Denver Catholic Register*, the Irish lass remains a mystery." [242]

Actually the *Register* itself had identified an Irish woman — though hardly a "lass," since she was 75 years old — whose corpse was found to be incorrupt. She was Mrs. Honora Gleason (1806-1881), who died in Leadville Sept. 15, 1881.[243] Her body now rests at Mt. Olivet in sect.

---

[238] Wilma Gerspach to Fr. Kennedy, Denver, Oct. 29, 1977, Kennedy papers, AAD].
[239] DCR 2-22-1995.
[240] DCR 4-15-2009.
[241] Dennis Hawkins, phone interview by Burkey, Jan. 10, 2012.
[242] Mason 4.
[243] DCR 8-10-1950: "Efforts to discover further information about the life of Honora Gleason, whose incorrupt body, recently discovered in the course of disinterment operations at Mt. Calvary,

24, block 4, lot 6, grave 1, just on the other side of the road from Julia Greeley's grave.[244] Ms. Parsons may well have spoken of both Greeley and Gleason in the same few minutes of the tour.[245]

The Post-Kennedy Years

Since Fr. Kennedy's time, at least 27 articles in the *Denver Catholic Register* have mentioned Julia Greeley. Many of these were mere mentions. A handful of them, however, retold Julia's story. These will be listed here, but with a reference only to what distinguished them from other articles. One such article which added nothing was "Julia Greeley, 'Colored Angel of Charity'."[246]

Paul H. Hallett published a lengthy article entitled "An Ex-Slave Known for Her Sanctity" in which he said that the *Register*'s funeral article in 1918 was "perhaps the only time a major newspaper devoted its first page to the obituary of someone who was celebrated for nothing but for the fact that in the eyes of all who knew her she had died in the odor of sanctity." Hallett also aptly spoke of Julia as setting "herself up as a one woman St. Vincent de Paul Society" and later called her a "fairy godmother" to the "Cinderellas" of her acquaintance.[247]

In "Ramblings: Joys of the Business," James Fiedler told with much satisfaction of a letter received from Marjorie Urqurath Simpson praising Hallett's recent article.[248]

February's annual African-American history month prompted two articles. Charlene Scott wrote "Julia Greeley 'a Beloved Figure',"[249] and Mary O'Sullivan "African-American history month:

Denver, have proved unsuccessful. The story of the discovery was carried in the National Edition of the Register (p. 3 issue dated Aug. 13, 1950). A promising start was made in the quest for information when a small news item was discovered in the Sept. 17, 1881, issue of the Rocky Mountain News. The item stated: 'The remains of Honora Gleason of Leadville were shipped to Undertaker Browne's establishment yesterday morning. The funeral will take place from that place at 10 o'clock this morning.' (The Mass was probably in Leadville). Accuracy of the news item was confirmed by a copy of the Leadville Directory for 1880, which listed a Mrs. Honora Gleason residing at 408 E. 10th. Also listed at the same address were Thomas Gleason and William Gleason, miners.... Honora Gleason had been born in Ireland and had died in Leadville Sept. 15, 1881."

[244] Annette Fugita, Mt. Olivet Cemetery, phone interview by Burkey, Jan. 11, 2012.
[245] Report of possibly another incorrupt body comes from Msgr. Robert Amundsen, pastor in Lafayette, Colo., who said one of the funeral directors involved in moving the bodies from Mt. Calvary to Mt. Olivet told him years ago that a young girl's body was found to be incorrupt and was reinterred in the magnificent mausoleum of Verner Zevola Reed's family in sect. 15, block 1. Cemetery records indicate there are no other bodies in that mausoleum than those of Reed family members.[245] Records do show there is another body buried seven foot behind the mausoleum on the Reed lot, but it is that of a Reed descendant, "Baby Fisher," put there on Dec. 29, 1934. [Annette Fugita, Mt. Olivet Cemetery, phone interview by Burkey, Jan. 17, 2012.
[246] DCR 3-17-1976.
[247] DCR 10-13-1982.
[248] DCR 11-17-1982.
[249] DCR 2-7-1990.

Recalling Julia Greeley"[250] Without any further explanation, O'Sullivan said <u>little is known about Greeley's early travels in Pennsylvania and Wisconsin</u>, and she debuted the legend of the incorrupt body.[251]

O'Sullivan's article, however, brought responses from John J. Erger and Mary Anderson, published under one title: "Thanks for the 'Beloved Julia Greeley' article."[252] Both used the occasion to speak further of Julia:

> My mother Agnes Erger, often spoke of visits by Julia to my godmother, Rose Fisher, who lived across from St. Elizabeth Church. "Aunt Rose" often gave Julia dinner when Julia came over to the west side.
> My godmother was a saint like Julia on feeding and clothing the poor—that is why they all got along so well.
> Julia, whose eye was put out by a slave owner, gave a wonderful lesson to blacks and whites that forgiveness, not revenge, is the Catholic-Christian response to injustice.
> Among the many stories my mother told me of Julia was that of a rose picked from the coffin of Julia at her funeral by Ellen Weckbaugh. The rose did not wither, but remained fresh and fragrant for years. Perhaps the Weckbaugh family can shed more light on the subject.
> Julia, let us never forget your legacy of love, forgiveness, and joy! I've heard there was always a smile on your face.
>
> John J. Erger
> Denver

There indeed was such a rose saved by Mrs. Edward Wechbaugh<u>, but it had nothing to do with Julia Greeley.</u> It was taken from Fr. Leo Heinrich's coffin in 1908. Paul Hallett later wrote about its involvement in a cure believed to have been worked in 1921 through Leo's intercession.[253] Hallett noted the rose had been mentioned in a much earlier Register article.[254]

The second response to O'Sullivan's article successfully proposed action to remember Julia:

> I have many African American friends in various denominations who never heard about her. With your permission, I intend to copy this article and distribute it widely throughout the Denver area.
> For any of you who might be interested in visiting the grave of this friend of the Sacred Heart, it is in block 8, section 7 at Mt. Olivet Cemetery in Golden.
> It would be wonderful if we could have a Mass said in her honor, at the cemetery or at the Church of the Sacred Heart on the Feast of the Sacred Heart of Jesus, June 23, 1995.
>
> Mary Anderson, Arvada

---

[250] DCR 2-22-1995.
[251] The present study has found nothing about such travels. Cannon 270 does speak of Mrs. Gilpin being in New York with her children before her marriage to the ex-governor, but Julia was definitely not with them.
[252] DCR 3-15-1995.
[253] Hallett (1983) 7.
[254] DCR 4-24-1919.

And a couple of months later, the paper carried notices of a special Mass at Sacred Heart Church on Sunday, June 25, in honor of Julia Greeley and her devotion to the Sacred Heart.[255] The first said "Julia lived across the street from Sacred Heart Church, which was not really the case, and was a daily communicant," and the second urged, "Please come to give honor to this modern day saint in THANKSGIVING for her generosity of giving and working for the poor and the needy of Sacred Heart parish for many years."

In 1996, the first notice was given of scholarships being offered to high school graduates in honor of Julia Greeley. They were offered by the ladies auxiliary of Charles Bright Court 261 of the Knights of Peter Claver.[256] Among other things the article said of Julia "Upon her death, thousands attended the funeral, including nearly every elected official in the state." This of course was a gross exaggeration. In subsequent years, additional stories have revealed that the Julia Greeley Scholarships are still being offered.[257] Linda M. Chase and Shirley Johnson established the scholarship program through the inspiration of Mary Frances O'Sullivan in 1994. Recipients of the scholarships are expected to exemplify their Catholic faith through Mass attendance, community service, academic standing, and a willingness to give back to the community. The first scholarship was given on June 24, 1995, and additional ones have been given every year since then. In 2011, seven scholarships in the amount of $1,200 each were awarded.[258]

Mary Frances O'Sullivan has played major roles in keeping Julia Greeley's fame alive. She saw to it that Fr. Kennedy's essential work was preserved, she wrote an article for the Register, and she inspired the dames of St. Peter Claver to offer scholarships in Julia's honor.

Following a visit to Denver by Rome-based Cardinal J. Francis Stafford in the spring of 1998, the Register noted that the cardinal had announced his interest in supporting the cause for Julia's canonization and then reran in its entirety Paul H. Hallett's article from 1982.[259]

Cardinal J. Francis Stafford

To a wire story on preparations for the 2002 National Black Catholic Congress, which merely listed a number of exemplary black Catholics worldwide, the Denver Catholic Register added "In Denver, Julia Greeley was a devout and saintly Catholic who worked tirelessly for the poor out of Sacred Heart Church, Denver's oldest Jesuit church."[260]

Another series of articles mentioning Julia began in 2006, when Endow, an organization founded in Denver in 2003 and dedicated to Educating on the Nature and Dignity of Women, named Julia Greeley its model in recognizing the "Genius of Women" and began bestowing the annual Julia

---

[255] DCR 5-24-1995 and 6-7-1995.
[256] DCR 10-2-1996.
[257] DCR 11-22-2000, 10-23-2003, 2-27-2008, 5-25-2011.
[258] Linda Chase to Burkey, Denver, 7-9-2011.
[259] DCR 4-15-1998.
[260] DCR 11-14-2001.

Greeley Award on a stellar array of extraordinary Catholic women exemplifying the feminine genius.[261] The 2007 article told of a CD-video Endow had produced about Julia, and quoted Sr. Prudence Allen, R.S.M., as saying of Julia on the video, "She was full of creative ways of loving people."

Later on in the decade, Pam Pedler wrote both "Denver's Saintly Woman: Julia Greeley"[262] and "Ex-Slave Was an Angel of Charity in Early Denver."[263]

And finally two articles on tours of Mt. Olivet Cemetery noted that Julia Greeley was buried there.[264]

Some Special Surprises

This study's extensive survey of *Register* articles was made possible by the Denver archdiocese's posting on line in 2005-2007 its entire collection of back issues. A powerful search engine located not only the scores of articles published since Julia's death, but also found four articles which appeared during her life time.

The first was in 1903, when the paper published a huge list of Sacred Heart parishioners who contributed to special Christmas and Easter collections. Julia gave $1 to each.[265] Later that same year, a full page report on the parish's Charter Bazaar revealed that Miss Julia Greeley had raised the highest amount in the sale of tickets. Her $87 was followed by her friend Mrs. Thomas Lee's $65. The next highest among the many participating was $28.[266]

In subsequent years, Julia's donations to the parish were reported in a parish magazine. These included an annual $8 pew rent, Easter collection and the Aid Society. From 1905 till 1916, her annual donations averaged $24. This is put in better perspective by realizing the largest annual contribution reported for anyone in the parish was $250. During 1917, Julia's contributions dropped to $10 and she moved to a new location, possibly a sign of failing resources.[267]

In 1913, Julia's name appeared in a list of 85 people from all across Colorado who contributed to a fund being raised by the *Register* itself to fund an appeal of a local judge's decision to place a Catholic orphan in the care of a nonreligious person in opposition to the expressed will of her dying parents. Julia contributed 25 cents, which was a considerable amount at that time. The same issue of the paper advertised a new typewriter for $5.[268]

---

[261] DCR 5-17-2006, 5-9-2007, and 4-7-2010.

[262] DCR 4-15-2009.

[263] DCR 3-24-2010.

[264] DCR 9-8-2008 and 9-29-2010.

[265] DCR 5-9-1903.

[266] DCR 11-7-1903.

[267] Sacred Heart Church and School Monitor, 1:2 (Jan. 1906) 17; 1:4 (Jan. 1907) 20; 2:1 (Jan. 1909) 17; 2:3 (Jan. 1910) 21; 2:5 (Jan. 1911) 26; 2:7 (Jan. 1912) 35; 3:2 (Jan. 1913) 31; 3:4 (Jan. 1914) 27; 3:6 (Jan. 1915) 24; 3:8 (Jan. 1916) 24; 4:2 (Jan. 1917) 38; 4:4 (Jan. 1918) 24].

[268] DCR 1-23-1913.

Mother Pancratia Bonfils SL.

The fourth article was about Julia's friendship with Mother Pancratia Bonfils, S.L. (1852-1915), former principal of St. Mary's Academy and foundress of Loretto Heights College. Titled "Colored Lady Had Mass of Requiem for Mother M. Pancratia," it reported from Sacred Heart Parish, "Last Tuesday, on the octave of her funeral, a requiem high mass was sung for the late Mother Pancratia on the part of Julia Greeley, 'colored Julia,' to whom the saintly sister was ever a 'white angel' as she was to the Indians of earlier days."[269]

Discovery of this item led to Mother Pancratia's extensive obituary in the *Denver Post*, which held still another surprise:

> Mother Pancratia's charitable acts, her compassion for the poor, her repeated kindnesses to the unfortunate, ever will live in the hearts of those with whom she came in contact.
> In the early days over in the old St. Mary's academy, the sisters had an old negro cook—"Black Julie" the sisters called her. Julie formerly was in the service of Governor Gilpin of Colorado.
> A few days ago, old "Black Julie," almost forgotten by most of the sisters, appeared at the hospital where Mother Pancratia lay facing death. Julie asked to see Mother Pancratia. The physicians had left strict orders that day for no one to see her. Mother Dolorine [Morrison] told Mother Pancratia that "Black Julie" wanted to see her. "Send everyone else out of the room," Mother Pancratia declared. "Let old 'Black Julie' in if everyone else in Denver is excluded. Her affection for me is too clearly shown from the long walk she must have made to visit me."
> And old "Black Julie" toddled into the quiet room.[270]

And that, dear friends, is all that till now has been found about Julia Greeley. Those who might have been able to tell more have all joined Julia in the hereafter.

---

[269] DCR 10-28-1915. Mother is buried in the center of the Loretto Sisters' cemetery on the northwest corner of the campus of Colorado Heights University on South Federal.
[270] Denver Post 10-12-1915.

In Superior and Supreme Courts

When this study had reached this point in August of 2011, Mrs. Stephens' report (No. 40 on p. 63) that Julia Greeley had testified at the Gilpin divorce trial in superior court and been blackballed by Colonel Gilpin finally percolated the thought that Julia's testimony might still be available. What a find that would be!

Yes indeed, what a find it was! A visit to the Colorado State Archives quickly produced a stack of transcripts half a foot high and two volumes of briefs.[271] Among the thousands of pages, Julia's sworn testimony was immediately found, almost as if Julia herself were guiding the way. This testimony quickly raised the realization that Julia was there not to testify about the Gilpin marriage, but about herself. Colonel Gilpin's reported blackballing her was not the result of her testifying, but was actually at the root of her need to testify.

The ex-governor had accused Julia of being a "lewd and unprincipled woman," and subsequent sworn testimony both refuted Colonel Gilpin on this subject and quite to the contrary attested to Julia's inherent goodness. Though not essential to the trial, the transcripts also produced details about Julia Greeley's pre-1887 history which were quite different from what Professors Cannon and Karnes, and many others, reported in this study's earlier pages. What sweet irony that the Colonel's meanness toward Julia now (125 years later) provides so much wonderful new information about Julia's earlier years.

Due to this study's purpose of gathering all available information about Julia, it will be necessary to reproduce this sworn testimony extensively, without any concern of being repetitious.

It is also absolutely necessary, however, to sum up what the trial was about, since only about two percent of the trial's documents are being reproduced here, namely those on the hundred or so pages that actually dealt with Julia Greeley. A summary is needed also to assist present-day readers not accustomed to reading large amounts of legalese. The summary is admittedly the compiler's own understanding, and the full records remain at the state archives for anyone to examine further.[272]

The Divorce Case in a Nutshell

After 13 years of married life, Colonel Gilpin decided to file for divorce from Julia Pratte Gilpin on the grounds of extreme cruelty, and he asked that he be given custody of his own three children by Mrs. Gilpin.

Mrs. Gilpin was unwilling to agree to the divorce; but, faced with the possibility of the Colonel's winning his request for custody of the children, she countersued for their custody accusing the

---

[271] Gilpin vs. Gilpin, Case No. 1726 in the Superior Court of the City and County of Denver, and Case No. 2210 in the Colorado Supreme Court, boxes 38422, 38770, 38771, 40895 and 45460.
[272] See also Karnes 334-336, Cannon 272-273.

Colonel of extreme cruelty and asking for alimony. As she contested the divorce, the case by the law then in force was taken before a jury.

Colonel Gilpin had 24 major complaints against Mrs. Gilpin, including that she had turned the affections of Gilpin's children against him, that she had done much to dissipate his fortune, that she was scheming to deprive him of his fortune and his children, and even that she was planning to kidnap his children and murder him.

Included in his complaints was no. 15: that Mrs. Gilpin had threatened the morality of his household by forcing into it Julia Greeley, whom Colonel Gilpin described as "a negress" and "a lewd and unprincipled woman," who was a threat to the morality of his children. He also claimed she had conspired with others to kidnap the children and murder the Colonel.

The trial ended with the Colonel being granted the divorce and custody of the children, without any alimony for Mrs. Gilpin.[273]

Mrs. Gilpin's lawyers appealed the verdict to the Colorado Supreme Court *on error*, that is contending that errors had been made in the trial. The Supreme Court reversed the opinion of Superior Court in April 1889 and remanded the case for possible retrial— which never happened.

In May of 1891, the Gilpins became reconciled and lived together the last three years of the Colonel's life in the house at 1321 Bannock St. (then known as S. 14th St.).

The only part of the case with which the present study is concerned is what was said about Julia Greeley. She was not on trial, of course, but Colonel Gilpin's accusations regarding her, in a very real sense, threatened to stain her reputation.

The Colonel's accusations about Julia were answered one by one by Mrs. Gilpin. Her testimony on the stand, however, turned out to be somewhat confusing, especially on the question of whether Julia Greeley had been dismissed and, if so, by whom and for what reason.

In her initial counter-complaint, Mrs. Gilpin had accused the Colonel of dismissing Julia out of spite because of her affection for Mrs. Gilpin. On the stand she was not sure who had dismissed Julia or even whether she had been dismissed. At one point she thought maybe she herself had dismissed Julia for keeping an untidy kitchen. Later she seemed to remember that the Colonel had told her she could take Miss Greeley back as a cook, but that Julia herself was afraid to come back because the Colonel had said that she was trying to poison him. The Colonel himself was just as foggy as to who dismissed Julia. All this would seem to explain why Miss Greeley herself testified she "left because I was tired of staying." This matter was not resolved, and it never will be, but it really has no bearing on whether Julia Greeley was "a lewd and unprincipled woman."

---

[273] It seems only fair to note that, at the time, trials were somewhat stacked against women. William Gilpin was a well-known statesman, and all the jurors were men. Colorado women would not have the right to vote for another six years, and none were able to serve as jurors until 1944. [Varnell 106].

Most important for the present study, Mrs. Gilpin's lawyers relentlessly challenged in court the Colonel's accusations about Julia Greeley, and he was unable to produce any credible evidence that Julia was "a lewd and unprincipled woman."

As a special bonus to the present study, in further sworn testimony, Mrs. Gilpin's witnesses spoke extremely positively of Julia Greeley's reputation; and none of Col. Gilpin's witnesses said anything that would suggest that Julia Greeley was "a lewd and unprincipled woman." As the present readers might conceivably be worn out long before they read these testimonies on pp. 100-104, **bold facing will be used to highlight them.**

Ironically, the following testimony is the latest find on Julia Greeley and rightly appears here near the end of this study. In both its origin and content, however, it predates almost all of the material presented earlier.

It is only fair to point out that the material which follows will not have the spiritual character of what has preceded. This was a civil trial, and Colonel Gilpin's complaints set the agenda for what would be discussed. As far as Julia Greeley was concerned, the defense lawyers were content to prove that she was not a lewd and unprincipled woman. Religion entered the trial only in regards to the Gilpins' relationship with one another, since the Colonel, a Quaker, complained that Mrs. Gilpin was more apt to obey her priest friends than him and was seeking to control the religious bent of their children.

Julia's pre-1887 History

Sworn testimony revealed that Julia was indeed a former slave, whose home had been in Hannibal, Mo. She had never been married and did not know how old she was. At that time, she could read a little, but not write.[274]

Julia Gilpin did not bring Julia Greeley to Denver, nor did she come to Denver in 1874. She brought herself to Denver sometime between 1878 and 1880, having first received a promise she would be received in the Gilpin home on Champa Street.[275] Julia's closest friends may have known this. At the time of her death, Horan's records listed her as being a resident of Colorado for 35 years. While 38 to 40 years would have been more accurate, 35 still suggests she did not come with Mrs. Gilpin as claimed by Cannon and Karnes and others.

Miss Greeley had served the family of Mrs. Gilpin's sister, Lee or Lina Robinson, in St. Louis for nine years before coming to Denver. She left that position because of a difference with another servant in the Robinson home.[276]

---

[274] Brief p. 736-737, folio 2077.
[275] By this time all of the Gilpin children had been baptized, so Julia was not present at any of the baptisms of Mrs. Gilpin's children.
[276] Possibly one of the three hired hands living with the Robinsons at the time of the 1880 U.S. Census: Amy Darkson, black, aged 65, a widow, a servant: Peter Stewart, white, 35, a coachman; and Nellie Helzel, white, 15, a servant.

The Gilpin home which Julia Greeley served stood at 1743 Champa. A Residence Inn by Mariott now occupies the site. This engraving first appeared in Vickers' 1880 history of Denver.

Dr. Robinson wrote the letter for Julia asking for employment with the Gilpins.

It has already been known that Julia was definitely at the Gilpin house in Denver at the time of the 1880 U.S. census on June 1, 1880, and was received into the Catholic Church on the 26th of that same month.

She was employed by the Gilpins for approximately two years, at first doing the washing and ironing and later serving as cook.

In the summer of 1882, Julia stayed with the Gilpin family at Teachout's Ranch in Edgerton, a railroad stop 67 miles south of Denver and 8 miles north of Colorado Springs.[277]

---

[277] David Edgerton homesteaded a tract of land along Monument River (or Creek) in 1862. According to the 1884 Colorado Business Directory, the town known as Edgerton was settled in 1865 in an area variously called "Monument Park" and "Among the Pines." Lydia "Leafy" Teachout and her son Harlow M. Teachout owned land next to Edgerton. According to the El Paso County GenCom's history of El Paso County, Teachout's ranch was the site of the most serious Indian

This ad for Teachout's Ranch at Edgerton appeared in Gaff's 1878 travel guide for Kansas and Colorado

Sometime in 1883, possibly in April or May, Julia's service with the Gilpins was ended.

About June 1, 1883, on Mrs. Gilpin's recommendation, Julia Greeley was hired as a cook by Mrs. May Teachout, who ran the hotel in Edgerton. Julia was there two or three months.[278] She then returned to Denver. Mrs. Gilpin said she recommended Greeley "solely … to make amends for the persecution" Julia had sustained from the Governor.

After that Julia went to Cimarron, N. Mex., where she cooked for Mrs. Gilpin's daughter Louise "Lulu" Dickerson, who had recently married Frank Sherwin. Mrs. Gilpin thought she went there in September and stayed a month or six weeks.[279]

Not being able to find work anywhere else, Julia cooked for approximately two weeks at a brothel on Holladay St., now known as Market St.[280] During that time, she roomed on Lawrence St. just across from the church.[281] Julia said this event happened "a good while after I left Mrs. Gilpin's house."[282] Mrs. Gilpin was more definite in saying it

---

depredation in the county. In 1872, Cheyenne and Arapahoes drove off about 100 horses from Teachout's herd. It is not clear on whose property the town evolved, but by 1877 it was a railroad station along General William Jackson Palmer's Denver and Rio Grande railroad. According to Jeanne Davant, during the 1870s, "Leafy" Teachout opened her property to TB sufferers. As many as 200 tents would be set up in the great Colorado outdoors and air. An advertisement for this Teachout recreational opportunity in the Gazette newspaper in 1874 cited, "Fine riding horses, plenty of sweet cream and milk, board $7.00 a week." The eight-room hotel was already in operation by 1878, and an engraving of the inn appeared in Gaff's *Rambles through the Great Kansas Valley and in Eastern Colorado*, pp. 69 & 84. The post office was opened in 1881. By that time, the hotel was operated by Harlow and his wife May. Besides running the post office, which had daily mail service, Harlow was into livestock as were several other men among the 40 residents of the town. Edgerton was located just to the southeast of the present [Air Force] Academy High School, and the remains of Teachout's stone barn are still there. [Colorado … Almanac and Business Directory 157, Cunningham 1-4, Anthony, Summers, and both Davant articles].

[278] Brief p. 891, folio 2659.
[279] Brief p. 675, folio 1844a.
[280] Before that it had been named McGaa St. after one of the founders of Denver. McGaa proved to be such a disreputable character that the street was renamed Holladay after Ben Holladay, proprietor of the Overland Mail Express said to have been the country's largest private employer. It was later renamed a second time in an attempt to bury the street's reputation as a red light district. [Grace 45-48] See also Mrs. Simpson's testimony, No. 11 on p. 45.
[281] Transcript, folio 2081.
[282] Transcript, folio 2079.

happened in 1884 after Miss Greeley returned to Denver from Cimarron.[283] When Mrs. Gilpin found out, she urged Julia to quit there and recommended her to various people.

After she left the place on Holladay St., Julia was a laundress in the drying room of the Albany Hotel[284] at 17th and Stout.

Though Julia Greeley was no longer employed by the Gilpins, that did not keep her away from their house. Already in early 1883, Colonel Gilpin — Mrs. Gilpin thought out of jealous spite — had spread vicious rumors about Greeley's moral probity which often prevented her from gaining employment. And when she was unemployed and homeless she often came back to the house on Champa Street. The Colonel made it clear he did not appreciate her coming, but Mrs. Gilpin did appreciate it, and even longed for it, and seems to have encouraged it, since Julia Greeley was the sole adult contact with Mrs. Gilpin's family in St. Louis.

At one point, from necessity, Julia spent a night sleeping in the Gilpins' donkey shed.

For a while, Julia went to Cheyenne, Wyoming, where she worked for Priscilla McCrum Snyder (1840-1910), wife of Postmaster Albert C. Snyder (1844-1891).[285]

President Grover Cleveland named A.C. Snyder as postmaster on May 13, 1885, and on June 3 he received his commission and assumed the office.[286] Snyder was no new-comer to Cheyenne. He and Priscilla McCrum had married in Altoona, Penna., and by 1870 were residents of Cheyenne. Between then and 1885, seven children arrived in their house on Seventeenth Street:[287] — Otto,

Albert Snyder   Priscilla Snyder

---

[283] Brief p. 675, folio 1843.
[284] Transcript, folio 2081-2082.
[285] During the time period between Julia's employment at the Albany Hotel in 1884 and her working for Lt. Tyson in 1886, Cheyenne City had two postmasters, John W. Jones and Albert C. Snyder, either of whom could have had wives that Julia worked for. — However, 'Timberline" Jones' lengthy obituary in 1889 was quite detailed and gave no reason to think that he was ever married [Daily Sun (Cheyenne) 6-28-1889]. But even if he were, there is a more serious reason for saying Julia did not work for his wife. Jones was appointed from Iowa by President Chester Alan Arthur in the latter half of March of 1884 [Democratic Leader (Cheyenne) 3-23-1884] and resigned his commission and returned to Iowa upon the election of Grover Cleveland as president in early November of 1884. [Daily Sun (Cheyenne) 6-28-1889] This was over a full year before Julia worked for Tyson, and her own testimony is that she went from the postmaster's wife to Ft. D.A. Russell.
[286] Democratic Leader (Cheyenne) 5-14-1885, Weekly Boomerang (Laramie) 6-4-1885.
[287] It is not clear where on Seventeenth St. the Snyders lived while Julia was there in the second half of 1885. The 1884-85 Cheyenne city directory lists "Snyder, A.C., meat market, 455 17th St." The 1887 directory has "Snyder, A.C., postmaster, 423 E. 17th." Albert's 1889 obituary says he died at his home on the corner of 17th and Seymour, which would be somewhere between 622 and 703 E. 17th. After that Albert's widow is consistently listed at 423 17th St.

Edith, Isabel, Roscoe, Karl, Howard, and Kent.[288] By the time that Julia would have come into the Snyder home, Edith had died as an infant,[289] and there were five children aged 14 to 6 running around the house, with baby Kent either in the womb or the crib.[290]

A.C. Snyder came to Cheyenne as manager of the Western Union office. He and others later started their own telegraph office, and he ran a meat market before become postmaster. He was also a trustee of the public schools, a deacon in the Congregational Church, and superintendent of their Sunday school. Both he and his wife were highly respected members of the community and known for their magnanimous and charitable dispositions. Otto and Howard grew up to be physicians, and Kent a banker.[291]

From the Snyder family in Cheyenne, Julia moved out to Fort D.A. Russell, on the west side of Cheyenne, and served 2nd Lieutenant Lawrence David Tyson of the 9th U.S. Infantry. Tyson had married Bettie McGhee on Feb. 10, 1886, and she had joined him at Fort Russell at that time. Sometime after that, they employed Julia Greeley. By the time Tyson was deployed to Arizona in July, it seems Julia's employment at Fort D.A. Russell was finished. The sole reference to Julia in the Tysons' extensive correspondence was on July 30, 1886. At the end of one of her love letters to Lawrence, Bettie wrote: "Julia returned from Denver last night — I have payed [sic] her and feel rather relieved. We have just had a delicious watermelon. It was the best one I ever tasted in this country. I do so wish you could have had some with us." There is no way of knowing, of course, why Bettie was relieved. It probably was not because she was glad to see Julia go, as Julia had already been gone for some time before. It could have been because Bettie was worried about what had happened to Julia or because she had been afraid Julia would not get paid. In any event, there is no way of knowing. Nor do we know whether

Lt. Lawrence D. Tyson at West Point graduation in 1883. He later was a decorated World War I general and U.S. senator from Tennessee. Julia Greeley worked for him and his wife in the first half of 1886.

One of the laundresses' quarters at Ft. D.A. Russell was possibly Julia's living quarters while there.

---

[288] Otto Kerr Snyder, M.D. (1871-1963), Edith Margaret Snyder (1873-1875), Isabel Snyder Draper (1875-1951), Roscoe Palmer Snyder (1877-1942), Karl Snyder (1879-1905), Maj. Gen. Howard McCrum Snyder, M.D. (1881-1970), and Kent Barton Snyder (1885-1994).

[289] Wanda Wade to Burkey, Cheyenne, 11-11-2011.

[290] 1880 U.S. Census for Cheyenne, 1920 U.S. Census for Wheatland, Wyo.

[291] Cheyenne Sun 3-24-1891, Wyoming Tribune (Cheyenne) 5-24-1910. Howard McCrum Snyder, M.D., moreover, became a Major General and served as President Eisenhower's personal physician, both during World War II and throughout his presidency. His elder son, Howard McCrum Snyder, Jr., was also a major general who served on the staff of Gen. George C. Patton. Howard McCrum Snyder III, M.D., is a professor at the University of Pennsylvania and world-renowned surgeon in childhood urology.

Julia had anything to with the watermelon. In later letters to Lawrence, Bettie spoke several times of a need to find a servant, and there is no further reference to Julia.[292]

After that Julia went to Laramie, but could not remember the name of the family she worked for.[293] According to Governor Gilpin, his detectives were checking on Julia in 1886, during her stay in Cheyenne and Laramie.[294]

In 1887, Julia was subpoenaed to testify in Gilpin vs. Gilpin, case no. 1726 before the Superior Court of the City and County of Denver.

Testimony of the Gilpins

Colonel Gilpin's 15th Complaint

The following is extracted verbatim from William Gilpin's original complaint in his plea for a divorce and custody of his children. In these and following extracts William Gilpin is consistently referred to as Petitioner and Julia Gilpin as Defendant.

---

[292] Transcript, folio 2085. Lawrence David Tyson (1861-1929) entered the army in 1883 [Heitman 977] and was stationed almost immediately at Fort D.A. Russell. It was there that he met his future his wife, Bettie Humes McGhee (1865-1933), sister of Margaret McGhee (1858-1942), wife of Col. George W. Baxter (1855-1929), in 1886 territorial governor of Wyoming. [Hale 5: 1474-1475] Tyson later served in the campaign against Geronimo's Apaches, served as military instructor at the University of Tennessee, and after resigning from the army in 1896, went into law and business. During the Spanish-American War, Tyson was commanding colonel of the 6th U.S. Volunteer Infantry and for a while governor of an occupied part of Puerto Rico. During World War I, he was awarded the Distinguished Service Cross for his command as a brigadier general of the 59th Brigade of the 30th Infantry Division, which helped break through the Hindenberg Line. He also served as state representative and U.S. Senator from Tennessee. About 18,000 of his documents are in the University of North Carolina at Chapel Hill, including 49 folders of letters between Tyson and his wife, both before and after their marriage on Feb. 10, 1886. During most of the time of their courtship, Tyson was deployed in field camps away from Fort Russell, and Bettie was living with her sister or was at home in Knoxville, Tenn. After the wedding Bettie joined Tyson at Fort Russell, and the correspondence ceased until July of 1886, when Tyson was deployed to Arizona in the campaign against the Apaches. It was during the time when the Tysons were together in the first half of 1886, that they employed Julia Greeley. As there was no correspondence at the time, there was no opportunity to speak of Julia. The sole reference to Julia was found in Bettie McGhee Tyson to Lawrence D. Tyson, Cheyenne, July 30, 1886, Lawrence Davis Tyson Papers #1174, Folder 24, Wilson Special Collections Library, University of North Carolina at Chapel Hill.

[293] This seems strange, but probably meant only that Julia did not know their family name.

[294] Brief p. 771, folio 2220. The present compiler was particularly struck by the fact that not a single witness alluded in any way to Julia's blind eye. One might wonder if the blindness wasn't sustained until sometime between the trial in 1887 and her employment with the O'Donnells in 1893, but still Mrs. Erger told Fr. Kennedy that Julia herself had told her an infuriated slave master had destroyed her eye. See No. 28 on p. 55. All the more reason to point out that the trial was only indirectly concerned with Julia Greeley and the details of her life.

Brief p. 14-15, folios 524-527:

[Page 14, folio 524] In 1880 or '81, there was sent out from St. Louis, under the auspices of said Celeste Tracey, or some other of her kinsfolk, a negress[295] named Julia Greely <sic!>, a lewd and unprincipled woman, after the strictest sort a Jesuit,[296] for the purpose and intention that she should become a servant in plaintiff's family, who, upon her arrival, defendant received as a servant, and demanded that another faithful and long tried servant should be discharged, and the woman Greely taken in her place, which plaintiff, being advised of the bad character and vicious habits of the woman Greely, refused to do or admit her into the [folio 525] service of his family, but notwithstanding defendant persisted in admitting the negress [p. 15] into plaintiff's house, held long conversations with her, and after being advised of the nefarious character, and when she well knew at the time that said woman Greeley was employed as cook in a house of prostitution or assignation on Holladay street, in Denver; and not only did defendant admit said negress into plaintiff's house and hold conversations with her, well knowing the character of said negress and her infamous associations, but allowed her to detail in the presence of said defendant and her children, scenes of [folio 526] lewdness which were taking place in brothels in Denver, until finally plaintiff forbade defendant to admit said woman into his house; and hoped he had got rid of said negress; but to his great surprise, when soon after he caused his family to be carried to Edgerton, where, he was accustomed to send them to spend the summer, he found said negress in the employ of the mistress of the hotel, where defendant had procured said negress a situation, [folio 527] and where defendant received said negress upon the most intimate terms and treated her in the most considerate and affectionate manner, and allowed the children of plaintiff to associate with her upon the most familiar and intimate terms, whereby said children were subjected to the pernicious influence of portrayals of lewd and wanton scenes made by said negress to them.

Julia Gilpin's Replies

Defendant's Answer to Plaintiff's Complaints pp. 29-32:

[p. 29] This defendant further answering admits that the said Julia Greeley, in the complaint mentioned, was by defendant received into plaintiff's house as a servant; denies that defendant demanded that any other servant whatsoever in plaintiff's [p. 30] family, should be discharged

---

[295] The fact that Gilpin's complaint refers to Julia as "said negress" nine times in the space of 22 lines might suggest the possibility the Colonel was somewhat racially motivated in his opposition to Greeley's presence in his house. The other people involved in the trial seldom referred to Julia's color and never more than once. Bonnie Garramone, who has studied the entire 1885 state census for the Denver area, noted that there were four white servants living with the Gilpins in 1885 (Eliza McCarty, nurse; Fannie Madden, laundress; Mary Swanson, cook; and Bertha Ruton, seamstress) and added, "As you know, black/mulatto servants didn't usually live with the white families." [Garramone to Burkey, Littleton, Sept. 1, 2011] Nothing can fairly be made of this, however, as the complaint was probably not written by the plaintiff, but by his lawyers.

[296] The Jesuit community with which Julia was closely connected was a strictly male society. Merriam-Webster Collegiate Dictionary, 11th edition, 2003, p. 672, has as its second definition of Jesuit "one given to intrigue or equivocation."

and the said Julia Greeley taken in her place; denies that any servant was discharged to give place to the said Julia Greeley; denies that the said Julia Greeley was sent out from the city of St. Louis under the auspices of the said Celeste Tracy, or any other of plaintiff's[297] kinfolk; denies that she was a lewd or unprincipled woman, or a Jesuit of any sort; avers that the said Julia Greeley had been long a servant in the family of defendant and was known by defendant to be a faithful, honest, and virtuous woman; that the said Julia Greeley was received into plaintiff's house by and with the knowledge and consent of plaintiff; denies that the said plaintiff at that time believed, or pretended to believe, that the said Julia Greeley was a woman of bad character; denies that the plaintiff at that time protested or objected against the defendant's receiving the said Julia Greeley into her household; admits that the said Julia Greeley having been long a servant in the family of defendant, being much attached to defendant and her family, and the children of defendant, was accustomed to and did on occasions of her leisure, come to defendant and hold conversation with defendant touching her family, and other members thereof, and that said defendant permitted and indulged the said Julia to engage in such conversations solely because defendant knew of her affection for defendant, and defendant's family and children; denies that the defendant at the time of receiving the said Julia Greeley into her household, or at the time of holding such conversations with her, or at any time during the stay of the said Julia Greeley in the house of defendant, had been advised that the said Julia Greeley was a woman of nefarious character; denies that the fact was so.

[p. 31] Defendant further answering saith that some time after the said Julia Greeley had been in the service of defendant in the household of plaintiff, as before set forth, plaintiff having observed the great affection and regard of the said Julia Greeley for defendant, and thereupon solely for that reason, as defendant on information and belief avers, conceived a violent dislike to, and prejudice against, the said Julia Greeley, and animated solely by such unreasonable and groundless dislike, and in order to annoy and wound defendant, discharged the said Julia from his service and employment, and excluded her from the house, and began to and afterwards did persecute her by circulating reports that the said Julia Greeley was a woman of bad character and immoral life, and by reason of said unjust persecution and false accusation, made by plaintiff, the said Julia Greeley was for a long time prevented from obtaining service elsewhere; and as defendant on information and belief avers did (solely because of such inability, by reason of plaintiff's defamation) take service as a cook in a house of ill fame at the said city of Denver, but at what place in particular, or whether on Holliday street, or elsewhere, defendant hath no knowledge or information sufficient to found a belief; admits that defendant after being informed of the premises aforesaid did receive the said negress into plaintiff's house, and did hold conversations with her; avers that defendant having ascertained from reluctant admission of the said Julia the character of the house where she was so employed, urged and enjoined upon her to quit service at said improper place; denies that defendant held other conversations with her; denies that defendant allowed the said Julia to detail in the presence of defendant and her children, [p. 32] or any of them, any scenes whatsoever taking place in brothels or houses of prostitution in the said city of Denver; denies that the said Julia Greeley ever did so; admits that plaintiff did forbid defendant to admit the said negro woman into his house; admits that plaintiff did find the said negress employed by the mistress of the hotel or boarding house where plaintiff had caused his family to be carried to spend the summer, as in the said complaint mentioned; admits that defendant had recommended the said negress to the mistress of said house; avers that

---

[297] Should read "defendant's."

in so doing she was animated solely by the desire to make amends to the said negress for the persecution she had sustained from plaintiff; denies that defendant received the said negress upon the most intimate terms, or any intimate terms whatsoever; admits that the defendant treated her in an affectionate and considerate manner; admits that defendant allowed the children of plaintiff and defendant to associate with the said negress, but not upon intimate or familiar terms; denies that the said children were thereby subject to any pernicious influences whatsoever;

Cross Complaints of Defendant pp. 61-62:

[p.61] …shortly thereafter plaintiff falsely pretending to believe that a conspiracy had been entered into between plaintiff,[298] and the said Celeste Tracy, and one Julia Greeley, a colored woman, to abduct the children of them two, plaintiff brought from the city of Denver to Edgerton aforesaid a certain posse of detectives or sheriff's officers, by him levied for that purpose, and an attorney, and that there by threats at time, that if the defendant should not go with him she should be compelled to go, and at other times that he would seize and take with him the children of them two, plaintiff caused and compelled defendant to quit and leave the said hotel at Edgerton, and travel in company with the said posse to the city of Denver, and that while at Edgerton aforesaid to excuse his conduct in [p. 62] that behalf, plaintiff proclaimed and declared publicly that defendant had entered into a conspiracy with the said Celeste Tracy and the said Julia Greeley, to abduct the said children; and among the false and scandalous accusations plaintiff then and there at another time charged in the presence of others that defendant had murdered her husband the said John H. Bickerson,[299] and as he believed would do the same to him, or was intending so to do.

William Gilpin's Counter reply to Mrs. Gilpin's Complaints

[p. 134, folio 352] Denies that plaintiff knew that said Julia Greeley had long been a servant in defendant's family, and on information, etc., denies that said Greeley had long been a servant in the [p. 135] family of defendant, or was known by defendant to be a faithful, virtuous woman; plaintiff believes it to be true that said Greeley was much attached to defendant; avers defendant [folio 353] was much attached to said Greeley, and that it was the custom of said Greeley, when she was at liberty from employment on said Holladay street, to spend her spare time with defendant, holding conversations with defendant, and plaintiff submits it was a strange way defendant had of permitting said base negress to manifest her affection for defendant, to allow her to hold conversations and communications with said children; denies that plaintiff, observing the affection and regard of said negress for defendant, on that account conceived a violent dislike for said [folio 354] Greeley, or that, animated by such unreasonable dislike, in order to annoy defendant, he discharged said Greeley from his service, and, excluded her from their house, and began and afterwards, or did, persecute said Greeley by circulating reports that she was a woman of bad character and immoral life; denies that by reason of said unjust accusations made by plaintiff, the said Greeley was a long time, or for any time, prevented from obtaining services

---

[298] Should read "defendant."
[299] Should read "Dickerson."

elsewhere; and upon information, [folio 355] etc., saith that the character and reputation of said Greeley was such as exactly fitted and commended her to employment of those upon [p. 136] Holladay street, in whose service she was engaged.

Direct and Cross-Examination of Plaintiff's Complaint

[**Editor's Note**: In their later appeal, defense lawyers asked the Supreme Court to study carefully the following testimony in light of the plaintiff's 15th specification. The defense lawyers quoted all of the following, except for the four sections that the present study has indicated by using italics. The defense's request to the Supreme Court will be given following the plaintiff's original testimony.]

[Brief p. 234, folio 702] *Direct Examination*

Q. Do you remember a negro woman by the name of Greeley
A. Perfectly well.
Q. Where did you know her, Governor?
A. I had often seen her in St. Louis; often when I called in at Dr. Robertson's[300] house where she was a nurse or in some capacity, that is all I saw of her.
[folio 703] Q. State who Dr. Robertson was?
A. He was the first husband of Helena Pratt, my wife's younger sister residing in St. Louis.
Q. Mrs. Robertson is now dead?
A. Dead three years ago.
Q. Was this negress, Julia, a family servant of the Pratt family while slavery prevailed in [p. 235] Missouri?
A. That I do not know.[301]
Q. You first came to know her in the family of Dr. Robertson?
A. Yes

Q. In what year was that, Governor?
A. I was passing through St. Louis and on visits there I was in the habit of calling on them. I cannot state the year.
[folio 704] Q. Can you state when you first saw her, approximately what year?

---

[300] The Doctor's family name was Robinson [Beckwith 107-110].
[301] This question was not asked of any other witnesses who might have been able to answer. The U.S. Census for 1860 does indicate that both Julia Gilpin's father and grandfather were slave owners. Bernard Pratte Sr. of St. Genevieve County had five slaves, including a 17-year-old girl, who would have been 44 at the time of the trial and a one-year-old girl who would have been 28. [1850 Missouri Slave Schedule, p. 312, nos. 7a & 9a]. Bernard Pratte Jr. in St. Louis had two slaves, one a 14 year-old girl who would have been 41 in 1887 [1850 Missouri Slave Schedule, p. 345, no. 20b] It does not seem likely, however, that any of these was Julia, since she herself testified that she first became acquainted with Mrs. Gilpin while she was living with Mrs. Robinson in approximately 1871-1880.

A. Very well; probably 1876 or 1877; I had gone on to Philadelphia on this business matter and was returning.
Q. Do you know in what capacity she was in the service of Dr. Robertson's family?
A. I do not except as a servant.
Q. Did this woman Greeley afterwards come to this city?
A. She came here unannounced to me and with a letter from Dr. Robertson that he had paid all her expenses.
Q. Can you state what year it was she came here in?
A. I cannot from my recollection, but I can discover it.
[folio 705] Q. Can you state approximately, Governor?
A. It was six or seven years ago; about 1879 or 1880.
Q. What was the age of this woman, Governor?
A. I should judge her to be about 30, or between 30 and 35.
Q. You say that the first you knew of <her> was when she presented herself at your house; on coming here I mean?
A. Yes.
Q. What did you wife say about her presence here?
A. She said she was an old and faithful servant of the Pratt family and that she had been, and that she wished to employ [p. 236] her in her house, and so she remained, and I [folio 706] paid those expenses which I was asked to pay.

Q. What, if any, request was made by Mrs. Gilpin to have any other servant, if any such was made, turned out of the house in order to make a place for this woman.
A. Now I cannot remember. On one occasion she disappeared and a white woman was brought in her place, and I asked where she had gone to, and my wife said she had been insolent to her and had displeased her, and she afterwards came back.
Q. What did Mrs. Gilpin say to you, if anything, about removing a servant you already had to make room for this negro [folio 707] woman?
A. She endeavored to force me to displace a faithful servant to make an opening for her.
Q. What servant was that she tried to have displaced?
A. The most prominent effort on her part was against the one who is now the cook of our establishment.
Q. What is her name?
A. Mary Larson.
Q. Did you learn something or anything about the moral character of this woman, Greely, about that time?
A. I did from several sources.
[folio 708] Q. Did you report what you had learned to your wife, Mrs. Gilpin?
A. Yes.
Q. What did your wife do then in respect to this woman?
A. She continued to retain her for a time.
Q. For a time; for about what length of time, Governor?
A. Very well, I insisted [p. 237] upon her departing from our household before going a trip I made to New York.
Q. Well, what did your wife do?
A. This I think was in April or May, 1883, I think so.

[folio 709] Q. And you still — she still retained her in her service after that time, after you made the report of what you learned of this woman's character.

A. She still entertained her as a visitor.

Q. She still retained her in her service?

A. No.

Q. What did you learn?

A. I learned from the grocerykeeper, Mr. Slayback, I was examining my accounts —

Q. I spoke of the woman's character, her reputation and chastity. What did you learn of the woman's character?

A. That she was very loose and wasteful.

[folio 710] Q. Did you learn anything from any other source of her reputation for morality?

A. I did.

Q. What did you learn?

A. I learned that she was in the habit of visiting houses of assignation on Holladay street.

Q. Did you retail[302] that fact to your wife?

A. I did.

Q. Did the woman thereafter visit your house?

A. Yes, sir.

Q. On how many occasions, if more than one occasion, did that take place?

A. These visits were timed to take place when I was not at home. I cannot say. I know frequently, I found them in my wife's sitting [folio 711] room absorbed in conversation.

Q. Who would be present on those occasions [p. 238] when this woman was there holding conversation?

A. Just my wife and her.

Q. Was there ever any occasion after you had informed your wife — was not there any occasion after you had informed your wife that she was allowed to hold conversation with your family?

A. Oh, yes, and on one occasion I met her entering the house and, passing from my room, I stopped her. I said "you have my peremptory orders not to come near [folio 712] this house and among my children."

Q. Where did this negro woman go after she left your house?

A. I have learned since —

Q. Do you know of your own knowledge?

A. That she was employed as a cook at a house of assignation on Holladay street.

Q. Where did you next meet this negress after she had left your house in connection with your family.

A. Without knowing why, I know this, that her visits had ceased, and afterwards visited Edgerton after taking my family down there I found her there as cook.

[folio 713] Q. Was it not your custom to carry your family to Edgerton to spend the summer?

A. Yes.

Q. For how many years had you been in the habit?

A. Six or seven years — I cannot say — every summer up until two years ago, this is the third year.

Q. She then was at Edgerton when you got there?

---

[302] Merriam-Webster's Collegiate Dictionary, 11th edition, 2005, p. 1063, gives as the second meaning of retail "TELL, RETELL."

A. Yes.
Q. Did you learn from your wife in what way the woman had gained employment at [p. 239] Edgerton?
A. Yes; it was on application of Mrs. Gilpin. She sent her to her.

[p. 239, folio 714] What was the association between your wife and this negress, and in what manner did they receive one another when they met at Edgerton, or how did they conduct themselves while they were there together, as to social relations?
A. With perfect and unreserved familiarity.
Q. In what manner, if at all, was this negro woman allowed to associate and converse with your children?
A. Freely, and I have seen her stoop down, and one of my children kissed her in the door where I happened to be approaching.
Q. State whether or not she was allowed free converse with them so far as your wife was concerned.
A. I saw nothing to interfere with that.

[p. 368, folio 953] *Cross-Examination*

Q. You say that Julia Greely was a very lewd, vicious, bad woman?
A. Yes.
Q. When did you find that out first?
A. In various ways.
Q. I say when?
A. After my attention was attracted to her and her conduct and her conversation between my wife and herself.
Q. When was that?
A. After she had been for a time a cook in my house.
Q You discovered from her conversation with your wife and with your children that she was a lewd, bad woman?
A. Yes.
Q. Will you tell anything she said in the presence of your wife in your hearing or in the presence of your children that satisfied you that she was a lewd, bad woman?
A. They were just in the change of conduct, of manners.
[folio 954]Q. Change of what conduct?
A. That I had I think come in contact with before.
Q. Tell the jury what you heard Julia Greely say either to your wife or in the hearing of your children of a lewd and vicious character.
A. I saw it.
Q. What did you see?
A. She was visiting these houses of assignation.
Q. You saw her visiting houses of assignation?
[p. 369] A. I got positive proof she had been there.
Q. I asked you what you saw or heard in your house, from Julia Greely that satisfied you that she was a lewd woman.
A. I saw it continually.

Q. What did you hear her say in your house?
A. That I saw these things.
Q. I asked you what you heard her say that was lewd or indecent, in the hearing of your wife and children?
[folio 955] A. She was very careful. I was watched and all that thing was carefully kept from me.
Q. So you did not hear anything, did you?
A. No, I could not. She was sent from the room or disappeared when she thought I would see her.
Q. But you will not pretend to say that you ever heard Julia Greely say anything lewd of indecent to your wife, will you?
A. I have seen her —
Q. Will you pretend to say that you ever heard Julia Greely say anything lewd or indecent in your house?
A. She never spoke to her in conversation when I was present.
Q. Did you ever hear her say anything lewd or indecent to your children?
A. I have seen her act, and the effect it had on them.
[folio 956] Q. What did you see her do?
A. I saw her take them off to accompany her in the street at night.
Q. Did you interfere?
A. Yes.
Q. What did you do?
A. I forbade them to go.
[p. 370] Q. Did they go?
A. Well, I mentioned it to their mother.
Q. I asked you what they did when you forbade them to go away with Julia Greely?
A. I took possession of them.
Q. Then they did not go?
A. No.
Q. Did you know where they were going?
A. I did not.
Q. You took that as evidence of her lewd talk in their presence?
[folio 957] A. No, because they were warned, and she was warned not to go with them. (956)
Q. Did you discover that she visited houses of assignation or ill fame while she was a servant at your house?
A. Yes.
Q. While she was a servant at your house?
A. Yes.
Q. How did you learn this?
A. I learned it from parties that, at my quest, ascertained.
Q. At your request?
A. Yes.
Q. While she was living as a servant in your family you had detectives watch her?
A. No I had not. I had friends who informed me of it, and then I traced her into them.
Q. You had friends who informed you while she was a servant in your house that she was accustomed to visit these houses of assignation?
A. Yes.

Q. Who told you so?
A. I cannot remember — it is so long ago, and it was a matter of interest for me to know, and I was informed by parties without asking.
[folio 958] Q. You say that you were so informed, and [p. 371] then to satisfy yourself you watched her and discovered it; where did you find her?
A. I was on Blake street and I saw her going.
Q. While she was a cook in your family you saw her going where?
A. I cannot say it was while she was a cook in our family.

Q. That is what I am asking you about. Did you ever hear or know that she visited a house of assignation, or other disreputable place, before she ceased to be a member of your family?
A. I had positive information from a party, but he is dead. [folio 959]

Court. — *You understand that Mr. McNeal is enquiring during the period this colored woman was a servant and an inmate of your family, and not after she left. Understand that all the time — that so far Mr. McNeal is indicating the time when this colored woman was an inmate of your family.*

Q. I want to know if during the time you became aware that she visited houses of ill-fame or assignation?
A. I did become aware.
Q. Did you discharge her from the family on that account?
A. I did discharge her and my wife herself discharged her, saying that she had been insolent to her, and had rebelled against her, and she was afterwards brought back.
Q. She was a second time a servant in your family?
A. Yes.
Q. Did you tell your wife at that time you discharged her that the reason you did it was because she visited houses of ill-fame?
A. My [p. 372] wife discharged her the first time and then it was for this reason.
[folio 960] Q. Your wife first discharged her for insolence to her?
A. She told me so.
Q. She was re-employed — who re-employed her?
A. My wife.
Q. How long was she in your employment a second time?
A. That I cannot tell. Not long.
Q. How long was she in your employment the first time?
A. That I cannot remember.
Q. How long was she in your employment altogether — about how long?
A. I cannot at all remember possibly several months.
Q. Cannot you give any better answer than that?
A. No, sir.
Q. Possibly several months?
A. Yes.

[folio 961] Q. You say the party who told you about her bad character is dead. Who was that?
A. I was in settling my accounts with my grocer.

Q. I asked you who it was that told you that Julia was a lewd, bad woman, that you say is dead — who told you that, that is now dead?

A. It was Mr. Slayback, a partner in the firm of Humphrey and Slayback.

Q. You say that Mr. Slayback told you that Julia was a lewd woman?

A. An extravagant woman and a careless woman.

Q. Did Slayback tell you that Julia was a lewd woman and visited houses of assignation?

A. I can not say to that extent, but he did tell me — My question was this — I was asking some settlement with him and several matters of account appeared to me extravagant [p. 373] and unnecessary, and I asked him to help me restrict them, and he said, "How is it possible for me to do that, when this lewd and extravagant woman is constantly running here and in the name of her mistress getting these things and carrying them off."

[folio 962] Q. And that is all you ever heard of her character about lewdness?

A. It was a confirmation of what I found elsewhere.

Q. Can you remember who else had told you before than she was lewd?

A. I am not sure that I can.

Q. Is it not a fact that you first knew of her being in a house of ill fame or assignation as a cook after she had ceased to be a servant in your family?

A. I cannot tell. I learned positively of it at that time. But I believe — from information I was satisfied that she frequented those rooms before my wife had discharged her.

[folio 963] Q. You did not tell your wife that, did you?

A. I do not know — I expect I did.

Q. Cannot you remember whether you told your wife that she had a servant in the house who frequented houses of assignation? Would you not be likely to tell her?

A. I told my wife it was very unsatisfactory to me to have a woman of such a very uncertain character and bringing her in the perpetual companionship of the young ladies and my little children.

Q. You knew where she was brought up before she came there?

[p. 374] A. I did not.

Q. You knew she had been a servant in the family in St. Louis?

A. I knew she had been with Mrs. Robertson.

Q. Yes, Mrs. Gilpin's sister; how long had she been there?

A. I do not know.

Q. Did you understand she had been a servant for several years?

A. I have learned since.

Q. Did you know from your visits to the family that she had been a servant for several years?

A. I did not. When passing [folio 964] through St. Louis I called on Mrs. Robertson, and she met me at the front door.

Q. That is all you know of her previous history?

A. Yes.

Q. Did she come here with your consent or knowledge?

A. No; she came here, and my wife said she came with the best recommendations as an old servant of the family.

Q. You furnished the money to pay the expenses of bringing her?

A. Dr. Robertson wrote, stating he had paid her fare here, and he wanted the money refunded, as he was a poor man.

Q. You did not know she was expected until she arrived in town?

A. Yes, sir.
Q. You never heard of her until she came?
[folio 965] A. Yes, and then I was told by my wife she was an old family servant and that she had been very attentive to Mrs. Robertson's children; part of the time servant there and attending to front door, and part of the time, and that she wanted to have her <sic!>.
[p. 375] Q. And you consented.
A. I made no objection.
Q. How long had she been there when you did commence to object, if you ever did?
A. I have always disliked her presence there, but it was a concession I made to the wish of my wife not to separate her with our family (not heard).
Q. You understand, then, that on account of the long service of this negro woman in the family of your wife's sister, she would like to have her there in the house?
A. She told me so.
Q. There was a sort of family attachment between them?
A. It was a slave state until recently <sic!>.
Q. Did you understand your wife desired to have Julia there because of the family [folio 966] relation that had existed between them — she had been a servant in the family?
A. She told me so.

Q. And you had not any reason to doubt it at the time?
A. I neither doubted it or otherwise; but because she wished it, I made no objection.
Q. You cannot tell how long she had been in the family, but you insisted she should leave as a lewd woman?
A. It was not a great while before I suspected her, but my wife always defended her, and said she would see that nothing of the kind worked mischief.
Q. After you advised her she was a lewd woman, and attended these houses of assignation, she continued to keep her?
A. She sent [p. 376, folio 967] her to Edgerton after that without my knowledge.
Q. Did she discharge her from her own service after you told her she was a lewd bad woman, — because you told her?
A. She had been discharged, and while roaming about I did not know what had become of her, except making these visits to which I objected; and it was after that time that she was sent to Edgerton.
Q. And it was when you discovered her making visits there that you told your wife she was a lewd, bad woman?
A. She defended her, and complained that I wanted to banish her from the last link she had with her kinsfolk at the distance.
Q. She claimed you wanted to banish her because of her devotion to her?
A. She said (not heard)
Q. She did not know any reason why the woman should not come there and see her and the children.
A. Yes.
Q. The next thing you heard of her, she was at Edgerton?
A. Yes.
[folio 968] Q. And your wife sent her there and that was one of the evidences of the conspiracy that you talk about? A. Yes.

Additional Testimony of Governor Gilpin (Brief p. 770-771, folio 2219-2220):

[p. 770, folio 2219] Q. Did you have anybody look up Julia Greeley anywhere, and do any service in connection with her?
A. Yes; she entered my house against my orders, and I think Mr. Hawley [a detective] ascertained.
[p. 771, folio 2220] He reported to me from time to time where she was, whether she was in the city or elsewhere.
Q. Did you have her looked up in Cheyenne and Laramie?
A. Yes; wherever she might be.
Q. When was that done?
A. During a particular time.
Q. Of what year?
A. 1886.

Plaintiff's Complaint Reexamined

Request that Supreme Court Examine Col. Gilpin's 15th Specification, pp. 21-27:

[p. 21] we asked the court to examine the 15th specification of plaintiff's complaint, containing the grave charge that defendant, without his consent, introduced into his family as a servant a colored woman of whose lewd character and vicious habits he was advised: but defendant received her and held long conversations with her, knowing her to be employed as a cook in a house of prostitution, and allowed her to detail in the presence of herself and children scenes of lewdness; and when he forbade the woman his house, defendant secured employment for her at a hotel in Edgerton where he was accustomed to go with his family. Where defendant treated her in an affectionate manner, etc. **Following is the testimony offered by plaintiff on direct and cross-examination to sustain this charge**:

> [The testimony given on pp. 85-92 was quoted at length here]

No other evidence of the truth of these charges against this woman's character was offered, though it appears in evidence that detectives had been following the old woman and looking her up for months before the trial. The whole of the proof is that a dead man told Gilpin the woman was extravagant, and for a few weeks she cooked in a Holladay street place, sleeping elsewhere, and when Mrs. Gilpin discovered it, she had her leave.

Defendant's Case

Direct Examination (Brief pp. 557-559, folios 1475-1484):

[p. 557, folio 1475] I first knew Julia Greeley twelve or fourteen years ago. At that time she was servant in the family of my sister, at St. Louis. She [folio 1476] was nine years with her as her nurse. I think I first saw her in Denver in 1880. I received a letter saying she wanted to come here to my employment. I did not want my sister [folio 1477] to think I had coaxed her away, because she was believed to be a valuable and good servant, and I wrote to Mr. Robinson and asked if Julia had left his service or had been dismissed. I asked the governor if I might have her, and he told me to write to Doctor Robinson, and she came out. [folio 1478] She came to my house as a cook, and remained there in that capacity for two years. I do not think the governor objected to her while she lived with me as a servant. She was an exceptionally good cook, and I always found her perfectly honest. She was [folio 1479] a little noisy, she would laugh and sing in the kitchen, but I never knew her to say an ugly word. When she got through her kitchen work, she would come into my room, sit on the floor and talk about the family and children.

I never discovered anything immoral in her language or conduct; she would not dare to indicate anything immoral to me. I never heard of her doing so with my children. I never heard her accused of that by any of them, even the Governor, until this unfortunate case. He didn't like her, and he told me [p. 557, folio 1481] she should not come to the house; that was after she left my service. He said she was a lewd woman, a thief, had stolen my watch, had been in conspiracy with the negro, Bob Twining, to let him into the house. She had been nine years with my sister and two years with me, and I knew it could not be true, and the Governor never told me from whom he heard these things; he merely asserted them, and I didn't suppose he went into those places to find out, so I didn't know who she was with. The children loved her just as the little Southern children love their mammies. She would kiss and hug them and play with them, and give them candy. I never knew of her taking the children out at night on the streets; think I should know. After she left me she went as a cook to Mrs. Teachout's in the country. She had written to me to send her a cook, and this girl being out of a situation, I sent her; I knew she was honest. She went there and stayed with Mrs. Teachout until she went to Mrs. Sherwin's service down in Cimarron. She stayed there until October. She came up here again, and I believe [folio 1482] she worked around by the day; she came to my house when she could not find work, to get something to eat. I have known her in bitter coldness to sleep in my donkey's stable, because she had no shelter. I tried to get her some work, and asked Mrs. Clough to take her as a cook. I tried two different places, acquaintances of mine. There was an influence [folio 1483] used that prevented her getting employment; I got the information from the parties [p. 559] that I went to. One day she came to see me looking a little more tidy, better dressed than usual, and I asked her if she was working and she said she was. I asked her where, and she seemed to be a little embarrassed, and said, "Mrs. Gilpin, I am doing some cooking on Holladay street." I said, "Oh, for God's sake, you must come out of such a place as that." She said she couldn't get a thing to [folio 1484] do, but would come away from there as soon as she could get a place. I did not even ask her the name of the person with whom she was staying.

Cross-Examination of Defendant

Brief, pp. 672-677, 685-686, 695 , folios 1834-1851, 1879-1882, 1922:

[p. 672, folio 1834] I think Julia Greeley came to our house in the winter or summer of 1878; am not quite sure. When I say she wrote a letter, I mean she had someone write for her, asking me to take her into my service. She had been nine years in the house of my sister, Mrs. Robinson; had not seen very much of her, because I had not lived in St. Louis. I knew [folio 1835] she had been a faithful servant, and what I saw of her I liked, as a good, simple, kind woman. I wrote to Dr.

Robinson, and wanted to know whether Julia had left his services, or had been dismissed; did that because if she had been dismissed for any misconduct I should not have engaged her, and didn't want [folio 1836] my sister and brother-in-law to suppose I had taken her from their service to my own. My sister Celeste did not write the letter for Julia. Julia came in the winter of 1878 or '79, and stayed until 1881, I think.

Q. What was the occasion of her leaving?
A. I believe she was not very tidy in the kitchen; do not know whether I dismissed her, or whether she left. No, I do not. You need not look at me in that way, Mr. Patterson.
Q. You do not know whether you dismissed her or whether she left?
A. No, I really don't.
Q. Had the Governor found any fault with her?
A. I do not know whether he did or not. I do not think so.
Q. Then according to your recollection the [p. 673] Governor was not at all instrumental in her leaving?
A. Wait a minute. I asked him if I could take her back, and that makes me think he sent her away; but I remember he said in his answer to me, "take Julia." I remember that perfectly well.
Q. Why were you a moment ago in such a maze of doubt whether you dismissed her or she left?
A. It just occurred to me.
Q. This is not a new subject to you?
A. Oh, no.
Q. Why were you a moment ago in such a maze of doubt whether you dismissed her?
[folio 1838] A. What do you suppose.
Q. I am just endeavoring to reach the truth.
A. I am giving you a fair opportunity.
Q. Why were you in such a maze of doubt a moment ago as to whether she left herself or was dismissed by you?
A. I will say, I do not remember, or whether the Governor dismissed her, I say that truthfully.
Q. Did you take her back into your service after she left first?
A. No, I did not; although I dispatched.
Q. You say that you dispatched to the Governor?
A. I did, and I remember that he was East at the time.
Q. And he dispatched "yes?"
[folio 1839] A. The Governor had said that she was trying to poison him; somebody had told him [p. 673] so, and she was afraid to come back; think she had been a few weeks away when I telegraphed for permission to take her back. The reason I telegraphed him was he had always said something she was not virtuous, and a lewd woman, and was trying to poison him. He had said this occasionally the first [folio 1840] year she was there. She made application for me to take her back, and I telegraphed the Governor, and he telegraphed "yes," and she wouldn't come back because she was afraid; found the influences at work that kept Julia from getting a place at Mrs. Speer's and Mr. Clough's; didn't try at any other places. They told me the Governor [folio 1841] had spoken about it.
Q. In your sworn answer you make this statement with reference to Julia: I will ask you so that you may aver it or deny it "Defendant further avers that sometime after the said Julia Greeley had been in the service of defendant in the house of plaintiff, as before set forth, plaintiff having observed the great affection and regard of said Julia, etc., conceived a violent dislike to and

prejudice against the said Julia Greeley, and animated [folio 1842] solely by such unreasonable and groundless dislike, and in order to annoy defendant, discharged the said Julia Greeley from his service and employment?"
A. I have just said I do not remember.
Q. In your sworn answer he discharged her because he observed that there was a great affection and regard of Julia for you?
[p. 675] A. I believe that he never liked anybody that liked me.
Q. You swore positively he discharged her for that reason; now you swear you do not know?
A. When I said that there was only one person talking. You have asked me so many questions that I do not know exactly.

   I do not deny that the Governor discharged [folio 1843] her. I just now said that the reason I thought the Governor discharged her, was his giving permission to take her back. I do not know that he forbade her coming to the house at the time she left. I know that he has very often. I do not know that it was after she went to work on Holladay street; he did not know it at the time. She didn't go there after she left me, but after she left Mrs. Sherwin's service in 1884, the year after Mrs. Sherwin was married. I do not know where she went after she left me; I [folio 1844] know she lived in Denver. She went to Edgerton to work in the summer of 1883, after I discharged her must have been right away; think she went there in May, and stayed until August or September; do not know when she went to Cimarron. She [folio 1844a] went in September, to stay a month or six weeks, then she came back to Denver, and I think it was shortly after she came back that she went to Holladay street. The Governor forbade her to come to the house all the time; he didn't wait for occasions. I cannot fix the date when she went to work on Holladay street. The Governor did not tell me [p. 676] she was working there; after she left there he told me of it; she left there after three week's service. He didn't tell me he had seen her in lewd positions in play with the children; have heard it since, but never [folio 1846] before, and if I had heard it, I never should have believed it; she had been nine years my sister's nurse, and had lived with me two years, and I knew it could not be true. When the Governor told me he did not want her to visit the house, I may have told him I didn't believe all he said about her; don't know [folio 1847] what I said. I may have said she could come if she wanted to; knew her so well. She came to my house, and went around singing with the children; always came where I was; the children could play and romp with her, and she would bring them candy, and I knew those things could not be true. Besides I had other things to form my opinion on. I knew how the Governor had talked about other people to me. I thought it was just a [folio 1848] notion of his and he had a great many. He displayed considerable feeling about it: I just let her come. I didn't think he was right, and I stood by my own judgment against his dictation until I had some reason to believe he was right. I knew all my life he had taken prejudices against gentlemen and ladies. [folio 1849] I did not consult Father Raverdy as to whether Julia should come to the house. She often came in through the alley, but I do not think she came in that way to avoid being seen. I heard one of the witnesses here say that she concealed herself so that he could [p. 677] not see her but I did not know it at the time. [folio 1850] He always had an opportunity of knowing she was in the house, because she was around laughing and talking. Everybody else knew she was there for the same reason. I never concealed it from him. She came up to my sitting-room, and would go all over the house, except, perhaps to his sitting room; if he didn't see her, he could not help hearing her. I think he gave me to understand three or four times that he disapproved of her coming. [folio 1851] It may have been oftener.

[p. 685, folio 1879] Julia Greeley was not working at Edgerton in 1882, it was the summer of 1883; in 1882, she was with me in my employment. Think she had not been discharged by me at that time. [folio 1880] The Governor took us all down in 1883. Think [p. 686] we left here for Edgerton on the 26th of June; before we had usually left about the [folio 1881] first of June. We sometimes went in May and made arrangements, and then took the family in June. Think in 1883 I was detained in Denver later than usual by my sewing or something of that kind. We were there but a little while, and came up about the fifth of July.

Think Julia Greeley was there when we [folio 1882] went down. Think she went down in May or the beginning of June. Mrs. Teachout wrote me she wanted a trusty servant, and I recommended Julia. My sister Celeste came not very long after we arrived there.

[p. 695, folio 1922] I think I returned from Cimarron in Sept. 1883; have said I thought Mr. Sherwin's trouble began in Oct. '83. When I was in Cimarron, I think no one was there who was interested in this suit except myself. My sister, Celeste, and Julia Greeley were there, and Mr. and Mrs. Sherwin. Julia Greeley was there because Mrs. Sherwin wrote that she wanted her.

Other Witnesses

for the Plaintiff

Mary Larson (Brief p. 478-484, folios 1199-1232):

[p. 478, folio 1199] My name is Bertha Mary Ann Larson; I am a Swede; have been living in the family of Governor Gilpin for about three years, as cook; in addition I clean the dining room and the governor's sitting room….

[p.484, folio 1229] I have seen the negro woman Julia Greeley in the house. She didn't work there while I was there. [folio 1230] I have seen her come there quite a number of times, but I do not know how often, she came to see Mrs. Gilpin and the children. Mrs. Gilpin received her in her sitting room upstairs. I was never present when this woman was talking to Mrs. Gilpin. She took the children about sometimes — went back and forth through the house. I don't know where she took them, only I know they have gone out with her sometimes. I never knew [folio 1231] her to take them out at night, but in the afternoon. She has taken Miss Lizzie and the small children, Marie, Willie and Louis. She has taken the boys separate once or twice, don't know how often. I don't know [folio 1232] where she was living at the time. I don't remember that Mrs. Gilpin said anything about it.

[p. 490, folio 1257] I remember her [folio 1258] taking the boys out one day by themselves. When she took the girls, she took Miss Lizzie and Louis. The boys were not there, and she just took Miss Marie and Lizzie. She would go out in the afternoon, about 3 o'clock; she didn't go out very often. I suppose she took them with Mrs. Gilpin's consent. I don't know whether they went on errands or not. I didn't pay much attention, but I knew she took them out by seeing them going — seeing them twice or three times. They were always home for tea or dinner. I did not notice [folio 1260] which way they went. I knew they were on the streets because I heard them talk about whatever amused them on the street.

Re-direct Examination by Mr. Dillon

I do not know, and did not hear Mrs. Gilpin say where Julia was working at that time, but I heard it in the house. She did [folio 1261] not appear to be very old, about thirty years of age.

Eliza McCarthy (Brief p. 470-471, folios 1168-1171):

[p. 468, folio 1160] My name is Eliza McCarthy, have lived eight years in Governor Gilpin's family; have been a nurse and a kind of waitress to the ladies. My duties are around the nursery and sometimes in the dining room. …

[p. 470, folio 1168] I remember a negro servant in the family by name of Julia Greeley, and her leaving, but I did not know at the time she was discharged. [folio 1169] She was not there when Mrs. Speer had charge of the house in Mrs. Gilpin's absence; she had left before. She came in and out of the house very frequently whenever she felt like it, to see Madame and the children. When she came to see Mrs. Gilpin and went to Mrs. Gilpin's own room, I was never present at any of the conversations, [folio 1170] and never heard any of their conversations. Julia always played with the children — she seemed like a child; she would run back and forth and play with them all the time just like one of them — screaming and jumping. At such times the governor would be down in the sitting-room if he was in. These frolics were sometimes upstairs and sometime [folio 1171] down. She came in at the alley and sometimes at the front door; after the Governor didn't seem to like to have her come there, she came through the alley mostly; I think he always knew if she fooled with the children if he was around. When she came there she said she was working on Holladay [p. 471] street. I never asked her the character of the house; I knew it was not a very good place. I never heard Mrs. Gilpin say what the character of the house was. I never told the governor she was going in through the alley. After sometimes the governor observed her presence in the house, and he told us girls, one or two, "let her go, let her go, don't detain her," so she went to see the children and the Madame. She didn't come many times after he said, "let her go, don't detain her." I never saw anything more of her.

Elizabeth Owens (Brief pp. 503-505, folio 1323-1331):

[p. 503, folio 1323] I have lived seven years in Denver; two years of that time with the family of governor Gilpin, I do not remember the year, but I think it was in 1883-84.

[folio 1324] I knew the colored woman named Julia Greeley during that time; do not think she worked in the family, but I think she had done so. I understood from her she had been forbidden the house. I asked her why she should hide herself and she said she hid from governor Gilpin, who did not allow her to come to the house. I was never aware of her coming in until she was in the house, and I would hear her laughing [1325] and roaming with the children, and I would ask if that was Julia, and they would say it was. I was going to the cellar, and she hid on the cellar steps. I don't remember that she was there more than three or four times. I guess she went through Mrs. Gilpin's room and through the house whenever she liked to go. I think she generally went to her sitting room [folio 1326] upstairs. Sometimes she would stay three or four hours running around the house. I do not know how long she would be with Mrs. Gilpin. I have not known of her and Mrs. Gilpin holding private interviews when the children were not present; nor have I known of her receiving her into [p. 504] her room and talking with her when the children were present. I do not think there was any particular arrangement. Sometimes [folio 1327] she and the children were dancing, laughing and singing in the parlor and Miss Julia playing for them. They told me she was drunk on one of these occasions when I asked why she was so boisterous.[303] I do not know [folio 1328] whether liquor had been given her in the house or not; I could not tell whether she was drunk when she came there, nor do I know whether she was drunk when she went away. I suppose she was drunk; I didn't hear Mrs. Gilpin say anything about it; I didn't pay much attention to it. I didn't go near enough to detect the smell of liquor on [folio 1329] her breath. I should say she was between 30 and 40 years of age. I saw the governor drive her out of the yard when he discovered her there. I never heard anything said, not a word. I saw him motion to her when she was playing in the yard with the children. I don't remember anything said in her talks with the children; I never paid much [folio 1330] attention, **Her manner when she was with the children was a kind of jolly, laughing and dancing**. One occasion I heard her hollering about the yard. Don't remember what she said at such times. I never knew her to take any of the children away from the house upon any of those occasions; I think I have known her to go down town with little [folio 1331] Marie. **I remember when Mrs. Speer was there in charge of the house in Mrs. Gilpin's absence. I don't remember that I reported [p. 505] to her any bad conduct on Julia Greeley's part**; I may have done so. Don't remember whether this was after or before the governor had forbidden her in the house; didn't know where she was working at the time, [folio 1332] and didn't hear Mrs. Gilpin say.

Mrs. Bertha Router Johnson, seamstress (Brief p. 738, 2088-2089)

[p. 519, folio 1381] I have resided in Denver six years. Before marriage I lived in the family of Governor Gilpin. My maiden name was Bertha Router. I lived about five years in the family….

[p. 738, folio 2088] Julia Greeley was there, and she nursed Mrs. Sherwin's baby. [folio 2089] She was working there when I went to the house. She was about the house nursing Mrs. Sherwin's baby about six months. Saw her frequently. **Saw nothing wrong about her conduct. She never did anything but funny — making fun.**

for the Defendant

May D. Teachout (Brief p. 889-892, folios 2648-2650, 2653, 2655, 2657-2664):[304]

---

[303] This, of course, is hearsay evidence; and there is no way of knowing that the children were serious.
[304] See information on Teachout's Ranch in footnotes to Julia's pre-1887 History on p. 78. Mrs. Teachout gave her deposition at Colorado Springs, Mar. 26, 1887.

[p. 889, folio 2648] My name is May D. Teachout, age 32, residence Edgerton, El Paso county. … [folio 2649] Was residing at Edgerton in the summer seasons of 1882 and '83; my husband was keeping a public house; that is a station on the Rio Grande railroad. Mrs. [folio 2650] Gilpin and her children were there during the summer of 1882 about three months, and in the summer of 1883 a very short time — about three weeks. … [folio 2651] Mrs. Celeste Tracy … came to our house during Mrs. Gilpin's stay there in the summer of 1883. … [p. 890, folio 2653] The governor and Mrs. Gilpin went to Denver within two or three days after that; did not know for what purpose; they left within two or three days. Three or four gentleman came to our house that night. I afterwards learned they were officers from Denver. I was informed the next day that Governor Gilpin had brought the officers to take Mrs. Gilpin and the children to Denver. He said he [2655] thought his children unsafe there; he thought there was some conspiracy by Mrs. Tracy and Julia Greeley to kidnap them. This was in the forenoon, my husband and self were present. I remember being in the post office in the afternoon with the governor and Mrs. Gilpin and my husband; there was a general conversation about what had happened that day. Governor Gilpin said he believed Mrs. Gilpin had murdered her first husband and wanted to treat him the same way. Mrs. Gilpin said she had shed more tears over the death of her first husband than there were drops of water in the creek. Afterwards the [p. 891] governor apologized for the statement…. He said he was very sorry — did not believe it was so — asked Mrs. Gilpin to forgive [folio 2657] him. Mrs. Gilpin said she thought that bringing the officers there was an insult to her; she did not know of any reason why she should be treated so. The whole family went away on the same train…. Julia Greeley [folio 2658] was a cook; she was in my service about three months; **she was a good, constant servant; her conduct and demeanor was proper so far as I know; modest and proper so far as I am aware.**

Cross-examination:

Julia Greeley came to me about June 1st, 1883, and lived with me two or three months [folio 2659] as cook; she was one of Mrs. Gilpin's servants before that, and I saw her, as I did the other servants, at Edgerton; she was there in the employ of Mrs. Gilpin in 1882; I knew [p. 892, folio 2660] nothing of her before that. **I never heard anything but that her reputation was good; she was recommended to me, and I know nothing more than that** — Mrs. Gilpin recommended her; I do not know whether it was by letter or verbally; do not know whether [folio 2662] at that time it was understood that the family would spend the summer at Edgerton; so [folio 2663] understood it.

Re-direct Examination:

Julia Greeley remained at my house six or seven weeks, perhaps, after Governor Gilpin and his family had left; she then went to Denver, I think, and next took service with Mrs. Sherwin in New Mexico. During the time that I was acquainted with Julia Greeley, both in her capacity as my servant and as Mrs. Gilpin's servant, **I never heard her character brought in question.**

Second Cross-examination:

[folio 2664] I don't know exactly how long it was after she left me that she took service with Mrs. Sherwin; it was very soon. Mrs. Sherwin lived on a ranch near Cimarron. I do not know where this woman was between the time she left my service and took service with Mrs. Sherwin.

Mrs. Louise Pratte (Brief, p. 892-895, 901-902, folio 2664-2690, 2764-2766):

[p. 892, folio 2664] I am eighty years old; reside in St. Louis, Missouri. I am the defendant's mother; have [p. 893] paid two visits to her in Denver; the first in October, 1873, until January or February, '74… On my first visit I brought Mrs. Gilpin's three little girls, Louise, Julie and Lizzie from Pendleton, Missouri, where they had remained during the absence of their mother in California. …. [p. 894, folio 2689] I know Julia Greeley well; saw her off and on for nine years.

She was a cook in Dr. Robinson's [folio 2690] house, afterwards a nurse.

Int. 19. State whether you were acquainted with the general reputation of said Julia Greeley among her acquaintance and those with whom she resided, in respect to whether she was a modest, virtuous and proper woman or otherwise. If yea, state what was such reputation.

Answer: **She was an honest, good faithful servant.** During my stay at Dr. Robinson's she seldom went out of the house**; I never knew her to keep company with man or woman.** The way she went to Denver was this: Defendant wrote me to send Julia Greeley to her as cook; Dr. Robinson furnished Julia with the money, which was afterwards returned to her by plaintiff.

Second deposition:

[p. 901, folio 2764] Ans. 5**. I have made particular enquiries as to Julia Greeley, and learned her associates and friends were among the most respectable colored people in St. Louis. They have known her eighteen years, and never knew her to have a male friend. They all testify to her** [folio 2765] **good character, and state that her reputation for modesty and virtue were never questioned.**

Ans. 6**. I have known her personally more than thirteen years. I lived in the house with her several months at a time on different** [p. 902] **occasions, and I never knew or heard of** [folio 2766] **her having a male companion. I can testify to her modest deportment on all occasions.**

Mrs. Celeste Pratte Tracy (Brief, p. 898, folio 2717-2719):[305]

[p. 898, folio 2717] Julia Greeley was a faithful servant in my family for nine years. Before going to Edgerton, I wrote her occasionally in answer to her letters enquiring about the children of Dr. Robinson, to whom she was fondly attached. My letters constituted the trivial sayings and

---

[305] Celeste Tracy had served as Julia Greeley's baptismal sponsor in 1880.

doings of the children in the family, such letters as would only be interesting to a servant. I never at any time [folio 2718] entered into any combination with any persons to steal, abduct or carry away the children of Mrs. Gilpin, or to assist in so doing, nor did I at any time know or hear of any such design or combination on the part of any person or persons. I did not send Julia Greeley to Colorado, neither was I privy to her going, nor did I aid, advise or suggest her going; the first information I had of it was from a letter sent from my mother while I was in South Carolina. I have known [folio 2719] Julia Greeley since about the year 1875. When first acquainted with her she was employed by my sister as nurse, afterwards she served in the capacity of cook. **Upon inquiry among respectable colored people in St. Louis, I learn that her general reputation for modesty and virtue is excellent, and from my personal observation I concur in the general good reputation she bears.**

Dr. Paul Gervais Robinson [1834-1913] (Brief, p. 899-900, folio 2739-2741):[306]

[p. 899, folio 2739] I am 52 years old, reside in St. Louis, Missouri. I married the youngest sister of Mrs. Julia P. Gilpin, the defendant. Lina, my wife, sister of the defendant, died at my house in St. Louis, January 31st, 1882…[307] I knew a negro girl whom we called Julia Greeley, who was employed by me for about seven years, in the capacity of child's nurse generally though she did a variety of work about the house. **She was remarkable for her fidelity, honesty and devotion to the inmates of my household and especially to my children.** To the best of my knowledge she left our service on account of some difference [folio 2740] with another servant. She was then taken into defendant's employ with good understanding on all sides. I was requested to pay her passage to Denver by the defendant, with the promise on her part that the amount [p. 900] would be refunded to me by Governor Gilpin. I did as requested, and the amount was refunded to me by Governor Gilpin. I have no record or letters from Governor Gilpin relating to this matter. I know nothing [folio 2741] of the reputation Julia Greeley bore among her acquaintance, as I never had occasion to enquire, and never had reason to suspect that she was not what she ought to be in every respect. **As I said before I thought her a remarkable good negro, and we valued her services very highly.**

Russell Riley (Brief, p. 900, folio 2742):

[p. 900, folio 2742] I am 42 years of age: a druggist; reside 1500 Olive street, St. Louis, Missouri. I have known Julia Greeley about six or seven years. **Her reputation among her acquaintances in St. Louis for modesty and virtue is excellent.**

---

[306] Dr. Robinson had been a surgeon in the Confederate army [Beckwith 110] He was married twice — first in 1858, to Elizabeth R. Dickson, who died in 1861, leaving no children; then to Miss Lina Pratte, daughter of Bernard Pratte of St. Louis, in 1869. [Hyde v. 4, pp. 1931-1931].

[307] The Robinson house was at 3411 Washington St., the site now of part of a parking lot for the St. Louis Symphony Orchestra. Shortly after Julia Greeley left St. Louis, the 1880 U.S. Census listed the Doctor and Mrs. Robinson with five children: Paul G., 9; Nina, 7; Maria, 5; [Francis] Lee, 4; and Adele, 2. A daughter, Margaret listed on the 1870 census as born in 1865, must have died before 1880.

Col. Clay Taylor (Brief, p. 900-901, folio 2742-2743):[308]

[p. 900, folio 2742] I am sixty years of age; reside in Warren county, Missouri; I have known Julia Greeley fifteen or twenty years, **I know the general reputation which she bore among her acquaintances in St. Louis during her residence there for modesty and virtue; it was good. I consider her one of the most honest, truthful and faithful servants I ever saw, and would trust her with my children under all circumstances, or even with my own life. I never heard a word of suspicion against her character.**

Julia Greeley's Own Sworn Testimony

[Julia's testimony was presented in Brief p. 736-738. Since it is the only "writing" of Julia's known to be in existence,[309] her testimony will be presented here in full from the transcript itself, rather than the Brief.][310]

Folios 2076-2086:

[folio 2076] JULIA GREELEY being duly sworn testified as follows:

Direct examination by Mr. Taylor

Q. What is your full name? A. Julia Greeley.

Q. Were you a slave? A. Yes sir.

Q. Where was your home? A. In Hannibal, Missouri.

Q. How old are you? A. I do not know, I never was told?

Q. Can you read or write? A. Well, a little, I can read, I cannot write.

[Folio 2077] Q. When did you first become acquainted with Mrs. Gilpin. A. I knew Miss Julia when I was back in St. Louis when I was living with Mrs. Robertson.

Q. How long was it? A. I do not remember.

---

[308] Clay was married to Julia Gilpin's sister, Louise Pratte. Their children were Bernard Pratte Taylor and Porter Taylor. [Beckwith 108]. Bernard served as Julia Greeley's baptismal sponsor in 1880.

[309] Another possibility would be the letter that she had Fr. Swift take down for her (see No. 3 on p. 37), but since it is not known to whom she may have written, there is no way to even begin looking for it. Julia also had someone write letters for her to Celeste Tracy (cf. p. 102)..

[310] Transcript pp. 721-726, folios 2076-2086, in Archives Box 38771.

Q. How long did you live with Mrs. Robertson? A. 9 years.

Q. Did you see Mrs. Gilpin then frequently? A. Frequently, yes sir.

Q. How did you happen to come out to Colorado. A. I came out because I wanted to.

Q. Did you communicate with Mrs. Gilpin about coming to her service? A. I got a friend of mine to write and ask her.

Q. And you got a favorable reply and that is what brought you out? A. Yes sir.

[folio 2078] Q. When did you first go to work for Mrs. Gilpin? A. Just as soon as I came to Denver.

Q. What year? A. I do not remember.

Q. How long did you live with her? A. 2 years.

Q. What were your duties? A. When I first went there I did the washing and the ironing.

Q. How long did you work for her? A. Two years.

Q. How did you happen to leave? A. I left because I was tired of staying. I didn't care to stay any longer.

Q. Did you have anything to do with the children while you were there? A. Oh yes, (not heard) I would see to them.

Q. During this time was there any attachment between you and the children; did you get fond of them? A. Yes, I got real fond of them.

Q. You cannot tell the jury when you left Mrs. Gilpin's service can you? A. No, I cannot tell.

[folio 2079] Q. You cannot tell exactly when you came? A. No sir, I cannot tell the year I came. I know it was the 20th. I do not know the month. I think it was the 20th of March, but I do not remember what year it was in.

Q. Did you ever work on Holladay street? A. Yes.

Q. How long was that after you left Mrs. Gilpin's house? A. It was a good while when I went there.

Q. What did you do when you went down on Holladay street? A. I cooked there.

Q. How did you happen to go there? A. I did not have no other place to work at and I went there to work.

[folio 2080] Q. Did you ever tell Mrs. Gilpin about it? A. When I came round I said ..

Objected to, objection sustained.

Q. Did Mrs. Gilpin at this time you told her, admonish you or tell you to leave that place?

Objected to, objection overruled.

A. Yes sir, she said I must get out of that place.

Q. How long did you work there? A. I worked there 2 weeks.

Q. Have you ever been married? A. No sir.

Q. Describe what you did when you were cooking down there, when you went there, and when you came away, where you slept, what part you took in it? A. When I went to cook.

[folio 2081] Q. Yes? A. I took the cooking and stayed just in the kitchen, and did the cooking and I set the table there, and washed the dishes there, and set the table.

Q. Where had you a room? A. A room on Lawrence street right across from the church.

Q. What time did you go to work? A. At eight o'clock and sometimes half past ten, sometimes 11, and sometimes ½ past 11.

Q. When did you come away? A. Sometimes supper was about ½ past 4, or 4 o'clock and there was table set for lunch, and would go away about 5 ½.

Q. Where did you go to work when you left this place? A. I went to the Albany hotel.

[folio 2082] Q. What were you doing there? A. I was in the drying room, was a laundress there, had six dollars a week.

Q. Did you ever go to work for Mrs. Teachout? A. Yes.

Q. When? A. I do not know the year; it was in May; I was there a good while.

Q. Were you there one or two seasons? A. Two seasons.

Q. You were there in 1882 and 1883 were you not? A. I cannot tell the year but I was there two seasons.

Q. About this time, let me ask you if you were in the habit of drinking? A. No sir, I never drank anything in my life.

Q. Were you ever under the influence of liquor in Mrs. Gilpin's house? A. No sir, never in my life.

[folio 2083] Q. Did you ever go out with the children while you were there. A. Yes sir, I used to go out very often.

Q. What time? A. Well, in the evening.

Q. When you say in the evening, do you mean in the afternoon? A. Yes, in the afternoon.

Q. Did you ever take then out at night? A. No sir, I never took them out at night.

Q. Do you remember being in Mrs. Gilpin's house when she was away and when Mrs. Speer was there with the children? A. Yes.

Q. I will ask you again whether on that occasion you were under the influence of drink? A. No sir.

Q. Did you ever have any trouble with Governor Gilpin? A. No sir, he never spoke to me at all.

Q. Did he ever tell you not to come to the house? A. Oh yes, when he told me not to come to the house.

[folio 2084] Q. Was that after you had left the house? A. Yes, after I had left.

Q. What did he say to you? A. He said he wanted me to go out of the house; he did not want me to come into the house.

Q. What were you doing there at that time, visiting? A. Oh yes sir, just there visiting.

Q. After that did you ever sleep on the place? A. Yes, once. I was out of a place, and did not have any place to go, and slept in the shed where the donkey was kept in. One night because the place where I was staying at they went to bed early, and I wasn't there, they was all in bed, and I didn't wake them up. I just slept in the stable that night.

Q. Your relations with the children were very friendly. A. Yes sir.

Cross-examination by Mr. Patterson

Q. You went down to Cimmaron [sic]? A. Yes sir.

Q. And then came back to Denver? A. Yes sir.

Q. And then did you go away from Denver again? A. After I came from Cimmaron [sic] – no sir.

[folio 2085] Q. Have you been living in Denver since? A. No sir.

Q. Where did you go? A. After I left Denver?

Q. Yes, A. I went to Cheyenne.

Q. What were you doing there? A. I worked with the postmaster's wife there, and then from there I went out to the post, and went with Lieutenant Tyson. He was a brother of the Governor up there. His brother in law was elected Governor.[311]

Q. Elected Governor in Wyoming? A. Yes.

Q. What did you say the name was? A. Lieutenant Tyson.

Q. Where did you go to from Cheyenne? A. Up to Laramie City.

Q. When did you come back here? A. Last Wednesday.

Q. Where did you come from? A. From Laramie City.

Q. Who were you working for there? A. For a private family but I forget the man's name, I cannot think of his name.

Q. You came back to attend this trial? A. I did not know what I was coming for.

Q. You were cent [sic] for? A. Yes, I was sent for.

Q. When you went down to Cimmaron [sic] whom did you go with ? A. I went by myself.

Q. You know Mrs. Tracy? A. Yes, sir, I know Mrs. Tracy.

Q. Did you go shortly after the Governor left? A. I stayed a week after the Governor and the children left?

Q. Stayed down at Edgerton? A. Yes, a week after the Governor and the children had left; then when my week was up I came here and stayed a week, and then I went down to Cimmaron [sic].

Q. How did you come to go down to Cimmaron[sic] ? A. I went down to Mrs. Sherwin's to cook.

---

[311] George W. Baxter was married to the sister of Lt. Tyson's wife. [Hale 5: 1474-1475] He was not elected to the office, but appointed by President Grover Cleveland and served only for 39 days: from Nov. 1, 1886, till Dec. 20, 1886.

*****

And once again, dear friend, that is all the information that has been found — so far!

Julia and the Church Courts?

So now the question remains. Is there a possibility that Julia will ever be canonized? People have talked about that since the time when she died. Some have even spoken as if her cause was being considered in the 1970s.[312] The short answer is: there is no official cause. Father Kennedy worked hard at seeking those who could testify, possibly with the hope that an official cause would materialize, but Kennedy in both of his articles underscored that what he wrote "was submitted to the judgment of the Church."[313] There never was an official cause introduced, however, and now it is rather unlikely that any contemporaries of Julia can be found to testify.

The only one who can begin an official cause for Julia is the local bishop, and to date none of the local ordinaries are known to have expressed their mind publicly on the subject. Cardinal J. Francis Stafford was reported to have "announced that he was interested in supporting the cause for canonization of Julia Greeley."[314] However, by the time he said this, he was no longer the local ordinary, and what is more to the point there was no official cause to support. Archbishop Charles Chaput has also expressed his hope that Julia's cause can be begun. By then, however, he was already archbishop-designate of Philadelphia.[315]

Blessed Pope John Paul II said in the most recent papal norms, promulgated in 1983, "It is the right of diocesan Bishops... within the limits of their own jurisdiction, either ex officio or upon the request of individual members of the faithful or of legitimate groups and their representatives, to inquire about the life, virtues or martyrdom and reputation of sanctity or martyrdom, alleged miracles, as well as, if it be the case, ancient cult of the Servant of God, whose canonization is sought."[316]

Before he could do so, however, the local ordinary would need to ask Rome's Congregation for the Cause of Saints for clearance (nihil obstat) to introduce a cause. If this is given, the person in thereafter referred to as a Servant of God.

The virtues specially examined would be the theological virtues of faith, hope, and charity, the cardinal virtues of justice, prudence, courage, and temperance, and other virtues particular to a

---

[312] DCR 2-7-1990, 2-22-1995.
[313] Kennedy 1974, p. 13; 1979, p. 30 in Kennedy papers, AAD.
[314] Tarkelson, RMN 3-3-1998, Hallett, DCR 4-15-1998.
[315] Chaput to Burkey, private conversation, St. Francis Friary, 8-24-2011.
[316] John Paul II, Divinus Perfectionis Magister, Jan. 25, 1983.

person's state of life. The reader might find it instructive to reread the present study with these virtues in mind.

Since Julia was illiterate, there are no writings to be examined. Just how the examination would deal with the lack of living witnesses is not clear, but the Congregation does have provision for historical cases.

There are two major concerns for the archdiocesan ordinary and anyone who might wish to promote a cause:

1. Before the ordinary would be likely to pursue a cause, he would want to see that there really is a widespread interest in the Archdiocese and elsewhere in pursuing the cause.

2. Pursuing a cause would involve the labor of many people who would need to be remunerated for their work, and it would need to be clear how this would be covered.

So back to the question, is there a possibility that Julia will ever be canonized? The answer seems to lie in the answer to another question: Can the faithful, possibly through an organization of some sort, demonstrate an authentic groundswell of interest in pursuing a cause and in providing for its pursuit?

Recently a group of people, representing a number of larger groups interested in moving Julia's case forward, gathered in Sacred Heart Parish's Julia Greeley Room. After discussing the situation at length, they joined themselves into a loose knit consortium called the Julia Greeley Guild and planned a number of concrete steps aimed at promoting Julia Greeley's fame. Present at this first meeting on August 1, 2011, were representatives of ENDOW, the Ladies Auxiliary of the Knights of St. Peter Claver, the Secular Franciscan Order, Sacred Heart Parish, Cure d'Ars Parish, the Archdiocese Office for Black Catholics, the Capuchin Franciscan Order, and the Religious Sisters of Mercy. Representatives from Loyola Parish, the Jesuits, and the Archdiocesan Liturgical Office expressed interest in being at this first meeting, but for various reasons were unable to attend. By a second meeting in September, representatives of Holy Name Parish, the Catholic firemen, and New Advent Ministries had also joined the Guild.

In the meantime, the present study has no intention of presuming or anticipating any decision of the Church concerning Julia's holiness.

It is important to remember, however, that whether or not the Church decides to move forward on Julia's case, she will always remain a stellar role model for all those who have been placed in challenging situations in life, as well as those who have been blessed with everything. Both the Ladies of Peter Claver and ENDOW have already made it perfectly clear that they embrace Julia Greeley as their role model.

Chronology of Julia's Life

1815 — William Gilpin born.

Sometime between 1833 & 1848 — Julia Greeley born, daughter of George and Cerilda, slaves, reportedly in Hannibal, Missouri (but also reportedly in the Carolinas).

1836 Mar. 6 — Julia Pratte born in St. Louis, the daughter of Bernard Pratte, Jr., and Marie Louise Chenie.

1857 (circa) — William Gilpin first proposed marriage to Julia.

1860 Mar. 27— Julia Pratte married Capt. (Bvt. Maj.) John H. Dickerson.

1860 Dec. 25 — Fr. Joseph Projectus Machebeuf celebrated the first Mass in St. Mary's Church, corner of 15th and Stout.

1861 May 27 — Colonel Gilpin arrived in Denver as the newly appointed first governor of Colorado territory.

1862 Mar. 31 — Gov. Gilpin replaced by John Evans as governor of the Colorado territory.

1864 Mar. 31 — Dickerson resigned his commission.

1865 Feb. 15 — Louise E. Dickerson born [later married Frank Sherwin].

1866 Nov. 20 — Sidney Dickerson born.

1868 Aug. 16 — Machebeuf ordained bishop as Vicar Apostolic of Colorado. St. Mary's became a cathedral.

1868 Sept. — Julia Dickerson born [later married Lee Allen].

1871 (circa) — Julia Greeley began working for the family of Dr. Gervais Paul Robinson, brother-in-law of Julia Gilpin.

1871 Apr. 12 — Elizabeth Dickerson born [later married Otis B. Spencer and Edward D.S. Southwork, Jr.; children: Allen B. Spencer, Mrs. Abbott Oberndorfer, and Mrs. Louis Sherwin].

1872 Mar. 2 — Captain Dickerson died in St. Vincent Hospital, St. Louis, of mental illness. Julia and the children had been living in New York for about two years.

1874 Feb. 16 — Julia Pratte Dickerson married ex-governor William Gilpin in St. Louis.

1874 Feb. 19 — Julia Gilpin arrived in Colorado.

1874 — The Gilpins spent several weeks in California.

1875 May 12 — Willie Gilpin & Marie Louise Gilpin, twins, born.

1876 — St. Joseph's Hospital built on land donated by the Gilpins.

1877 July 10 — Louis Bogy Gilpin born.

1878 — St. Elizabeth Parish begun.

1878-1880 — Julia Greeley came to Denver.

1879 — Sacred Heart Parish begun.

1880 April 25 — Sacred Heart Church dedicated.

1880 June 1 — Julia Greeley was living with the Gilpins on Champa St.

1880 June 26 — Julia was conditionally baptized at Sacred Heart Church.

1882 summer — Julia was living with the Gilpins at Teachout Hotel in Edgerton, Colo.

1883 Apr. or May — Julia's service with Gilpin ended.

1883 June 1 — Julia began cooking at Teachout's Hotel in Edgerton.

1883 — Julia Gilpin's daughter Louise married Frank Sherwin.

1883 Sept. — Julia worked for Mrs. Sherwin in Cimarron, New Mexico..

1884 — Worked briefly as a cook at brothel on Halloway (now Market) Street.

1885 — Sidney Dickerson graduated from Notre Dame University.

1885 or 1886 — Julia worked in Cheyenne for the postmaster's wife.

1886 (first half) — Julia worked at Ft. D.A. Russell for Lt. Tyson and his wife.

1886 or 1887 — Julia worked in Laramie.

1887 Mar. 17 — Col. Gilpin filed for divorce. Accused Julia Greeley of being lewd and unprincipled.

1887 Aug. 7 — Denver raised from a Vicariate Apostolic to a Diocese.

1887 Oct. 28 — Nicholas Matz ordained coadjutor bishop of Denver.

1887 Dec. 8 — Col. Gilpin received his divorce and the same day purchased house at 1321 S. 14th St. and took his children there by force.

1889 — Colorado supreme court reverses superior court's divorce decision.

1889 July 10 — Bp. Machebeuf died. Succeeded by Bp. Matz.

1890 — Bishop Matz built a four-story brick and sandstone school at 1842 Logan St. and moved his cathedral to the basement thereof.

1891 — Gilpins reconciled, reunited at 1321 S. 14th St.

1892 June 16 — Willie Gilpin killed in fall from cliff — buried from pro-cathedral at 1842 Logan — one of first persons buried in Mt. Olivet Cemetery.

1893 Nov. — Julia Greeley began working at the O'Donnell home at 5th and Federal. Worked there till about June 15, 1894.

1894 Jan. 19/20 — Gov. Gilpin died without a will and was buried from St. Mark's Episcopal Church in unconsecrated ground in Mt. Olivet Cemetery.

1896 — Julia Greeley cooked at Ft. Logan for Capt. George Young, attended St. Patrick's Church, now Holy Name Church.

1898 Apr. — Capt. Young deployed to Cuba.

1898 May 1 — present St. Elizabeth Church dedicated.

1898 — Julia cooked at the Sliney Hotel on Lowell Blvd., north of Mansfield Ave.

1899 — Julia Greeley, colored, living at 1421 28th St. — 1899 city directory.

1900 — First St. Mary's Cathedral demolished.

1901 Feb. 24 — Julia Greeley received into the Secular Franciscan Order (O.F.S.) as Sr. Elizabeth, by Fr. Francis Koch O.F.M., at St. Elizabeth Church..

1902 — ground broken for present cathedral.

1902 — Ryan Sisters moved from 2720 Lawrence to 5127 Homer (Lowell) Blvd.

1904 — Julia listed as cook, rooming at 2913 Walnut in 1904 & 1905 Denver city directories and in Monitors till 1917.

1904 — William Urquhart died.

1905 Fall — Julia Greeley named Francis Xavier Lee.

1906 — Julia living at 2913 Walnut.

1908 — Servant of God Leo Heinrichs murdered at St. Elizabeth's Church.

1910 — Julia cooking for the Ryan sisters at 5127 Homer (Lowell) Boulevard.

1910 Jan. 16 — Sacred Heart Parish's Loyola Chapel at 25th and Ogden blessed by Bp. Matz.

1910 Apr. 23 — Julia is listed on the U.S. Census in a boarding house at 2913 Walnut St.

1910 May 28 — Julia Greeley brought bouquet from 5127 Lowell to First Communion at St. John the Evangelist Church at 5th and Josephine.

1912 Oct. 27 — present Denver cathedral dedicated.

1912 Dec. 21 — Mrs. Gilpin died at 4337 Maryland St., St. Louis, Mo. [near the site of that city's present cathedral.

1912 Dec. 24 — Mrs. Gilpin buried from Denver cathedral at Mt. Olivet Cemetery.

1912 Dec. 30 — Julia Greeley told she might receive $100 from Mrs. Gilpin's estate.

1913 — Ryan sisters moved to 2459 Lafayette.

1913 — Julia rooms at 2913 Walnut — 1913 Denver city directory.

1914 — Julia first visited the Urquhart home at 4270 Hooker Street.

1915 Sept. 11 — Marjorie Urquhart born. Julia soon began caring for her.

1916 Apr. — photo of Julia Greeley and Marjorie Urquhart, taken in McDonough Park on Federal Boulevard.

1916 — Julia living at 2913 Walnut.

1917 Aug. 9 — Bp. Matz died.

1917 Oct. 12 — Julia's friend Mother Pancratia Bonfils died in St. Joseph's Hospital, shortly after Julia visited her. Pancratia revealed that Julia had once cooked for the Loretto Sisters at St. Mary's Academy.

1917 Dec. 21 — Bishop J. Henry Tihen installed as bishop.

1917 — Julia living at 2821 Walnut; same address given for Mrs. John Golden.

1918 June 7 — Julia Greeley died, St. Joseph Hospital, Room 407.

1918 June 9 — Julia's body lay in state, Loyola Chapel, Ogden Street.

1918 June 10 — funeral at Sacred Heart Church, Larimer Street, with burial as Mt. Olivet.

1922 May 12 — Julia's friend Jennie J. Ryan died.

Signs of Julia's Cultus through the Years

1918 June 7 — Julia Greeley died.

1918 June 10 — "A plain casket under a blanket of flowers was rolled in place before the altar of the Church of the Sacred Heart Sunday afternoon at 3 o'clock. Then came a quiet crowd of men and women and children, some with flowers in their hands, to pay their last respects to the one who had closed life's accounts and entered into 'the sleep that knows no waking' and whose body was lying in state before the church altar." (*Denver Post*)

1918 June 11 — "From a childhood of slavery in a Southern cotton field, to genuine honors in death, signalized by the body's reposing in state for forty-eight hours, while a thousand white people filed by to pay tribute, is a far swing." (*Rocky Mountain News*)

1918 June 13 — "Her life reads like that of a canonized saint…. When her body lay in state, limousines and giant touring cars came carrying the rich to see her. The poor flocked to the chapel in throngs. When Father McDonnell recited the Rosary for her soul at 7:30, the chapel was well filled. The Sacred Heart church was crowded Monday morning at her funeral. The prosperous and the poor, the educated and the uneducated, the prominent and the unknown were there—proud to pay homage to the aged negress." (*Denver Catholic Register*)

1918 July 18 — A month after Julia's funeral, the *Register* carried two more items relating to Julia. The one took notice of an article in *Ave Maria* magazine, which, commenting on the honors paid Julia, said: "Worldly philosophers will see in the demonstrations thus recorded a striking instance of the democracy of the American Catholic Church; Scripture students will look on them as exemplification of the dictum of Proverbs: 'Favor is deceitful and beauty is vain; the woman that fears the Lord, she shall be praised'." The other was a short piece titled, "People Deem It Honor to Distribute Leaflets Colored Julia Handed Out." It told how several people wanted to take over Julia's ministry of distributing leaflets of the League of the Sacred Heart to the firehouses of the city and other places that "the saintly old colored woman" used to care for every month. "It is no small thing to visit every firehouse in Denver monthly," the Register noted. (*Denver Catholic Register*)

1918 July — "Old 'colored' Julia is gone to her reward. She died a beautiful death on the Feast of the Sacred Heart — a fitting close to forty years of untiring labor as an apostle of the Sacred Heart." (*Sacred Heart Church and School Monitor*)

1922 Dec. 21 — "When death claimed Julia Greeley..., priests who had known her well declared her the most saintly character they had ever met." (*Denver Catholic Register*)

1928 June 14 — The *Register* noted that the "last issue of the St. Elizabeth chronicle, magazine of a St. Louis [Missouri] Negro parish" had reprinted verbatim the *Register*'s own lengthy 1918 obituary. The *Register* editor went on to call Julia "an ugly one-eyed woman" whose soul "was like a lily." He then gave some illustrations of her charity and apostolic spirit and revealed possibly for the first time that she made her rounds of the fire houses on foot. "After her death," he recalled, "there was a scramble to get a share of the work she had made eminent in the distribution of those leaflets." (*Denver Catholic Register*)

1939 March 2 — Julia's life was to be reviewed in a series of radio programs to be broadcast on a new radio program, The Sacred Heart Hour, which Fr. Murphy was about to begin airing on station WEW at St. Louis University in Missouri, beginning Sunday, March 19. "Her story will be used to exemplify the eleventh promise made to St. Margaret Mary: 'Those who shall promote this devotion shall have their names written in My Heart never to be blotted out'." The Register used the occasion to repeat much of the content of its 1918 article, adding a few new items, such as avowing, "When Julia Greeley died, Denver lost a woman whom everybody believed to be a saint," and calling her the Apostle of the Sacred Heart. (*Denver Catholic Register*)

1939 March 9 — The Register gave its younger readers their first glimpse of the visage of Julia Greeley — the now familiar photo of her in a white dress and her large black hat, seated and holding her "Little White Angel," as she called her tiny charge. The photo was accompanied by an article entitled, "Saintly Negress Nurse 'To Little White Angel'." (*Denver Catholic Register*)

1939 April 13 — An article, entitled "Secret Charities of Julia Greeley Are Recalled by Denver People," began, "In a world where saints are often forgotten sooner than sinners, the memory of Julia Greeley, saintly and beloved Negress, refuses to die. An example of the great respect this woman commands is revealed in the report of a Boulder resident that a novena was made in honor of Miss Greeley and a small favor resulted. Old-time Denverites, stirred by recent articles about Julia in the Denver Catholic Register, have disclosed hitherto unpublished anecdotes about this charitable apostle of the Sacred Heart." — The story ended: "Thus the tales of Julia Greeley continue to come to the fore. Many of her charitable acts will probably remain hidden forever, but the modest 'Nigger Julia,' as she called herself, continues to be a saint to hundreds of Denverites—and as one Denver woman put it, 'more of a saint every year'." (*Denver Catholic Register*)

1939 April 13 — The same issue of the paper carried "Mrs. Hagus Recalls Julia's Kind Deed," written by Rose M. Hagus.

1939 April — "There may, someday, be a Saint Julia Greeley of Denver. Another saint in the great catalogue of the Church is not so significant as the fact that Julia Greeley was a negro and a former slave. Julia's great charity is remembered tenderly by many Denverites, not because she did anything so great, but because she did so many little things with her whole heart. 'Love Thy Neighbor' wasn't just a platitude to Julia. It was a commandment. Second only to 'Love Thy God.' Everything she did, everything she said, found its roots in the two great commandments. And because love begets love, Julia's black and white friends would make her a saint [....] Pigment may be different, racial traits may be different, but difference does not mean inferiority. Julia Greeley knew that.

Julia was a real democrat. She ignored the barriers of color and gave help where help was needed. She ignored the barriers—so there were none. Julia may yet have to intercede before the throne of God, for those white people whose floors she scrubbed [....] We cannot be good citizens in this democracy unless we are willing to be catholic as well as Catholic. Unless we are able to throw aside our petty prejudices and acknowledge that the fatherhood of God and the brotherhood of man makes no stipulation whatsoever for the brotherhood of white with white and black with black. May Julia Greeley show us the way!" (Madelyn Nicholds in **T'Akra**)

1941 August — Dr. Currigan operated on Helen Noonan and diagnosed the case as hopeless — cancer throughout. He gave her a colostomy and told her mother to get the family together, that Helen had only about two weeks to live. When Currigan was driving home that rainy night, he kept seeing an ugly, black, scarred face in the windshield. He was terribly puzzled about who it was. Finally it dawned on him that it was the face of Julia Greeley, whom he hadn't thought of for years. He took care of her as a young intern in her last illness and is thought to have been with her when she died. He drove back to the hospital and told the family to have novenas of Masses said honoring Black Julia for Helen's recovery. Many parishes waved their present Masses so that these could be said immediately. Helen stayed in the hospital a couple of weeks, but at Dr. Currigan's insistence she went home. Dr. Cheley later operated and found no cancer. He diagnosed it as peritonitis of the intestines. He treated her, but did not close the colostomy until he was sure all was all right. He closed it in about two months. She led a very active life after that. [While not a verifiable miracle, this is still an example of private cultus towards Julia].

1942 Nov. — Sr. M. Lilliana Owens, S.L., teacher of history at St. Mary's Academy in Denver, had an article published in the *Sacred Heart Messenger* entitled "A Negro Apostle of the Sacred Heart," which told Julia's story.

1943 April 29 — The Register announced the publication of a pamphlet written by Fr. Murphy entitled *My Name Written in His Heart*. The pamphlet reviewed the career of Julia Greeley as an apostle of the Sacred Heart from the time of her coming to Denver "until her saintly death" in 1918 and again reflected on the 11th promise of the Sacred Heart to St. Margaret Mary Alocoque: "Those who promote this devotion shall have their names written in My Heart never to be blotted out."

1943 — Fr. John LaFarge, S.J. (1880-1963), an editor of *America* magazine and founder of the Catholic interracial movement in the United States, mentioned Julia Greeley in his seminal study of Catholic doctrine on interracial justice. He included her in his list of black "examples of that moral triumph which we call sanctity" and further called her and New York's Ven. Pierre Toussaint (1766/1780-1853) "hidden martyrs of charity." (The Racial Question and the Negro," by John LaFarge)

1958 — The 8th edition of Fr. Murphy's pamphlet was published with a press run of 39,000 copies.

1965 June 17 — "When Julia Greeley died, Denver lost a woman everybody believed to be a saint. [...] Long before the days when sympathy with Negroes became fashionable, people from all walks of society flocked to Loyola chapel to pray before the little Black body as it lay in state. This testimony was not to her race, but to sanctity. [...] Perhaps very few are alive today who remember Julia Greeley. When these are gone, her name may be known only from the yellow files of the Register. But the sanctity of her life can never become uninteresting, irrelevant, or unimportant." (Paul Hallett, in *Denver Catholic Register*)

1966 — Paul Hallett wrote a 28-page history of the Catholic Church in Colorado, which was added as an appendix to Hafen's Colorado general history text book. This expanded edition was meant for the Catholic schools of the state and was still being used at St. Therese School in Aurora as late as 2011. It contained a full page on the life of Julia Greeley.

1969 Sept. 21 — "She was old when I first knew her. She was very poor and worked at whatever she could get, most of the time for 50 cents a day. But Julia was happy and never complained. Every first Friday of the month she made the rounds of the fire houses (there weren't very many at that time), and she would distribute leaflets of the Sacred Heart. It made no difference to her whether the firemen were Catholics or not. She would always say, 'They are all God's children.' I called many people who knew her, and they would always say, 'Yes, I knew Julia, but I don't remember anything about her. It's too bad someone hasn't written about her.' So I thought perhaps you could fill in some of the details I'm sure we all would like to know." (Eleanor Castellan, to *Empire Magazine*)

1969 Oct. 26 — Wouldn't it be nice if all who knew her [Julia] would join into a circle or league of friends, donate a dollar a month or a week, have a Mass for her every First Friday and let the Jesuit fathers distribute any money left over for her own poor in their parish? (Theodora Arnold in *Empire Magazine*)

1974 — "I will pray for Julie as one of God's saints, canonized or not." (Theodora Arnold)

1974 — She was so cheerful — she had time to talk to kids — not many people do that — she was liked by kids — If there's ever a saint in heaven, she was out of this world. [...] I pray to that woman every night to intercede with Sacred Heart for me. I know she's not at that stage, but to me she is. (John McNulty)

1974 March 22 — "I am very happy & interested in anything concerning the saintly life of Old Black Julia Greeley." (Sr. Ellenora Louise Hilbers, S.C.)

1974 April 20 — "Was well thought of by the Sisters, the Priests, and the Laity. Well known in Denver. Most People thought Julie a Saint — So do I. To this day I never forgot Julie, although I never knew Julie personally. As everyone knew, Julie was a colored woman, a former slave, worked for the Sisters of Charity in their convent, for the Poor in Denver. I'll never forget her." (Francis O. Worland)

1974 December — Fr. Pacificus Kennedy, O.F.M., published, "Old Black Julia" in *Friar* magazine.

1978 Sept. 15 — "I have a very vivid boyhood recollection of her. […] God must have loved her greatly, because in her poverty she was always happy, seeking only to help others whom she considered less fortunate than herself. — It was incongruous to see that lovely smile while a tear dropped from her poor blind eye." (Judge Neil Horan)

1979 June — Fr. Pacificus Kennedy, O.F.M., published a sequel, "Beloved Old Black Julia" in *Friar* magazine.

1982 Oct. 13 — Paul H. Hallett published a lengthy article entitled "An Ex-Slave Known for Her Sanctity," in which he said that the *Register*'s funeral article in 1918 was "perhaps the only time a major newspaper devoted its first page to the obituary of someone who was celebrated for nothing but for the fact that in the eyes of all who knew her she had died in the odor of sanctity." Hallett also aptly spoke of Julia as setting "herself up as a one woman St. Vincent de Paul Society" and later called her a "fairy godmother" to the "Cinderellas" of her acquaintance.

1990-1995 — For a number of years in this time period, Fr. Marcus Medrano was invited to celebrate Mass at Julia's grave, on or near the feast of the Sacred Heart. No known records of this were kept, and the Masses were not publicly announced. About a dozen people attended, and the Mass of the Sacred Heart was used. At some point in the Mass the various people present announced intentions that they were committing to Julia's intercession. Mary Frances O'Sullivan remembers being there two years; Max Castillo three, and Dennis Hawkins was there at the last of the series. Russ Tafoya was also present. (Dennis Hawkins to Burkey by phone, 10 Jan. 2012; Mary Frances O'Sullivan to Burkey by phone, 3 Feb. 2012; Max Castillo to Burkey by phone, 3 Feb. 2012)

1992 — On the occasion of the centennial of Mt. Olivet Cemetery, a commemorative booklet told Julia's story and singled it out her grave as that of a saintly woman to be visited on a walking tour of the cemetery.

1992 — Shortly thereafter, Archbishop Stafford asked his secretary, Fr. Michael Glenn, to see what he could find out about Julia's fame for sanctity. This was the beginning of Glenn's interest in Julia (which was evidenced in Endow's DVD concerning Julia). (Msgr. Glenn, phone interview with Burkey, Jan. 23, 2012)

1994 Mar. 24 — At the request of Fr. Medrano, Mary Frances O'Sullivan requested copies of the materials collected by Fr. Kennedy and later saw to it that they were preserved. She also had enlargements made of the Greeley-Urquhart photo and presented them to Sacred Heart Church and Cure d'Ars Church.

1995 Mar. 15 — "Julia, let us never forget your legacy of love, forgiveness, and joy! I've heard there was always a smile on your face." (John Erger in **Denver Catholic Register**)

1995 Mar. 15 — "I have many African American friends in various denominations who never heard about her. With your permission, I intend to copy this article and distribute it widely throughout the Denver area. For any of you who might be interested in visiting the grave of this friend of the Sacred Heart, it is in block 8, section 7 at Mt. Olivet Cemetery in Golden. It would be wonderful if we could have a Mass said in her honor, at the cemetery or at the Church of the Sacred Heart on the Feast of the Sacred Heart of Jesus, June 23, 1995." (Mary Anderson, in *Denver Catholic Register*)

1995 May 24 — The Register carried a notice of a special Mass at Sacred Heart Church on Sunday, June 25, in honor of Julia Greeley and her devotion to the Sacred Heart.

1995 June 7 — Another notice of the same. This one urged, "Please come to give honor to this modern day saint in THANKSGIVING for her generosity of giving and working for the poor and the needy of Sacred Heart parish for many years."

1995 June 24 —Through the inspiration of Mary Frances O'Sullivan, Linda M. Chase, and Shirley Johnson, the Ladies of Peter Claver established a Julia Greeley scholarship program. Recipients of the scholarships are expected to exemplify their Catholic faith through Mass attendance, community service, academic standing, and a willingness to give back to the community. The first scholarship was given on June 24, 1995, and additional ones have been given every year since then. In 2011, seven scholarships in the amount of $1,200 each were awarded.

1997 — Dr. Michael Woodward became director of the library at St. John Vianney Seminary. During his first few months there he learned of Julia Greeley. "We housed the archives [of the archdiocese] at the time and the Greeley box was one of the most accessed by people. Such interest prompted me to begin looking over the archival materials on her wonderful story." (Woodward to Burkey, 2 Feb. 2012)

1998 April 15 — Following a visit to Denver by Rome-based Cardinal J. Francis Stafford, the Register noted that the cardinal had announced his interest in supporting the cause for Julia's canonization and then reran in its entirety Paul H. Hallett's article from 1982.

2000 Sept. 2 — Julia Greeley memorial added at Find A Grave web site by Rev. Dennis Hawkins, a non-denominational Christian minister.

2001 Nov. 18 — "Hello Miss Julia. Remember me, Russ Tafoya. I was the one who placed that cross in the upper left hand corner of your headstone. Me and Jim Smith prayed the rosary over your grave several times. Sept. 11 in the NYC was real bad. Love you, Miss Julia. Pray for me and our 'O' program." Lots of love. (Russ Tafoya on Hawkins web site)

2002 or 2003 — Dr. Woodward gave a faculty colloquium at St. John Vianney Seminary on Julia Greeley and four other famous Colorado Catholic women, from the draft of a paper he had written for an encyclopedia. (Woodward to Stephen Sweeney, 26 Jan. 2012) Sr.

Prudence Allen RSM first learned about Julia at the colloquium. (Sr. Prudence Allen to Burkey, 23 Jan. 2012)

2005 Spring — Fr. Christopher Hellstrom gave the Religious Sisters of Mercy a tour of Mt. Olivet Cemetery. At Julia Greeley's grave Sr. Prudence prayed interiorly to Julia for guidance to Endow, which was enfolding its mission in Denver. She interiorly heard the words, "Take me with you on pilgrimage," and responded, "Why should you go on pilgrimage? You are already in heaven." The words were repeated, "Take me with you on pilgrimage." (Ibid.)

2005 September — The Endow board made a pilgrimage to Siena and Rome, to study the Dialogues of St. Catherine of Siena and seek the Spirit's guidance for what direction it should take. In the hotel attached to St. Catherine's home, Sr. Prudence shared the story of Julia Greeley with the Endow board (Ibid.)

2005 later in the Fall — Sr. Prudence and Hanna Nevin met and shared their mutual admiration for Julia Greeley. Hanna said that she had learned about Julia from Sr. LaVonne Guidoni SCL (1932-2007), a well-known Denver advocate for children, and she gave Sr. Prudence several articles about her. (Ibid)

2006 May 17 — The Register announced that Endow, the three-year-old Denver-born organization dedicated to Educating on the Nature and Dignity of Women, had named Julia Greeley its model in recognizing the "Genius of Women" and would award a Julia Greeley Award in her honor. (This became an annual event honoring a stellar array of extraordinary Catholic women exemplifying the feminine genius).

2008 Jan. 12 — "What a wonderful woman you were, Julia? If only all of us could remember to follow the Golden Rule like you did. Rest in Peace. See you in heaven." (Mary on Hawkins web site).

2008 July 6 — You are already a Saint — bless you." (Brenda Joyce on Hawkins web site)

2010 June 7 — "Aunt Julia. On this day 92 years ago you returned to the Lord. Eternal rest be unto you, Julia." (Cookie and Doug on Hawkins web site)

2010 Dec. 21 — "Julia, I believe you are a Saint because of the holy life you led and I ask for healing of my body and feet and ankles. Ask Jesus to heal me of my affliction. Amen. Love you Julia." (Gino Acosta on Hawkins web site)

2011 Apr. 5 — Following an Archbishop's Lecture on Bishop Machebeuf by Bishop Joseph Francis Martino, Sr. Prudence briefly mentioned publicly that Julia Greeley was someone in Denver worthy of being canonized. This remark set off the chain of events which brought about the present study.

2011 May 30 — After Archbishop Chaput's Memorial Day Mass at Mt. Olivet Cemetery, the Religious Sisters of Mercy went to the grave of Julia Greeley and placed there a photo of

Robert Lemming, board member of Endow and past chairman of Seeds of Hope, who had suffered a life-threatening stroke on May 9, thereby intending to place him under the protection of Julia Greeley.

2011 Aug. 1 — A group of people, representing a number of larger groups interested in moving Julia's case forward, gathered at the invitation of Fr. Gene Emrisek, O.F.M.Cap., pastor of Sacred Heart Church, in the parish's Julia Greeley Room. After discussing the situation at length, they joined themselves into a loose knit consortium called the Julia Greeley Guild and planned a number of concrete steps aimed at promoting Julia Greeley's fame. Present at this first meeting on August 1, 2011, were representatives of Endow, the Ladies Auxiliary of the Knights of St. Peter Claver, the Secular Franciscan Order, Sacred Heart Parish, Cure d'Ars Parish, the Archdiocese Office for Black Catholics, the Capuchin Franciscan Order, and the Religious Sisters of Mercy. Representatives from Loyola Parish, the Jesuits, and the Archdiocesan Liturgical Office expressed interest in being at this first meeting, but for various reasons were unable to attend. By a second meeting in September, representatives of Holy Name Parish, the Catholic firemen, and New Advent Ministries had also joined the Guild.

2011 Sept. 8 — Bishop James Conley, apostolic administrator of Denver, approved a prayer asking Julia's intercession for an endeavor started by Fr. Regis Scanlon, O.F.M.Cap., to begin a much-needed shelter in Denver for homeless single women. Fr. Regis and the circle for lay people working to bring this project to reality had decided to name the shelter after Julia.

2011 Nov. 21 — "I have had a devotion to one-eyed Julia for a number of years. I would like to help with the book, and any efforts for her sainthood… I have had a number of profound interior experience through Julia. But no outward physical ones. She sustains me when I am feeling sorry for myself. I just think about her, and her struggles, and suddenly my problems seem so small. A couple of times I thought I heard her speak to me, words of guidance and consolation mostly. She was an incredible woman." (John B., email to Kevin Knight)

2011 Nov. 23 — "My mother's aunt, Rose Fisher, who was my godmother and was also a living saint, befriended Julia and often served her lunch and dinner. Once Rose's assistant told Julia, 'You'll have to pray for me.' Julia reportedly replied, 'I'll put you in the canoe (with many other people) but I pray for Mrs. Fisher all by herself.' […] Rest in peace, Julia! Keep us in your prayers — even if you put us in the 'canoe' with many others." (John Erger, in *Denver Catholic Register*)

2011 Nov 29 — "Much like her fellow African-Americans, Venerable Pierre Toussaint and Father Augustine Tolton, Julia Greeley experienced truly horrendous maltreatment by whites (including Catholic clergy) but without making her bitter. May her cause for beatification and ultimate sainthood be advanced to the Holy See as quickly as possible." (Anonymous on "Our Beloved Julia Greeley" website)

2012 Jan. 8 — "I would love to see her elevated to sainthood. The miracle to me, is that, with no bitterness in her heart, even though she was so looked down upon, she did not wallow in self-pity or anger, but became a blessing. She was pregnant with love and gave birth to the 'Christ' every day in her heart." (Jody Walker, Cumberland MD, to Burkey)

2012 Feb 12 — About 40 people made a bus pilgrimage sponsored by the Development and Mission Office of the Capuchin Province of Mid-America to 22 sites connected with the life of Julia Greeley. Fr. Blaine directed the pilgrimage.

The pilgrims visited, among many other sites, (top left) the interior of the building where Julia boarded with the Conway family for over a decade; (top right) the corner of 28th and Larimer which Julia crossed daily en route to Sacred Heart Church and on June 7, 1918, on her way to her death; and (bottom left and right) Julia's grave in Mt. Olivet Cemetery

To the above list one might add many more of the scores of articles mentioned in the Bibliography that follows on pp. 126-135.

Anyone receiving favors through the intercession of Julia Greeley are invited to notify the Julia Greeley Guild in writing at 2760 Larimer Street, Denver CO 80205.

Valued Generous Collaborators

Apostleship of Prayer: Fr. Jim Kubicki SJ / **Archdiocese of Denver:**, James Baca, Daniel Campbell, James Daniel Flynn, Roxanne King, Karyl Klein, Mary Leisring, Jeanette DeMelo, Tracy Murphy, J. Francis Card. Stafford / **Capuchin Province of Mid-America**: Br. Joseph Mary Elder OFMCap, Gina Francis, George Ketchel, Fr. John Lager, OFMCap., Rose Lane, Stephanie Pfeifer Pedersen, Fr. Charles Polifka OFMCap, Fr. Christopher Popravak OFMCap, Fr. Regis Scanlon OFMCap, Toni Schreivogel, Br. Ryan Tidball OFMCap / **Cheyenne Genealogical and Historical Society**: Wanda Wade / **Colorado Genealogical Society**: Bonnie Garramone / **Colorado State Archives:** entire search office staff / **Cumberland Card Club Copyreaders:** Jeanora Hare, Carolyn Neely, Virginia Plummer, Ann Thomas, Jody Walker / **Denver Catholic Register Readers:** Jackie Cugliat, Fr. Lawrence B. Kaiser, Fr. Martin Lally, Gwen Mayer, Diane Rodriguez / **Denver County Assessor's Office**: Walter Sorrentino / **Denver Firemen's Museum**: Winifred Ferrill / **Denver Public Library**: Jennifer Callaway, Coi Drummond-Gehrig, Bruce Hanson, James Jeffrey, Charleszine "Terry" Nelson / **Eleanore Mullen Weckbaugh Foundation** / **Ellis County (Kans.) Historical Society**: James D. Drees / **Endow**: Eileen Love, Hanna Nevin, Terry Polakovic / **Ft. Logan Historical Society**: Dr. Jack Ballard / **Franciscan Friars, Holy Name Province:** Fr. Vincent Grogan OFM, Fr. Pacificus Kennedy OFM, Jocelyn Thomas / **Holy Name Church, Sheridan:** Deacon Don Schaefer / **Independent Friends of Julia Greeley**: Donna Auguste, Lawrence A. Bowers III, Max L. Castillo, Michelle Wessling-Fisher, Terrance R. Kelly, Curtis Martin, Mary Frances O'Sullivan / **Ladies Auxiliary of Knights of St. Peter Claver**: Linda Marie Chase / **Mt. Olivet Cemetery**: Annette Fugita, Lloyd Swint / **Regis University**: Elizabeth Cook, Stan Ericson / **Relatives of Acquaintances of Julia Greeley**: Simon Alixopulos, Kathleen Cronin Bensman, James Castellan, Henry Davis, John Gibbons, Andrew Grosheider, Virginia Maroney Haddad, John J. Horan, Joanne Sesson, MaryAnne Simpson, Dr. Robert Simpson, Dr. Howard McCrum Snyder III, Col. Richard C. & Marie Snyder, Mimi Stephens / **Religious Sisters of Mercy:** Sr. Mary Prudence Allen RSM, Sr. Mary Pierre Wilson RSM / **Sacred Heart Church**: Fr. Gene Emrisek OFMCap, Maria Garcia de Chavez / **St. Joseph Hospital**: Margaret M. Bandy, Sr. Maureen Kehoe SCL / **St. Therese School, Aurora**: Laura Dement / **Secular Franciscan Order**: Michael O'Toole OFS / **Sheridan Historical Society**: Bonita Hutcheson / **Sisters of Charity of Cincinnati**: Sr. Benedicta Maloney SC / **Sisters of Charity of Leavenworth**: Sr. Kathleen Mary Connelly SCL, Sr. Barbara Sellers SCL / **Sisters of Loretto**: Sr. Janet Rabideau SL / **Sisters of the Blessed Sacrament**: Dr. Stephanie Morris / **Society of Jesus Missouri Province**: Fr. Tim McMahon SJ, Dr. David Miros, Mary Struckel / **Stafford Library**, St. John Vianney Seminary: Stephen Sweeney / **University of Colorado Denver**: Dr. Tom Noel / **University of North Carolina, Wilson Library, Southern History Collection**: Matt Turi – and possibly many others.

Photo Credits (by page numbers)

Simon **Alixopulos** 29 / **America** Magazine 30 / **Archives**, Archdiocese of Denver 32, 66a / Kathleen **Bensman** 52a / Blaine **Burkey** 2b, 3a, 7a, 18, 24b, 25b, 26, 27a-b, 41a, 41da, 47, 51, 56a-b, 57c, 60 / John **Camrud** Design 1 / Daniel **Ciucci** 56a, 124a,d / James **Castellan** 33 / **Denver** Catholic Register 2a, 9, 24a, 31a, 72b / **Denver** Firemen's Museum 52b, 61a / Joseph Mary **Elder** 59 / **Endow** 23a / **Fort D.A. Russell** web site 81b / **Fort Logan** Historical Society 25a / John **Gibbons** 37, 65a / Andrew **Grosheider** 57a-b / **History Colorado**, Denver 17a-b / **Holy Name** Church, Sheridan 65c / **Holy Name** Province, Franciscans 32c, 35 / John J. **Horan** 39c / Dick **Kreck** 53a / Jim **Kubicki** 21 / **Machebeuf** High School library 10b / **Midwest Jesuit** Archives, St. Louis 3b, 4, 7b, 10a, 22b, 38a, 50a / **North Carolina** University, Chapel Hill 81a / Mary Frances **O'Sullivan** 72a / **Regis** University archives 5a, 43, 50b / **Sacred Heart** Church 1 / **Saint Catherine** of Siena Church 23b, 41a / **Saint John Vianney** Seminary kitchen 22a / **Saint Joseph** Hospital archives 3c / **San Diego** Carmel 58 / Jacob **Schneider** 53b, 124 b-c/ Joanne **Sesson** 38c / **Sheridan** Historical Society 65d, 66b / Robert **Simpson** 41b-c, 42 / **Sisters of Charity**, Cincinnati 37b, 39a-b, 39d, 48, 64 / **Sisters of Charity** of Leavenworth 40, 67a / **Sisters of Loretto** 46a-b, 61b, 74 / Howard **Snyder** 80a-b / Mimi **Stephens** 38b, 62a-b / Jim **Tipton** 54 / **Western History** Collection, Denver Public Library 5b, 32b, 44, 65b, 67b, 78-79.

Bibliography

Archival Collections

Archdiocese of Denver Archives, Denver CO:
    Baptismal Records, St. Mary's Church, Denver CO
    Fr. Pacificus Kennedy Collection

Blair-Caldwell African-American Research Library, Denver Public Library, Denver CO:
    James Harrison Scrapbooks — 1910s-1970s — 9 vv. — C MSS ARL 31
    Thomas Jacob Noel — Research on Julia Greeley "Colored Angel of Charity" 1900-1994
        C MSS ARL 137

Capuchin Province of Mid-America Archives, Denver CO:
    Max L. Castillo — Collection of Papers of Fr. Pacificus Kennedy

Colorado Historical Society Library, Denver CO:
    Cannon, Helen. Governors' Wives — Collection 1861-1910 — MS 977
    Julia Pratte Gilpin —Collection 1886-1896 — MS 2544
    William Gilpin Collection. — MS 268

Colorado State Archives, Denver CO:
    Julia P. Gilpin Probate Case 15579, City & County of Denver
    William Gilpin v. Julia P. Gilpin Divorce Case 1726, Superior Court of Denver County
    William Gilpin v. Julia P. Gilpin Error in trial, Case 2210, Colorado Supreme Court

Jesuitica Collection, Regis University Archives, Denver CO:
    Album Mortuorum Societatis
    Fr. Edward Barry Scrapbooks, 1894-1921, 2 vv.
    House Diary, Sacred Heart College Denver CO, 1888-1980, 15 vv.
    House Diary, Jesuit Residence, Sacred Heart Parish, Denver CO, 1879-1923, 4 vv.
    Profile: Fr. Charles M. Ferrari, 1842-1914

Mt. Olivet Cemetery, Wheat Ridge CO:
    Interment Records

Sacred Heart Church, Denver CO:
    Baptismal, Marriage & Death Records

St. Joseph Hospital Archives, Denver CO:
    Letter from Sr. Ann Margaret Noonan, SCL, Leavenworth, to Sr. Perpetua McGrath SCL, April 28, 1998

Western History and Genealogy Department, Denver Public Library, Denver CO:
    Davis, Herndon Richard — portrait of Gov. William Gilpin — C69-23
    Denver Assessor's Lot Indexes 1860-1917
    Sanborn-Perris Map Co., Insurance Map of Denver CO, 1890-1928, 4 vv.
    Sanborn-Perris Map Co., Insurance Map of Denver CO, 1929-1962, 11 vv.
    William P. Horan Burial Records 1900-1994 — C 929.378883 W67

Wilson Special Collections Library, University of North Carolina, Chapel Hill NC:
    Lawrence Davis Tyson Papers, #1174

Books & Pamphlets

Adams, Gerald M. *Post Near Cheyenne: The History of Fort D.A. Russell, 1867-1930.* Boulder: Pruett Publ. Co., 1989, 271 pp.

Ballard, Jack Stokes. *Fort Logan.* Charleston SC: Arcadia Press, 2011, 127 pp.

Bancroft, Hubert Howe. *History of the Life of William Gilpin: a Character Study.* San Francisco: The History Company, 1889, 62 pp.

Beckwith, Paul Edmund. *The Creoles of St. Louis.* St. Louis: Nixon-Jones Printing Co., 1893, 169 pp.

Camp, Walter Mason. *On the Little Big Horn with Walter Camp: a collection of W.M. Camp's letters, notes and opinions on Custer's last fight,* compiled and edited by Richard G. Hardorff. El Segundo CA: Upton & Son, 2002, 267 pp.

Carr, Ralph Lawrence. "William Gilpin, Pioneer." *Westerners Brand Book* (Denver), 25 (1969) 423-443.

Catlett, Sharon R. *Farmlands, Forts, and Country Living: the Story of Southwest Denver.* Englewood: Westcliffe Publ., 2007, 240 pp.

Cicognani, Amleto Giovanni. *Sanctity in America: Lives of Saints and near-Saints, of these United States.* Paterson NJ: St. Anthony Guild Press, 1939, 156 pp.

Colorado, New Mexico, Utah, Nevada, Wyoming and Arizona Gazetteer and Business Directory, 1884-5, vol. 1. Chicago: R.L. Polk & Co., 1884, 888 pp.

Cullum, George W. *Biographical Register of the Officers and Graduates of the U.S. Military Academy at West Point, N.Y., from its Establishment in 1802 to 1890.* Boston: Houghton-Mifflin, 1891, 3 vv.

Cunningham, Sharon A. *The Good Old Days: The Early History of Academy District Twenty.* Colorado Springs: Academy School District Twenty, 2005, 120 pp.

Denver City Directories. Denver: Corbett, Hoye & Co., 1873-1880, 8 vv.; Denver: Corbett & Ballenger, 1881-1888, 8 vv.; Denver: Ballenger & Richards, 1889-1918, 30 vv.

Denver Householders Directory. Denver: The Gazetteer Publishing & Printing Co., 1924-56, 28 vv.

[Dorgan-Roos, Alex, editor] *Denver Fire Department Commemorative History 2009*. Denver: Denver Fire Department, 2009. 306 pp.

Field, Sharon Lass, editor. *History of Cheyenne, Wyoming*. Dallas: Curtis Media Corp., 1989, 546 pp.

Fishell, Dave. *Towers of Healing: the First 125 Years of Denver's Saint Joseph Hospital*. Denver: St. Joseph Hospital Foundation, 1999, 207 pp. (esp. pp. 100-101, "Former Slave Unshackles the Needy")

Gaff, pseudonym. *Rambles through the Great Kansas Valley, and in Eastern Colorado*. Kansas City: Ramsey, Millet & Hudson, 1878, 84 pp.

Gallagher, Dennis, Thomas J. Noel, and James Patrick Walsh. *Irish Denver*. Charleston SC: Arcadia Press, 2012, 128 pp.

Garrigan, Gilbert J. *The Jesuits of the Middle United States*. N.Y.: America Press, 1938, 3 vv.

Grace, Stephen. *It Happened in Denver*. Guilford, Conn.: TwoDot, 2007, 144 pp.

Hafen, LeRoy Reuben and Ann W. *Our State, Colorado: a History of Progress* (with a 37-page history by Paul H. Hallett of the Catholic Church in Colorado). Denver: Old West Publ. Co., 1966, 404 pp. (esp. p. 387, "Julia Greeley.")

Hale, Will Thomas. *A History of Tennessee and Tennesseeans: the Leaders and Representative Men in Commerce, Industry, and Modern Activities*. N.Y.: Lewis Publ. Co., 1913, 8 vv.

Heitman, Francis B. *Historical Register and Dictionary of the United States Army*. Washington: Government Printing Office, 1901, 2 vv.

Hyde, William, and Howard Louis Conard. *Encyclopedia of the History of St. Louis: a Compendium of History and Biography for Ready Reference*. N.Y.: The Southern History Co., 1899, 4 vv.

Karnes, Thomas L. *William Gilpin: Western Nationalist*. Austin: University of Texas, 1970, 383 pp.

Kreck, Dick. *Denver in Flames: Forging a New Mile High City*. Golden: Fulcrum Publ., 2000, 294 pp.

LaFarge, John, S.J. *The Race Question and the Negro: a Study of Catholic Doctrine on Interracial Justice.* New York: Longmans, Green & Co., 1943, 315 pp.

Leonard, Steven J., with Thomas J. Noel. *Denver: Mining Camp to Metropolis.* Niwot, Colo.: University Press of Colorado, 1990, 544 pp.

[Mason, Coleen Smith, editor] *Mount Olivet Cemetery 1892-1992: in Commemoration of the Centennial of Mount Olivet Cemetery.* Denver: Mt. Olivet Cemetery, 1992, 36 pp.

Mendizábal, Rufo, S.J. *Catalogus Defunctorum in renata Societatis Jesus.* Rome: Societas Jesu, 1972, xx-670-137 pp. [accessible on http://www.jesutmissouuri.org/arch/online.cfm]

Murphy, Eugene P., S.J. *My Name Written in His Heart: Thoughts on the Eleventh Promise of the Sacred Heart.* 1st edition, 1943; 8th edition, Huntington, Ind.: Our Sunday Visitor Press, 1958, 24 pp. (39,000 copies*) [copy in AAD]*

Noel, Thomas J. *Colorado Catholicism and the Archdiocese of Denver.* Niwot, Colo.: University Press of Colorado, 1989, 468 pp.

Porcchea, Paul (Baber Pathornee), "Catholic Music," pp. 100-104 in *The Musical History of Colorado.* Denver: Carles Wesley, 1889, 168 pp.

Smith, Herbert F. *Homilies on the Heart of Jesus and the Apostleship of Prayer for the world's Salvation.* N.Y.: Alba House, 2000, 224 pp.

Stansell, Harold L., S.J. *Regis: On the Crest of the West.* Denver: Regis Educational Corp., 1977, 238 pp.

State Historical Library of the Colorado State Historical Society. *Calendar of the Papers of William Gilpin, 1813-1893: a Holding of the Library of the State Historical Society of Colorado.* Denver: 1968, 10 leaves.

Stone, Wilbur Fiske. Biography of Dr. Martin Currigan pp. 868-869 in v. 2, of *History of Colorado,* Chicago: S.J. Clarke, 1918-1919, 2 vv.

Varnell, Jeanne. *Women of Consequence: the Colorado Women's Hall of Fame.* Boulder: Johnson Books, 1999, 312 pp.

Vickers, William B. *History of the City of Denver, Arapahoe County, and Colorado.* Chicago: Baskin and Co., 1880, 652 pp.

Signed Magazine & Newspaper Articles and Web Sites

Anthony, Jack. History. *Pikes Peak Road Runners* (esp. January: Woodmen to Ice Lake), (web site, cited Mar. 2, 2012) http://pprun.org/newsletter/HistoryTrailRun.pdf

Arnold, Theodora, "Julia Greeley's Compassion," *Empire Magazine* [of the *Denver Post*], Oct. 26, 1969.

Best, Allen. "Denver's Oldest Church Plugs Away at Restoration," DCR Sept. 16, 1998, pp. 18-19 & 26.

Cannon, Helen. "First Ladies of Colorado — Julia Pratte Gilpin," *The Colorado Magazine* 38:4 (Oct. 1961) 267-274.

Carberry, Jack. "Father Grace Asks Funeral in Denver," *Denver Post*, Jun. 1, 1934, pp. 1-2.

Castellan, Eleanor. "Letters," *Empire Magazine* [of the *Denver Post*], Sept. 21, 1969.

Davant, Jeanne. "'Chasing the Cure' led to Pikes Peak region," *Colorado Springs Gazette*, July 3, 2001.

Davant, Jeanne. "You won't find Gwillimville or Borst on local maps," *Colorado Springs Gazette*, Sept. 18, 2001.

Egan, Mary Lou. *Beloved Julia Greeley* (web site, posted Mar. 5, 2009, cited Mar. 2, 2012) http://sacredheartdenver.blogspot.com/2009/03/beloved-julia-greeley.html

Erger, John. "More on Julia Greeley," DCR Nov. 23, 2011.

Erger, John, and Mary Anderson, "Thanks for the 'Beloved Julia Greeley' article," DCR Mar. 15, 1995, p. 7, col. 1-2.

Fiedler, James. "Ramblings: Joys of the Business," DCR Nov. 17, 1982, p. 6, c. 1.

Gleason, John. "Cemetery tour: Revisiting History," DCR Sept. 29, 2010, p. 2.

Hagus, Rose M. "Mrs. Hagus Recalls Julia's Kind Deed," DCR Apr. 13, 1939.

Hallett, Paul H. "An Ex-Slave Known for Her Sanctity," DCR Oct. 13, 1982, pp. 5 & 16.

Hallett, Paul H. "Canonization May Be Pursued for Denver Woman," DCR Apr. 15, 1998, p. 3.

Hallett, Paul H. "Father Leo's Rose Recalled," DCR Nov. 21,1983.

Hallett, Paul H. "Registorials: Julia Greeley Saintly Negro," DCR Jun. 17, 1965, p. 5, col. 1-2.

Hardway, Roger D. "African-American Women on the Western Frontier," *Negro History Bulletin*, Jan.-Mar. 1997.

Hawkins, Dennis. *Julia Greeley* (Find A Grave web site, posted Sept. 2, 2000, cited Mar. 2, 2012) http://www.findagrave.com/cgi-bin/fg.cgi?page=gr&GRid=12678

Hutcheson, Bonita. *Before the Yellow Pages – Part 2* (web site, posted 2002, cited Mar. 2, 2012) http://www.rootsweb.ancestry.com/~coshs/ha_ypages2.htm

Hutcheson, Bonita. *A History of Sheridan, Colorado* (web site, posted 2002, cited Mar. 2, 2012) http://www.rootsweb.ancestry.com/~coshs/ha_morehistory.htm

Joyce, William, O.F.S. "Leo Heinrichs, O.F.M.—Protomartyr of Colorado, 1867-1908," *Troubadour* (Our Lady of the Angels Region, Secular Franciscan Order, New York) 40 (Fall 2007) 5-7.

Kennedy, Pacificus, O.F.M. "Old Black Julia," *Friar,* Dec. 1974, pp. 12-19.

Kennedy, Pacificus, O.F.M. "Beloved Old Back Julia," *Friar*, Jun. 1979, pp. 29-38.

King, Roxanne. "Boulder Woman Recipient of Inaugural Julia Greeley Award," DCR May 17, 2006, p. 8, col. 1-5.

King, Roxanne. "Cardinal Arinze to Speak at ENDOW Gala / Julia Greeley Award to be Given to Laywoman Sharon Post," DCR Apr. 7, 2010, p. 1, col. 2-4.

King, Roxanne. "Local Woman Honored for Overcoming Hardship with Faith to Live Life of Loving Service," DCR May 9, 2007, p. 10, col. 1-5.

King, Roxanne. "Msgr. Matthew Smith: Legacy of 'Msgr. Register' Continues," DCR Feb. 2, 2011.

King, Roxanne. "Sacred Heart Church Stands Tall on Larimer Street," DCR Dec. 15, 1999, pp. 3 & 18.

King, Roxanne. "Register's History is That of Faith in Action," DCR Mar. 4, 2009, pp. 9 & 16.

LaPoint, Nissa. "Saintly Denverite Julia Greeley Featured in Manuscript," DCR Nov. 9, 2011, pp. 1 & 5.

Leisring, Mary L. *The Inspiring Life of Julia Greeley* (web site, PDF version, posted Mar. 3, 2010, cited Mar. 2, 2012) http://www.archden.org/index.cfm/ID/3827?CFID=10347088&CFTOKEN=18975257

Leisring, Mary L. "Life of a Former Slave Continues to Inspire," *Catholic Review* (Baltimore) Feb. 18, p. A-25.

Matz, Nicholas. "Bishop Matz's Tribute: Words of Praise and Regret over the Body of Ex-Governor Gilpin," *Denver* Republican Jan. 25, 1894.

Naakkula, Al. "They also Died Bravely, in Line of Duty," *Rocky Mountain News*, May. 25, 1974, p. 55.

Neenan, W.S. "Saintly Catholic Woman Who Dies Here Had Taught 5000 in 40 Years," DCR May 17, 1923.

Nikolds, Madelyn. "Tolerance," *T'Akra* (Loretto Heights College, Denver), Apr. 1939, p. 3.

Noel, Thomas J. *Sacred Heart (1879): Sacred Heart is Denver's Oldest Still Used...* (web site, cited Mar. 2, 2012) www.archden.org/noel/07039.htm

O'Sullivan, Mary. "African-American History Month: Recalling Julia Greeley," DCR Feb. 22, 1995, pp. 1 & 11.

Owens, M. Lilliana, S.L., "Julia Greeley, 'Colored Angel of Charity'," *The Colorado Magazine* 20:5 (Sept. 1943) 176-178.

Owens, M. Lilliana, S.L. "A Negro Apostle of the Sacred Heart," *The Sacred Heart Messenger*, 77 (Nov. 1942) 34-35.

Pedler, Pam. "Denver's Saintly Woman: Julia Greeley" DCR Apr. 15, 2009.

Pedler, Pam. "Ex-Slave Was an Angel of Charity in Early Denver," DCR Mar. 24, 2010, p. 16.

Pratte, Bernard, Jr. "The Reminiscences of General Bernard Pratte, Jr.," *Missouri Historical Society Bulletin*, 6 (Oct. 1949) 59-71.

Raboteau, Albert J. "Black Catholic and Afro-American Religious History: Autobiographic Reflections," *U.S. Catholic* Historian 5 (1986) 119, 124.

Scott, Charlene. "Julia Greeley 'a Beloved Figure'," DCR Feb. 7, pp. 5 & 10.

Simpson, Mary Anne. *Our Beloved Julia Greeley* (web site, posted Sept. 4, 2005, cited Mar. 2, 2012) http://ourbelovedjuliagreeley.blogspot.com

[Smith, Matthew.] "Highest Honor Ever Paid to Dead Laic Goes to Negress," DCR Jun. 13, 1918, pp. 1 & 3.

Stone, Albert W. "Denver Catholic Clergy Honor 'Uncle Tom' Mullen, Ex-Slave," unknown paper, in Harrison scrapbook v. 1 at BCAARL.

Summers, Danny. "A Look Back at Edgerton," *Tri Lakes Tribune*, Mar. 30, 2011.

Tarkelson, Jean. "Cardinal Returns to Serve His Colorado Flock," *Rocky Mountain News*, Mar. 30, 1998.

Walsh, John. "Reflections on Colorado's Centennial in the Holy Year," DCR Jan. 2, 1975, p. 8, col. 1.

Wayne, Frances. "Tribute Paid to Memory of Julia Greeley, Negress," *Denver Post*, Jun. 10, 1918, p. 7, col. 4-5.

Woodward, Michael Scott. *Julia Greeley: Her Charity Knew No Bounds* (web site, posted 9-13-2011, cited 3-2-2012) http://endowgroups.org/2011/09/julia-greeley-her-charity-knew-no-bounds-2/

Unsigned Articles in Magazines and Newspapers:

Cheyenne Sun:
1891 Mar. 31, p. 5: "The Community's Loss: Albert C. Snyder Answers to the Summons of Death Last Evening"

The Claverite (New Orleans)
94 (Winter 2010-11) 21: [re scholarships]

Democratic Leader (Cheyenne)
1885 May 14, p. 3: "Wyoming's Turn: the President Appoints Two New Postmasters"

Denver Catholic Register:
1903 May 9: "Sacred Heart Church: Christmas and Easter Offerings"
1903 Nov. 7. p. 6: "Charter Bazaar, Benefit of Sacred Heart Church"
1913 Jan. 23. p. 1: "These People Identified with the Register in the Appeal of the Flannery Case"
1914 June 11, p. 1: "Father Ferrari, Pioneer Priest, Death's Victim"
1915 Oct. 28, p. 5: "Colored Lady Has Mass of Requiem for Mother M. Pancratia"
1918 July 18, p. 2: [re article on Julia in Ave Maria magazine]
1918 July 18, p. 8: "People Deem It Honor to Distribute Leaflets Colored Julia Handed Out"
1918 Oct. 3, p. 2: "Lived Weeks With No food Except Blessed Sacrament"
1919 Apr. 24, p. 45: "Rose from Casket of Denver Martyr Remains Together for Eleven Years."
1922 Dec. 21: "Two Laics Most Honored by Church at Burial in History of Denver Were Humble Negroes"
1927 March 1, p. 1, col. 6-7: "Father Stanislaus Lived For Ten Years With Priest Whose Cause He Is Putting Through"
1928 June 14, p. 1, col. 5: "Listening In" [re article re Julia in St. Louis magazine]
1939 March 2: "Radio to Dramatize Life of Saintly Negress / Ex-Slave Was Apostle of Sacred Heart"
1939 March 9, pp. 1 & 4:" Saintly Negress Nurse to 'Little White Angel'"

1939 April 13: "Secret Charities of Julia Greeley Are Recalled by Denver People"
1943 April 29, pp. 1 & 2: "Fame of Saintly Denver Negro Woman Spreads / 25th Anniversary of Julia Greeley's Death Occurs Next June / New Pamphlet Reviewing Career of Apostle of Sacred Heart Distributed by Director of Noted Radio Program"
1943 Dec. 30, p. 7, c. 3: [allusion to Julia's 25th anniversary of death]
1950 Aug. 3, p.1, cc. 1-5: "Mt. Calvary Cemetery Work Half Done"
1950 Aug. 10, p. 1: "No Information on Woman Whose Body Is Incorrupt"
1966 Apr. 28, p. 15, col. 5-6: "Best Books About Colorado" [mentions the Hafens' book and its Catholic insert by Paul H. Hallett]
1974 Dec. 12: [ad for Friar magazine's article on Julia]
1976 Mar. 17, p. 30: "Julia Greeley, 'Colored Angel of Charity'"
1995 May 24 [announced a special Mass in honor of Julia]
1995 June 7, p. 22, col. 4 [an ad for a special Mass in honor of Julia on June 25]
1996 Oct. 2, p. 19: "Scholarship celebrates memory of Father Peter Claver"
2000 Feb. 16, p. 3, col. 1-5: "Poor parish opens heart to Jubilee pilgrims"
2000 Nov. 22, p. 9, col. 3: "African-American order celebrates anniversary"
2001 Nov. 14, p. 9: "November Celebrates African-American Catholic history / Local
2003 Oct. 23:" Seven Students Awarded Julia Greeley Scholarships"
2008 Feb. 27, p. 7: "Knights and Ladies of Peter Claver: serving the African-American Catholic community"
2008 Sept. 8, pp. 1 & 3: "Burial sites of famous, saintly on Mount Olivet tour"
2009 Sept. 23, p. 1: "Venerable Sacred Heart Church marks 130 Years"

Denver Post:
1912 Dec. 23, p. 3: "Julia Pratt Gilpin, Governor's Widow, Dead in St. Louis"
1915 Oct. 12, p. 2" "Charity Guided Life of Mother Pancratia"
1918 June 8, p. 9: Died GREELEY
1918 June 9, p. 8: Died GREELEY
1923 May 13, sect. 1, p. 14: "Mrs. Jennie Ryan, Denver Teacher for 40 Years, Dies"

Denver Republican
1887 Dec. 9: "The Gilpin Divorce Case: Final Decree Promulgated Yesterday in the Superior Court."
1887 Dec. 9: "Scenes at the Gilpin House: The Ex-Governor Carries Away the Children by Force."
1892 July 17, pp. 1-2: "A Plunge to Death: Ex-Governor Gilpin's Eldest Son Falls Two Hundred Feet"
1894 Jan. 21, pp. 1-2: "William Gilpin Dead

New York Tribune:
1919 Jan. 8, p. 9: "Colonel George S. Young"

Rocky Mountain News:
1874 Feb. 20, p. 4, c. 2: "Personal Notes"
1874 Feb. 26, p. 4, c. 1: "City & Vicinity Brevities"
1874 Apr 7, p. 4, c. 3: "Personals"

1918 June 10: "Died"
1918 June 11, p. 10: "Former Slave Dies, Lies in State"

The Sacred Heart Church and School Monitor (Sacred Heart Parish, Denver):
v. 1 (1905-08) to v. 4 (1916-19) In DPL C 282-7881

Wyoming Tribune (Cheyenne):
1910 May 24, p. 3: "Mrs. Snyder Dead"

Unidentified Newspaper:
1922 date unknown: "Catholic Church Honors 'Uncle Tom,' Negro, at Impressive Funeral Service" (found in James Harrison scrapbooks, v. 1, in BCAARL)

Unsigned Web Sites

Greeley Family History (web site, cited 3-2-2012)
http://newcastlehs.org/historic-new-castleour-history/greeley-family

Julia Greeley. Endow, 2011, 10 min., 53 sec. [DVD, posted 9-15-2011, cited 3-2-2012)]
http://www.youtube.com/watch?v=cWuxEaXyTkg

The Knights of Peter Claver, Inc. *The Claverite* [PDF version] (esp.21)
home.catholicweb.com/kofpc/files/KPC_winter_2010_final.pdf

DVDs

2006 Endow Gala. Littleton CO: Good News Productions, 2006, 17 min.

Page numbers in *italics* indicate photographs.

ACPMA (Archives of the Capuchin Province of Mid-America), 36
Alia, Guiseppe, 32
Alixopulos, Madelyn Nicholds, 29, *29*, 117–118
Allen, Prudence, 73, 122
Altar and Rosary Society, 57n196, 58
Amundsen, Robert, 70n245
Anderson, Mary, 71, 121
Anthony of Padua, Saint, statue, *27*
Apostleship of Prayer, 20–22, *21*
3347 Arapahoe (Day Home), 57n195
Archdiocese Office for Black Catholics, 110, 123
Archives of the Capuchin Province of Mid-America (ACPMA), 36
Arkins, Mildred Connell, 47
Arnold, Theodora O'Donnell, 19, 34–35, 36–37, 48, 119
Auguste, Donna, back cover
Ave Maria Magazine, 20, 116
awards, 72–73

1361 Bannock St. (Urquhart home), 23
baptism, 13–14
Barry, Edward, 49, 63
BCAARL (Blair-Caldwell African-American Research Library), 36
Besson, Catherine Rita, 48, *48*
Blair-Caldwell African-American Research Library (BCAARL), 36
Blucher, Margaret Clare, 39, *39*
Bogy, Lewis V., 15
Bonfils, Pancratia, 13, 54, 61–62, 74, *74*
Brady, Richard, 26, 65–66, *66*
Brawles, Frederick, 54
Brown, John J., 58
Brownlee, Richard S., 14
Brucker, Aloysius, 7, 10–11, *10*
burial costs, 4
Burkey, Blaine, back cover

Cabrini Shrine, 13n37
1440 California St. (St. Mary's Academy), 22, 61–62, *61*, 74
Cannon, Helen, 16
canonization, 34, 72, 109–110
Capuchin Franciscan Order, 110, 123
Capuchin Province of Mid-America, 124
Casey, John E., 60n206
Castellan, Eleanor Pavella, 33–35, *33*, 37, 48–51, 119
Castillo, Max L., 36, 120
Catlett, Sharon, 25
Cerilda (Julia's mother), 14
1743 Champa Street (Gilpin Home), 16, *77*
3231 Champa St. (Gerspach home), *56*
3239 Champa (Lee home), *26*, 27n105
3241 Champa St. (Gerspach home), *56*
Chaput, Charles J., 109, 122
charity to the poor, 11–12
Chase, Linda M., 72, 121
Cheley, Dr., 67, 68, 118
children, Julia's love of, 12, 49
churches
    Catholic, in Denver, 58n200
    Cure d'Ars Church, 120
    Sacred Heart Church, 1, *1*, 3, 12–13, 60n206, 72, 120–121
    St. Catherine of Siena Church, 23, 24, *41*
    St. Elizabeth's Church, 13, 31–32, *31*, 51, *51*
    St. John the Evangelist Church, 57, *57*
    St. Mary's Cathedral, *10*, 17, 46
    St. Patrick's Church, 65–66, *65*
Clayton, George, 46
Colorado State Historical Society, 30
Conley, James, 123
Conway, John F., 7, 12, 45
Cronin, Ann Gertrude, 37–38, *37*
Cronin, Anna Catherine, 51
Cronin, Dan P., 52
Cronin, Daniel, 51n180
Cronin, Pat and Sarah, *52*
Cure d'Ars Church, 120
Cure d'Ars Parish, 110, 123
Currigan, Martin, Jr., 38
Currigan, Martin, Sr., 4, 66–69, *67*, 118
Curtis Park, 1
1528 Curtis St. (St. James Hotel), 54
2815 Curtis St. (Cronin home), *52*
3263 Curtis St. (Kennedy home), *56*

Dandridge, Richard, 54
Dave (handyman, Sacred Heart Church), 61
Day, Margaret Ducey, 57n196, *57*
Delaney, Asella, 68–69
Denver Catholic Register, 2,

136 Index

17, 19, 20, 22–23, 30, 44, 70–74, 116–117, 119–121, 123
  "Highest Honor Ever Paid to Dead Laic Here goes to Negress," 9–13
  incorrupt bodies, 69–70
  "Julia Greeley Saintly Negro," 31, 33
  "Mrs. Hagus Recalls Julia's Kind Deeds," 28
  "Saintly Negress Nurse 'To Little White Angel'," 24
  "Secret Charities of Julia Greeley are Recalled by Denver People," 25–27
Denver Post, 116
  Empire Magazine, 33–36, 119
  Julia Greeley obituary, 4–5
  Pancratia Bonfils obituary, 74
  "Tribute is Paid to Memory of Julia Greeley, Negress," 6–7
DeOrio, Ralph and Charles, 54
Devotion to the Sacred Heart of Jesus, 1, 11, 23
Dickerson, John H., 15
Dickerson, Julia. *See* Gilpin, Julia Pratte
Dickerson, Louise, 16, 79
donations, financial, by Julia Greeley, 73
Durkin, Helen Cecilia, 64n220

Echeverría, John, 3–4, *3*, 19, 51, 54, 61
Elizabeth (Julia's Third Order name), 31–32
Elizabeth of Hungary and Thuringia, Saint, 32
Empire Magazine, 33–36, 119

Emrisek, Gene, 60n206, 123
ENDOW, 72–73, 110, 122
Engine Company No. 3, *53*
Erger, Agnes Hines, 14, 54–55, 71
Erger, John J., 71, 120, 123
Eucharistic Adoration, 58

fasting, 12
Feast of the Portiuncula, 55
Feast of the Sacred Heart, 3–4, 13, 20n91
Ferrari, Charles, 13–14
Fiedler, James, 70
Find A Grave website, 69, 121, 122
Fire House #3 (2563 Glenarm), 54
fire stations, *53*
  Denver locations, 53
  Engine Company No. 3, *53*, 54
  Fire House #10 (33rd & Arapahoe), 53
  Julia's ministry to, 11, 22, 33, 38, 46, 48, 58–59
Fisher, Frank, 55
Fisher, Fred, 55n188
Fisher, Rose Stetter, 55, 71, 123
Five Points Neighborhood, 1
Fort D.A. Russell, 81, *81*
Fort Logan, *25*
Forty Hours' Devotion, 58
1321 14th St. (Gilpin home), 18
Frances Cabrini, Saint, 13n37, 40, 56
French, Florita, 39–40, *39*
Friar Magazine, 35, *36*, 66, 120
Ft. Logan Homes, 66n226
Fugita, Annette, 70n244–245
funeral, 4, 7, 12–13

Gallagher, Mrs. H.E., 25–26

Gautrelet, Francis X., 20
George (Julia's father), 14
Gerspach, Albert and Mary, 56n192
Gerspach, Otto and Julia, 56n192
Gerspach, Wilma, 55–56, 62–64, 63n215, 68
Gilpin, Julia Pratte, 10–11, 14–20, *17*, 30
  death of, 19
  divorce case, 75–77
  divorce testimony, 83–85, 94–98
  influence on Julia, 10–11, 17
  marriages of, 15
  separation from William of, 18
  will of, 19–20
Gilpin, William, *17*, 80
  death of, 19
  divorce case, 75–77
  divorce testimony, 82–83, 85–94
  marriage, 15
  separation from Julia of, 18
Gilpin, Willie, 18–19
Gilpin vs. Gilpin, 75n271, 82–108
Gleason, Honora, 69–70
2563 Glenarm (Engine Company No. 3), *53*, 54
Glenn, Michael, 120
Grace, Walter A., 7, 12
Graves, Anna, 62
Graves, Edward and Nora, 62n213, *62*
Graves, Madelyn G., 62n213
Greeley, Horace, 14
Greeley, Julia, *23*
  Apostle of the Sacred Heart, 10, 23, 30
  baptism of, 13–14
  birthplace of, 14
  charitable acts of, 11–12,

27, 28, 29, 49–50, 59
chronology, 111–115
church pew of, 50, 60n206, 73
as Confirmation sponsor, 64n220
conversion to Catholicism of, 10–11, 13–14, 17
death of, 4
description of, 1–2, 13, 23
employment of, 12, 79–82
eye deformity, 37, 40, 55, 64, 82n294
at Fort Logan, 25–26
and the Franciscans, 31–33
funeral of, 7, 12–13
and the Gilpins, 13–20, 75–77, 78–79
grave of, *54*, 69–70, *124*
illiteracy of, 21
large crowds attend wake of, 5
and legacy from Julia Gilpin, 19–20
miracles attributed to, 67–69
in Missouri, 77
musical ability of, 26, 74
in New Mexico, 79
origins of last name, 14
receives last Sacraments, 4, 12
testimony in Gilpin divorce case, 104–108
westward journey of, 77–78
in Wyoming, 80–82
Griffin, Helen Hyland, 56
Grosheider, Agnes Day, 57, *57*
Guida, John Baptiste, 56
Guidoni, LaVonne, 122

Haberl, Anthony, 46
Haberl, Fannie Darrah, 46
Haberl, Marie Anthony, 46, *46*
Hagus, Rose M., 28, 117
Hallett, Paul, 2, 31, *31*, 70, 71, 119, 120
Hartwell, Harold W., 54
Hawkins, Dennis, 69, 120, 121, 122
Hayden, Celine, 45, 57–59, *58*, 62–64, 63n215
Hayden, Charles K., 58
Hayden, Margaret R., 59n202
Hayden, Mr. & Mrs. Charles H., 58
Hayden, William H., 58
Healy, John F., Jr., 38
Healy, John F., Sr., *38*
Heinrichs, Leo, 31, 32, *32*, 71
Hellstrom, Christopher, 122
Higgins, Edward Cornelius and Catherine, 47n173
Higgins, John and Julie, 62n213
Higgins, William, 34
Hilbers, Ellenora Louise, 39, *39*, 46n169, 119
Hilbers, Mr. & Mrs. H.B., 39
Holy Name Parish, 110, 123
Honeyman, Frank, 60n204
Honeyman, Rose Ann, 59–60
4270 Hooker (Urquhart home), 24, *41*
Horan, Neil, 39, *39*, 120
Horan, William P., 4, 6n24, 12–13
Horan and Son Mortuary, 4, 5
Howard, Mrs. Michael, 26
3524 Humboldt St. (Honeyman home), *59*, 60n204

Imherr, Lucille Hagus, 60
incorrupt bodies, 69–70, 70n245
indulgences, plenary, 31

Jensen, Mary Hoolahan, 65n224, 66
Jesuits, 7, 9, 18, 20, 20–22, 32, 43–45, 57, 63, 83n296, 110, 123
John Paul II, 109
Johnson, Bertha Router, 100
Johnson, Shirley, 72, 121
2837 Josephine St. (Arkin home), *47*
Julia Greeley Award, 72–73, 122
Julia Greeley Guild, 110, 123
Julia Greeley Scholarship, 72, 121

Karnes, Thomas, 16
Katherine Drexel, Saint, 15n54
Kennedy, Mrs. Edward, 56
Kennedy, Pacificus, 14, 18, 19, 35–36, *35*, 66, 109, 120
letters to, 36–47
testimony collected by, 47–66
Klein, Antonita, 39–40
Koch, Francis, 31–32, *31*

Ladies Auxiliary of the Knights of Peter Claver, 72, 110, 121, 123
LaFarge, John, 30, *30*, 118
2459 Lafayette (Ryan Home), 44
Lally, M. Irene, 40, *40*
2640 Larimer St. (Pavella home), 51n179
2760 Larimer St. (Sacred Heart Church), 1, *1*, 3, 7, 12–13, 60n206, 72, 120–121
3311 Larimer St. (Hilbers home), 39
3320 Larimer St. (Hilbers home), 39
Larson, Mary, 98–99
2720 Lawrence (Ryan

Index

Home), 44
League of the Sacred Heart, 11, 20–22, 44
Lee, Ellen Madden, 26–27
Lee, Francis Xavier, 27
Lee, Mrs. Thomas, 73
Lemming, Robert, 123
Ligeste, Pierre de Laclede, 14
Lindblad, Carrie, 3
Logantown. *See* Fort Logan
Lonergan, William, 4, *4*, 6n24
Loretto Heights Academy, 29
Loretto Heights College, 74
5127 Lowell Blvd. (Ryan House), 43–45
Loyola Chapel (2536 Ogden), 5, *5*, 7, 44, 58n200
lying in state, 5–7, 10–11

Machebeuf, Joseph Projectus, 1
Margaret Mary Alocoque, Saint, 23, 30
de Marillac, Louise, 68
Marra, Joseph, 43
Martin, Curtis, back cover
Martin, Steve, 54
Martino, Joseph Francis, 122
Matz, Nicholas, 17–18, 19n78, 20n91, 64n220
McCallin, Fred, 67
McCarthy, Eliza, 99
McDonnell, Charles A., 4, 7, *7*, 12, 19
McDonough Park, 23
McMenamin, Hugh L., 67
McNulty, John, 60, 119
Medrano, Marcus, 60n206, 120
Messenger of the Sacred Heart, 11, 21
miracles, 67–69
Missionary Sisters of the Sacred Heart, 40
Morrison, Dolorine, 74

Mountain View Hotel, *66*
Mt. Calvary Cemetary, 69
Mt. Olivet Cemetary, 4, 19, 120, 122–123
  grave of Julia Greeley, *54*, 69–70, *124*
  graves of Ryan sisters, 45n165
  graves of William, Willie, Julia Gilpin, *18*
Mullen, "Uncle Tom," 22, *22*
Murphy, Eugene, 22–23, *22*, 30, 32, 117, 118
My Name Written in His Heart, 30, 118

National Black Catholic Congress (2002), 72
Neenan, W.S., 44
Nevin, Hanna, 4n15, 122
New Advent Ministries, 110, 123
Newman, Joe, 9
Noel, Thomas, 36, 69
Noonan, Emmett and Helen, 68–69
Noonan, Helen, 66n230, 67–69, 118
Noonan, Margaret Ann, 66–69, *67*

obituaries
  Julia Greeley, 4–5, 6–7, 22
  Pancratia Bonfils, 74
O'Donnell, Thomas, 34–35
2536 Ogden (Loyola Chapel), 5, *5*, 7, 44, 58n200
organ, purchased by Julia for St. Patrick's Church, 26, 66
O'Sullivan, Mary Frances, 19, 69, 70–71, 72, *72*, 120, 121
"Our Beloved Julia Greeley" website, 123
Owens, Elizabeth, 99–100
Owens, M. Lilliana, 29, 30,

118
Owens, Robert L., 19, 20
Owens, Terrance F., 61, *61*

Padan, Agnes, 65
Parsons, Jan, 69–70
Pavella, Emilie and Nicholas, 51n179
Pedler, Pam, 69, 73
pew, 50, 60n206, *60*, 73
pilgrimage, 124, *124*
plenary indulgences, 31
Pratte, Bernard, Jr., 15
Pratte, Bernard, Sr., 15
Pratte, Louise, 102
Prayer of the Good Thief, 10–11

racial attitudes
  and Julia's charity, 29, 59
  and Julia's "color" in heaven, 7, 13, 23
  towards black Catholics, 50n178, 63
  "white folk's pride," 9, 11
  of William Gilpin, 83n295
Radio League of the Sacred Heart, 22
Reed, Ruth L., 68
Reed, Verner Zevola, 70n245
Religious Sisters of Mercy, 110, 122–123
Renteria, Angelica, 3n13
Reynolds, Frank, 61
Riley, Russell, 103
Robinson, Lina, 77
Robinson, Paul Gervais, 78, 103
Roche, Alice Carlene, 61–62
Rocky Mountain News, 16, 116
  "Former Slave Dies; Body Lies in State," 8–9
  incorrupt bodies, 69n243
Ryan, Jennie J., 44–45, *44*
Ryan, John Patrick, 15

Ryan, Maggie A., 44
Ryan, Miss, 4
Ryan, William W., 23, *23*
Ryan House, 43–45, *43*, 58n198–199

Sacred Heart Apostolate, 20–22
Sacred Heart badge, *38*
Sacred Heart Church (2760 Larimer), 1, *1*, 3, 7, 12–13, 60n206, 72, 120–121
Sacred Heart Church and School Monitor, 116
Sacred Heart Messenger, 118
    "A Negro Apostle of the Sacred Heart," 29–30
Sacred Heart Parish, 110, 123
Sacred Heart statue, *27*
Scanlon, Regis, 123
scholarships, 72
Scott, Charlene, 70
Secular Franciscan Order, 31–32, 110, 123
Sherwin, Frank, 79
Signs of Cultus, 116–124
Simpson, Marjorie Ann Urquhart, 23–24, *23*, 41–42, *41*, *42*, 54, 70
Simpson, Mary Ann, 13n37, 19
Sisters of Loretto, 46–47, 59
slave roots, of Julia, 8, 10, 14
Sliney, Patrick, 66n227
Smith, Jim, 121
Smith, Matthew John Wilfred, 9, *9*
Snyder, Albert C., 80–81, *80*
Snyder, Priscilla McCrum, 80–81, *80*
Sorrentino, Walter, 3n12
St. Catherine of Siena Church, 23, 24, *41*
St. Elizabeth Chronicle, 22, 116
St. Elizabeth's Church, 13, 31–32, *31*, 51, *51*
St. Elizabeth's Friary, 35
St. Ignatius of Loyola Parish, 47
St. James Hotel (1528 Curtis St.), 54
St. John the Evangelist Church, 57, *57*
St. John Vianney Seminary, 121
St. Joseph's Hospital, *3*, 4, 17n64, 68
St. Louis University, 22–23
St. Mary's Academy (1440 California St.), 22, 61–62, *61*, 74
St. Mary's Cathedral, *10*, 17, 46
St. Patrick's Church, 65–66, *65*
Stafford, James Francis, 72, *72*, 109, 120, 121, back cover
Stansell, Harold L., 43
State Historical Society of Missouri, 14
Stephens, Marguerite Graves, 18, 62–64, *62*
Swift, Henry J., 37

Tafoya, Russ, 120, 121
T'Akra, 117–118
    "Tolerance" (excerpts), 29
Talle, M. Andrew, 67
Taylor, Bernard, 14
Taylor, Catherine Regina, 46, 64, *64*
Taylor, Clay, 104
Teachout, Harlow, 78n277
Teachout, May, 79, 100–102
Teachout's Ranch, 78, *79*
"The Sacred Heart Hour" (radio program), 22–23, 117
Third Order of St. Francis, 13, 31–32, 51
Toussaint, Pierre, 30
Tracy, Celeste, 14, 19, 102–103
1221 28th St. (C. Lindblad's home), 3, *3*
1421 28th St. (Julia's room), 2
Tyson, Bettie McGhee, 81–82
Tyson, Lawrence D., 81, *81*, 82n292

Urquhart, Agnes (Rooney), 23–24, *42*, 54
Urquhart, George Hill, 13, 23–24, *41*
Urquhart, William (Billy), 42
U.S. Census (1880), 16–17
U.S. Census (1910), 45

Van Hille, Benjamin Palmer, 64

Walker, Jody, 124
2821 Walnut St. (Julia's room), 2, 30
2913 Walnut St. (Julia's room), 2, *2*, 3n12, 45
Walsh, Agnes Gavaghan, 65, *65*
Walsh, Eva M., 37, *37*
Walsh, Joseph, 9, 37, *65*
Walsh, Mrs. Joseph, 4
Wayne, Frances Belford, 5–7, *5*, 19
Wechbaugh, Ellen, 71
Weinzapfel, Anthony, 65–66, *65*, 66
Wolff, Florence, 46–47, *46*
Woodward, Michael, 121
Worland, Francis O., 47, 119

Young, George Shaeffer, 25–26, *25*, 66n228

Julia Greeley Guild

The Julia Greeley Guild is a group of men and women dedicated to extending Julia's fame for sanctity, proposing her as a model of Christian virtue, and encouraging private devotion to her. For more information, see our web site, www.juliagreeley.org. To join in this effort and be aware of activities of the Guild, please send your name, postal address, email address, and phone number to the Guild at 2760 Larimer St., Denver CO 80205 or juliagreeleyguild@gmail.com.

A Prayer
Heavenly Father, your servant Julia Greeley
dedicated her life to honoring the Sacred Heart of your Son,
and to the humble service of your children, especially the poor.
If it be in accordance with your holy will,
please grant this favor I now ask through her intercession,
_____.
I ask also, in the Name of Jesus,
whose Sacred Heart filled Julia's heart with love for all she met,
that I may follow her example of humility and simplicity
in loving you and my neighbor. Amen.

Approved for private use by Bishop James D. Conley,
Apostolic Administrator of the Archdiocese of Denver,
March 16, 2012.

Please be so kind as to report all favors received, in writing, to Julia Greeley Guild at juliagreeleyguild@gmail.com or 2760 Larimer St., Denver CO 80205.

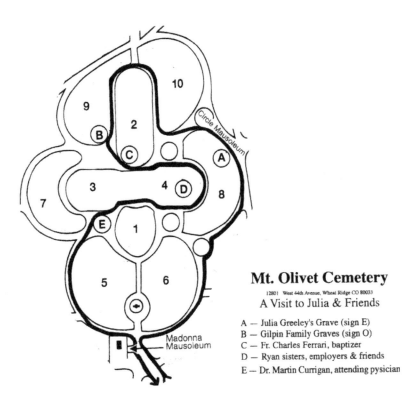

Mt. Olivet Cemetery
12801 West 44th Avenue, Wheat Ridge CO 80033

A Visit to Julia & Friends

A — Julia Greeley's Grave (sign E)
B — Gilpin Family Graves (sign O)
C — Fr. Charles Ferrari, baptizer
D — Ryan sisters, employers & friends
E — Dr. Martin Currigan, attending pysician

Julia Greeley at Fort Logan & Environs

1. Mother Pancratia's Grave
2. Colorado & Southern Depot
3. Sliney's Saloon & Hotel
4. Denver & Rio Grande Depot
5. St. Patrick's Church
6. Afro-American Settlement
7. Capt. Young's Officer's Quarters

(based on July 1901 W.C. Willits Map of Denver, Capital City of Colorado)